For my son, James, and all of his brothers in arms.
The Few. The Proud. The Marines.

By Ethan Cross

THE ACKERMAN THRILLERS

I Am the Night
I Am Fear
I Am Pain
I Am Wrath
I Am Hate
I Am Vengeance

I
AM
WRATH

ETHAN CROSS

HEAD
of
ZEUS

I Am Wrath
was previously published as
The Judas Game

First published as *The Judas Game* in the United States in 2016 by
The Story Plant, The Aronica-Miller Publishing Project, LLC

This edition first published in the United Kingdom by Head of Zeus in 2021
An Aries book

9 7 5 3 1 2 4 6 8

A CIP catalogue record for this book is available
from the British Library.

ISBN (PBO): 9781838931001
ISBN (E): 9781838930998

Printed and bound by CPI Group (UK) Ltd, Croydon, CR0 4YY

Aries
c/o Head of Zeus Ltd
First Floor East
5–8 Hardwick Street
London EC1R 4RG
WWW.HEADOFZEUS.COM

Episode 1

Francis Ackerman Jr. Admired his new face in the reflective side of the interrogation room window. The surgeons had done excellent work, better than he had expected. In fact, he hadn't initially been receptive to the idea. It wasn't that he had any qualms about getting a new face or worried that he would miss the original. It had nothing to do with vanity or sentimentality. His was a concern of practicality and offensive capability. He had been told by many women that his previous face was quite attractive and charming. What if he needed to seduce or charm someone of the fairer sex? His handsome face had always been a useful weapon in his arsenal—a helpful tool on his belt. What if his new face didn't possess whatever feature he had inherited to make the last one so disarming and seductive?

As he looked at his new face, he was happy that those concerns had proven to be a nonissue. His new face was at the very least as handsome as his last. Plus, this one had the added benefit of not appearing on wanted posters across the country.

Or at least, his face had been featured on the walls of every law enforcement facility in the United States. Now, he supposed they had taken the posters down. Stuffed them into drawers or wastebaskets or wherever the paper pushers stuck the posters that were no longer needed. Not needed because the men and women gracing their covers had been captured or killed. He was one of the latter.

According to the official story, Francis Ackerman Jr. had died in a shootout with the police nearly a year ago. His new friends at the Department of Justice and the CIA had dotted the i's and crossed all the t's to make it seem that Francis Ackerman Jr. was a dead man.

The whole thing made him a bit sad.

Not because he was now officially dead and locked up in some CIA black site usually reserved for terrorists and national security threats. And not because of how easily a person could be erased or how quickly a person could be forgotten. And not because they had taken down his posters.

Ackerman was sad at how mundane and simple they had made his death. He hated the way they had perverted his legacy, and he felt a burning to right that wrong.

His death should have been shocking and theatrical. He had even made some suggestions to what that might look like, but they had ignored him and carried out their own quaint little plans. Small minds, small thoughts.

They had faked a death scene with two cops pulling over a stolen car and being forced to take down the murderer behind the wheel. One of the most prolific and feared killers in the history of modern society, and they concoct a tale where two average state troopers gun him down over a routine traffic stop.

It was insulting, and a stain upon his memory and reputation.

But he supposed none of what he had done to build that reputation mattered now. All that mattered was being a good lab rat and staying alive long enough for his brother to get him out of this place, so that he could do what he had been born to do—hunt and kill.

The room was cold and gray and old, and the fluorescent lighting buzzed overhead like a bug zapper. The whole black site smelled like old paper and ink, like dust and graphite. Maybe the place used to print newspapers or housed a defunct post office?

The door buzzed open, and the CIA technician entered the room. The tech wore a dark polo shirt and was a diminutive sort of person; not to say that he was tiny or fragile. In reality, he appeared to be in above average physical condition. Ackerman found the man small in a way that was less quantifiable, as if Agent Polo Shirt added no substance to the space or sucked something from it, like a black hole. Polo entered and sat down across from him; yet Ackerman still felt like he was the only living being in the room.

They hadn't taken any chances with his restraints this time. Ackerman had been straightjacketed, restrained to a stand-up gurney from his head to his feet, and masked to keep from biting. He supposed that his last demonstration of escape artistry had made an impression.

A week earlier, he had freed himself and had drawn a maniacal happy face on a different CIA technician. He had done it just to prove a point.

Although, Ackerman couldn't exactly recall what that point had been.

Regardless of such trivial details, he felt a sense of

warmth recalling the event. A fond memory. The previous tech had cried for his family and begged for his life. Ackerman couldn't remember the man's name. Something beginning with an A. Austin, maybe? But he did remember how quickly Austin had lost control of his bladder. That had been good fun.

As Ackerman's gaze fell over the new tech, he wondered if this man would instead beg to be put out of his own misery. Agent Polo Shirt was talking to him; perhaps even trying to establish some connection with him or dominance over him. Ackerman couldn't tell which and didn't care.

"I won't answer any questions from this man. Roland, send me a different one." Ackerman shifted his eyes toward the two-way mirror, knowing that the tech's supervisor, Roland Green, was watching. He also knew that his old friend, Emily Morgan, occupied the space beyond the glass. "Better yet, Roland, just send in Emily. I'll do the test with her. The pod person here can still handle the machines, but I won't participate if I have to answer questions from him."

The tech finished hooking up all the medical equipment and monitors to Ackerman's body and then tried to continue with the test but, true to his word, Ackerman ignored Agent Polo Shirt.

Instead, he went inside himself. He imagined a huge hydroelectric dam bursting and flooding an entire small town. He watched the townsfolk being swept away and pinballing down the streets and alleyways, slamming into concrete walls and being impaled on tree branches. He watched an old man clawing the water for one last gasp of air. He watched a young mother futilely try to shove her children free from the smacking lips of the waves.

"Ackerman? Did you go to sleep on us, boy?"

Ackerman opened his eyes. "Good morning, Roland. So good to hear the smooth Texas twang of your voice. I just like the way that voice makes me feel. It brings to mind old Western movies. Hearing you speak makes me want to be a cowboy."

He intentionally tried to insert the CIA man's name as much as possible. It was a bit of a trick to keep Agent Green off balance. Ackerman had faintly heard someone in the corridor beyond the interrogation room call the agent in charge of the lab rat phase of his incarceration by his first name. Roland. The agent had introduced himself to Ackerman with his last name only without offering his first. This small nugget of information gave Ackerman a certain power over Agent Green. He could see the wheels turn in the other man's eyes every time he referred to him by that first name. Green would try to assume that the killer had just overheard it, or he had somehow let it slip, but he wouldn't know for sure. And, consciously or subconsciously, that question would gnaw at the back of Roland Green's mind.

Did Ackerman know where he lived? Where he slept? Where his kids went to school?

It was delicious.

Roland Green locked eyes with Ackerman and then gestured toward the technician. "What's wrong with him?" Green said.

Ackerman replied, "He depresses me, Roland. Just look at him. His eyes are like leaches. Stare at them too long, and they'll suck out your soul."

Green faced the tech, looked at him a moment, and

said, "Fair enough." Then he added, "I don't see the harm in letting her ask you the questions while the technician monitors the equipment, but if you cross me on this or try anything, if you so much as make her teary eyed, then the deal you have with the CIA is over. Do we understand each other?"

"Am I irritating you, Roland?"

"Of course not. Seeing you is the highlight of my day, Mr. Ackerman. Now, do we understand each other?"

"Carl Jung said, 'Everything that irritates us about others can lead us to an understanding of ourselves.'"

Roland Green nodded his head slowly for a moment and then said, "I'm just going to pretend you said 'yes' and move on. Emily, come on in."

Green pointed at Ackerman as he left and added, "Don't forget what I said."

"Of course not, Roland. To me your every word is like a drop of rain to a desert flower."

Roland raised his eyebrows and shook his head. "Whatever that means." The door opened, and Roland and Emily passed each other in its threshold. "You sure he ain't crazy, Doc?"

Emily tilted her head and said, "Crazy is a broad term used by the general populace, not a diagnosis. So it becomes a matter of perspective and definition."

The gray-haired Texan just nodded and said, "Sure thing, Doc."

Emily moved toward a pair of metal chairs which had been bolted to the floor–Ackerman had taught them that lesson as well. Agent Polo Shirt shifted over a seat as Emily slid into the chair directly facing Ackerman.

Emily's movements reminded Ackerman of a Siamese cat he had once seen in the home of a victim. It was the way he imagined a feline princess would move–confident but not boastful. Powerful. Graceful. But gentle. All at once.

Her features were pale with an odd mix of Asian and Irish heritage. Her skin was flawless and smooth like a child's. Like the harmful rays of the sun had never touched her skin.

If he recalled correctly, she had an Irish grandfather and a Japanese grandmother. Ackerman wondered when he had learned that piece of information.

Had Emily let that slip during one of her recent counseling sessions with him? Or had her husband told him that before Ackerman had murdered him?

He supposed that neither the source of that knowledge nor Emily's heritage mattered. What did matter was that he found Emily fascinating.

He had killed her husband, nearly killed her, and used her as human bait. Yet, she had always treated him with respect and had never shown him hatred. Actually, she had become a staunch ally in his brother's crusade to keep him alive and for him to be used as a resource in the hunt for other killers.

Perhaps by rehabilitating Ackerman she would give greater meaning to her husband's death? Perhaps she just wanted to make sure nothing like that ever happened to another family? Or maybe she just wholeheartedly believed in teachings of forgiveness and the turning of the other cheek?

Whatever it was, Ackerman found it remarkable. He found her remarkable. Unlike the way Polo Shirt sucked life from the space, she brightened it. She filled it with some kind of ethereal grace.

"I think I'm annoying poor Roland."

"I know what you're trying to do by using his first name."

"Whatever do you mean?"

"You're establishing dominance. Stealing power from him and bestowing it on yourself. With you, it's always about power. That and pain. Establishing power, experiencing pain in one form or another."

"You say all that as if I've never done any self-exploration of my own feelings and motives. I've lived most of my life in a cage. I've had ample time to plum my own depths."

"I never claimed otherwise. I was simply making an observation. Here's another. I know that your little trick with Special Agent Green's first name is very mundane in origin."

"How can you be so sure that I don't just know more about this facility than any of you could possibly imagine?"

"Because if it was something clever, you wouldn't have been able to resist telling us all about it by now."

Ackerman smiled. "I've missed you, Emily."

"I've been busy with other obligations."

"Obligations in regard to counseling or your field agent training?"

Emily had been given a counseling job within the Shepherd Organization after the courage she had displayed in her last encounter with him. It made sense. She had been a therapist in her pre-Ackerman life, and the Shepherd Organization was almost entirely made up of people who had displayed certain qualities during run-ins with serial killers. She fit right in as the counselor that this group desperately needed. But the thoughtful and deep-thinking Emily Morgan had shocked him by instead pursuing a position as a field agent. In fact, the argument of how to use Ackerman best had opened up another debate over the possibilities for Emily to serve as his liaison and babysitter.

"Obligations that are none of your concern," Emily said as a statement of fact, without a hint of emotion on the subject one way or another.

"Was it about the boy?" Ackerman said. "I hear he's having trouble adjusting to the new school."

Emily said, "His mother was murdered by your father, his grandfather. Then he was brainwashed and nearly killed by the same man. He's having a hard go of it after all that. I'm sure you can relate to how he's feeling."

Of course he could relate. Dylan's experience mirrored his own in many ways. Except that Dylan missed out on all the torture and manipulation for years on end.

"The boy needs to learn from the experience. Let it mold him. Make him stronger. We can't allow him to be a victim of his circumstance."

She held up a hand. "Let me handle the therapy. In your communication with Dylan, you should remain a positive, supportive listener. Nothing more. I monitor every word between the two of you. Every gesture. And if I ever have even the slightest suspicion that you are attempting to manipulate Dylan in any way, then your privileges with him will be revoked."

Ackerman involuntarily gritted his teeth. He hated that his jailers had something to hold over his head. He didn't like having something to lose.

He changed the subject. "So what new technology or technique is the CIA testing on me today? Are these electrodes to shock me or read my mind?"

"Neither," Emily said. "Nothing so dramatic. They're refining their new lie detection algorithms based upon the last test they did with you."

"That's a shame. I had been hoping for some electric shocks."

Agent Polo Shirt told Emily that they were ready to begin. With a nod, she glanced at her clipboard. Apparently, there was a list of predesigned questions she was supposed to ask. She said, "What species are you?"

Ackerman cleared his throat and said, "I am a meat Popsicle from the planet Galaktron."

Polo Shirt swore under his breath and said, "According to the system, he's telling the truth."

Emily said, "Just to be completely clear, I am directing these questions to Francis Ackerman Jr. and expecting a statement of fact in answer to my question. Mr. Ackerman, do you understand what we are doing and what is expected of you?"

Ackerman chuckled. Emily must have been trying to verify that he wasn't using some kind of mind trick or distancing to confuse the CIA's high-tech new toy. "I understand," he said. "And I, Francis Ackerman Jr., do hereby forswear to answer your questions to the best of my abilities and with the utmost respect and the most unimpeachable honesty."

"He's telling the truth," Agent Polo Shirt said.

Emily continued with the questions. "Please state your name and occupation." She rolled her eyes, possibly at the question's absurdity.

"I am the Ingenious Gentleman Don Quixote of La Mancha. And I am a knight."

Polo shirt sighed and said, "Telling the truth."

Ackerman watched hungrily as a ghost of a smile passed over Emily Morgan's porcelain features before she continued on to the next question.

As he climbed the ladder of Tower 3, a strange memory struck Ray Navarro. It was of his son. Ray had been sitting on their front porch after finishing the mowing, and a green blur had come zooming down the road. His little boy, in a bright green T-shirt, running full blast, and tugging along their cocker spaniel puppy, the dog's legs struggling to keep up with those of his son, Ian. A son he would probably never see again.

As Ray placed one hand in front of the next, his wedding ring kept clanging against the metal of the rungs. The echoes of metal on metal trickled down the concrete walls of Tower 3 like water. Each high-pitched sound sent shockwaves of regret and doubt down through Ray's soul.

He felt like the world was upside down, and he was actually climbing down into hell instead of ascending Tower 3 at Foxbury Correctional Treatment Facility.

The prison was actually an old work camp and mental hospital, which had recently been recommissioned as part of a pilot program for a private company's experimental prison. All of the guards, including himself, had been warned about the unique working conditions inside Foxbury. The program was voluntary. He had known the risks, but the money was just too good to pass up. He had bills to pay and mouths to feed.

Ray Navarro pushed open the hatch in the floor of the crow's nest and pulled himself up into the ten-by-ten space of the tower. The little room smelled like cigarettes, even though no one was supposed to smoke up there. A tiny window air conditioner squeaked and rumbled in the tower's back wall. He shed his jacket and rolled up his sleeves. The gun case was bolted to the left wall of the crow's nest. With almost robotic, instinctual movements, he watched himself unlock the case, grab the 30-06 rifle, and insert cartridges loaded with just the right mixture of chemicals and shrapnel, fire and steel, needed to blow a one-inch hole in a person's flesh. He had always excelled in the use of high-powered, long-range weapons. A pistol and a tactical shotgun also occupied the tower's gun cabinet. He was rated as an expert in their use as well, but he had taken to the 30-06 like a boy's hand to a well-oiled baseball glove.

Ray Navarro extended the rifle's bipod and started searching the prison yard for his first target.

The scope's line of sight slid effortlessly over each man's face. He noticed a pair of the prison's celebrity inmates. Leonard Lash, the infamous gang leader awaiting execution, and Oren Kimble, the madman responsible for a mall shooting five years ago. Then his eye stopped on two of the guards moving along the perimeter of inmates like cowboys watching over the herd. The men seemed to be having an in-depth conversation, a wiser silver-haired mentor teaching a younger pupil. He knew the older black man well. Bill Singer was a war veteran and a former sniper, just like Ray. When Ray returned from his last tour, he had been lost in doubt and fear and hadn't known where to turn. Until he had met Bill. Now, Ray Navarro was five years sober and had even patched things up with his wife, who had come very close to being an ex-wife before Bill had started counseling him.

Bill wasn't supposed to be on duty until Sunday, but something must have changed because there was his friend giving what seemed to be a mini-sermon to his younger counterpart.

The younger white man beside Bill, Jerry Dunn, had just come on with them. Jerry walked with a catch in his gait which made it seem like three of his steps were equal to two of a normal man's, but that wasn't the only aspect of Jerry Dunn which had earned him the nickname "Gimp" among his fellow correctional officers. Jerry also blinked about four times more than a normal person and often struggled to spit out more than a sentence or two.

Ray had no problem with Jerry and even felt sorry for the way many of the other guards treated him. A minor limp and a few tics didn't mean that Dunn couldn't do his job and, by all accounts, the young CO was more than competent.

Ray prayed that the next person up the tower's ladder after him wouldn't be Bill Singer or Jerry Dunn. Although, he didn't really want it to be anyone else either. It was one thing to kill enemy soldiers or even an inmate if there was no other choice. This was different. This was the outright murder of men who were his coworkers, his friends.

Ray threw up all over the floor of Tower 3.

He cursed under his breath and then said, "It's them or you."

He re-acquired his target. Slid the crosshairs over the man's heart and then up to his head. Normally, he would go for the chest, a larger target capable of accomplishing the same task. But since this was quite possibly one of his very last acts on the planet, he figured there was no harm in showing off and going for the true killshot.

"It's them or you."

He kept repeating that phrase like a mantra, over and over.

"It's them or you."

Bill Singer watched Jerry limp along in front of him. The more he watched, the more he noticed that the limp didn't seem to slow Jerry down a bit. Bill realized that from Jerry's perspective each step may have been painful or at the very least require twice as much effort. At his age, Bill realized the importance of pain management and the economy of movement, the debts that needed paying for each step, each incorrect dietary choice, each year with no trips to the gym, each time you tried to do something that you did easily ten years ago.

Knowing the difficulties faced by Jerry having been forced to start his life with inherent setbacks in that arena, Bill felt a soft spot for the kid and had taken the younger guard under his wing. Bill and his wife had neglected to have children, but he considered himself blessed to have some young men he had mentored who had become like sons to him. Jerry Dunn was one of those adopted sons. Another was Ray Navarro, who Bill knew was on overwatch in Tower 3 at that very moment. Then there were several others whom he had met through his volunteer work down at the clinic with his wife, Caroline.

Jerry Dunn actually reminded Bill more of one of those counseling patients than a correctional officer like Ray Navarro. Jerry was a wounded orphan while Ray was a wounded warrior. Both real problems that were no fault of either man, but whose differences were evident in each man's demeanor.

Jerry had shared his story around a table of hot wings and beers on the first night Bill met him. The kid had blinked ten times and twitched twice before explaining that his parents had been killed in a car accident when he was only eight months old.

Some of the others had sympathized but continued to mock Jerry behind his back. And, of course, there were a few assholes in the group, who referred to Jerry as Gimp even to his face. Bill had gone a different way. He had befriended the young officer quickly and learned that whatever its cause, Jerry lived with a lot of pain in his heart.

Jerry Dunn halted his half-gait mid-stride and turned on his heels to face the yard. Bill shook his head at the younger man's appearance. Jerry's shaggy, black, stick-straight hair hung over his ears and looked as if it hadn't been combed in days. Jerry's skin was as pale as Bill's was dark, and it had a certain smell about it. A mix of body odor and a cheap deodorant that acted as a substitute for bathing.

Jerry said, "I'm bored senseless. Let's make a bet. I bet you two bucks that the two big Aryan brotherhood type guys right there. See them, one benching a million pounds and the other spotting him and looking disinterested. I bet you two bucks that the big guy doesn't get it up and the smaller guy either makes fun of him about it or he barely even notices that the big guy dropped the thing on his chest."

Bill followed Jerry's gaze and shook his head again. This time at the younger man's assessment of the situation. Bill said, "I'll take that bet, but let's make it twenty bucks."

Jerry seemed worried by this raising of the stakes, but not worried enough to keep from saying, "You're on."

Bill let his gaze linger on the ABs and watched the scene play out just as he suspected it would. The bigger man dropped the bar, but his spotter didn't even let the bar touch the other man's chest before snatching it up onto the rack.

Bill said, "The spotter wasn't looking away because he wasn't paying attention. He was looking away because he was scanning the yard for threats."

"But they don't need to do that here. There are no physical threats."

"Old habits."

Crestfallen, Jerry continued along the perimeter, and Bill followed in step beside him.

"This group of one hundred," Bill said, referring to the first wave of prisoners being transferred to the refurbished and repurposed Foxbury prison, "has had to form bonds quickly in order to maintain their dominance when the next wave hits. I know we've only been here a few months, but I'm shocked that no one has been killed yet. This new 'experimental model' gives these guys way too much freedom."

As the bigger Aryan rose from the bench and took his place as spotter, the two locked fists, held the embrace for a breath, and released each other with a final squeeze of the shoulder. A strangely intimate public gesture that stretched the limits of the physical contact allowed at Foxbury. They may have even felt the jolt of a warning shock. Maybe that was the point. To bond through a little shared pain.

"It's in their nature to join together into packs. They're a group of hungry wolves thrown into a pen. The laws of nature take over. They're going to gang up and start establishing bonds and hierarchy. I don't care what they claim about this software and technology and cameras. It's nature of the beast out here. Always has been, always will be. Someone's going to get this place's number. There isn't a security system in the world that can't be bypassed. If one guy's smart enough to design it, then there's another guy out there hungry enough to bypass it."

"So far, it seems to be working. I think it's a glimpse of what the prison of the future could look like."

"Don't drink the Kool-Aid just yet. It's only been six months, kid. Trust me. 'So far' doesn't last that long."

Bill glanced back at the big Aryan, now standing solemn guard over his comrade like a stone sentinel.

Then Bill watched the big Aryan's head split down the middle. He saw the blood a heartbeat before he heard the crack of a high-powered rifle.

A millisecond of held breath followed the first man's death. A fraction of a heartbeat when the fight or flight instincts of every inmate twitched toward fight. After all, these men were all fighters in one way or another. It made time seem frozen somehow.

Then everyone, all at once, realized what had happened.

The inmates dropped to the ground, as they had been taught, and the guards struggled to keep their wits.

Bill analyzed the situation, years of training and drills all floating to the surface of his personal sea of memories. The training kicked in and won the battle over his instincts.

An inmate must have been putting the life of a guard in danger. That was the only reason a tower guard would have opened fire. His gaze had just enough time to slide over the yard, searching for what he had missed, when the second shot rang out.

This time one of the inmates with his belly to the ground jerked wildly and then lay still, a spray of blood splattering the man to his left.

Bill tried to work it out. Why would a tower guard shoot an inmate lying on the ground?

Unless this was something more.

An entirely different set of training and drills took over— from before he became a correctional officer, from back when he was a young army recruit—and those military-issued instincts helped Bill immediately recognize what this really was. A sniper attack. They were under assault.

"Everyone up!" Bill screamed. "Get inside the buildings. Get to cover!" The throng of prisoners scattered as they scrambled to find protection. The sound of a third shot spurred their legs to pump harder.

Bill didn't see the third man fall, but he did see from where the shot had originated. He had looked to the towers and walls first, scanning for the shooter. And up in Tower 3, he saw a man who looked like Ray Navarro, eye to his rifle, lining up another shot.

The yard was, looking down from above, the shape of

a giant stop sign. Guard towers topped four of the outer vertexes. The safety of the prison's main buildings was in the distance to Bill's left. But Tower 3 and the sniper who had become like a son to Bill was closer on the right.

Safety or friendship.

When Bill had served his tour of duty, he had learned and believed that it was all about the man on your right and on your left, your brothers.

Safety or friendship.

Saving his own ass or trying to keep his friend from being killed. The decision was an easy one for Bill Singer. Not even a choice really. Just another instinct; a natural result of all he'd learned and experienced.

He ran toward Tower 3.

Access to the outer perimeter of the yard and the guard towers was made possible via a barred gate in the old stone wall. The problem was that the gate was actually more modern than its surroundings, and it had no locks or keys. It could only be opened by one of the watchers—the name the guards had bestowed on the computer techs who constantly monitored the prison's thousands of cameras through some kind of special software. Amid the chaos of the yard, among the disorder of one hundred men running for their lives, one of those watchers would have to notice him and buzz him through the gate.

It was a long shot. Not to mention that he had to put himself squarely in Ray's crosshairs—if that really was Ray up there—just to reach the gate.

The Ray he knew would never fire on him. But the Ray he knew would never fire on anyone. If it really was Ray, then it wasn't the Ray he knew, and he had no way of anticipating the actions of this robot that had taken Ray's place, this creature that seemed to walk in Ray's skin.

Bill wasn't really surprised to see a pair of the other guards having the same idea. A pair of energetic thirty-something guards who Bill knew as Trent and Stuart were already pounding their fists on the shiny aluminum gate and shouting up at one of the prison's legion of cameras.

To his surprise, Bill was still twenty feet from the gate when he heard the buzz and clank of the lock disengaging. Big brother was watching. The other pair of guards pushed through and ran out of his view, but he knew where they were headed. He shot a glance to Tower 3 as he ran toward the now-open gate.

Ray had disappeared from the tower's window. Whether the shooting was over or Ray was just reloading, Bill couldn't be sure, but he did know that things would go better for his young friend if he was the first one up that ladder.

Bill shouted at the other guards to wait, to let him go up first, but he was so winded from the sprint across the yard that he couldn't make the sound come out with as much force as he wanted.

The younger guards didn't stop their assault. "Wait!" he shouted. The thought of Ray attacking the guards and escalating the situation spurred him forward, pumping his adrenaline to the next level.

Bill caught the gate before it could swing shut and relatch. He rounded the corner of the wall toward Tower 3 and looked up just as the parapet of the tower exploded in a searing ball of glass and fire.

★ ★ ★

The concussion wave slammed Bill to the ground like a swatted fly. Blackened and flaming chunks of concrete rained down around him. He looked back at Tower 3, and his eyes struggled to regain focus. The midday sun hung in the sky directly behind the watchtower. It looked to Bill as if the sun had simply absorbed the parapet of Tower 3 like some giant fiery PAC-MAN. He held his gaze into the sun just long enough to see that the tip of Tower 3 was gone, as if the crow's nest was the top of a dandelion blown away and scattered to the wind, there and then not.

He was still disoriented by the blast wave. His vision blurred and then came back into focus. Blurred and focused. Then, through the haze, Bill saw Ray Navarro stumbling toward the opening in the stone wall, heading back to the main building.

It was Ray. Bill was sure of it. Not some impostor or impersonator, but his friend. Had the kid completely snapped?

If something was happening in Ray's life that could have driven him to this, then Bill had no clue what it could have been. Maybe the kid had some kind of PTSD flashback? He couldn't have been in his right mind.

Bill's hearing suddenly returned. One second, it was a high-pitched ringing, a shrill otherworldly sound. Then the sound quickly merged back with the real world. The screams brought Bill back to the moment. He crawled, then stumbled, then ran toward the sound of the screaming. One of the men who had beaten him to the tower was on fire. He didn't see the other.

The man, or more of a boy to Bill's old eyes, rolled feebly

on the ground to smother the flames. Bill could smell the man's flesh cooking. It reminded him of sizzling bacon.

Bill shoved his hands through the flames to get to the boy. Just enough contact with the fire to singe off all the hair on Bill's arms, but also just enough contact with the boy's torso to shove him into a full roll.

He helped extinguish the last of the flames and then rolled the kid onto his back. His face was charred. He couldn't stop crying and coughing. And Bill could think of nothing he could do to help.

The sound of boots crushing sand and gravel announced the arrival of more guards. One pushed Bill back and started performing CPR on the burned man.

Bill hadn't even noticed that the kid had stopped breathing. He felt suddenly disoriented, as if he had just woken up from a bad dream, and his mind was struggling to realign with reality. All he could hear was the ringing, and it seemed to be growing in volume, swelling toward a climax.

He bent over and threw up. What could Ray have been thinking? Had he seen Ray heading back toward the prison? Had that been real? If so, where was Ray going? Had his young friend done this and then was trying to sneak away in the confusion?

Bill ran back toward the gate. The other guards shouted something about needing help, but Bill ignored them. He moved with a singular focus now.

One emotion drove him forward. Anger. One thought fueled his anger. That could have been me.

If Ray had premeditated this—and he obviously had, because he must have brought some kind of explosives with him and had at least some semblance of an escape plan—then that meant that Ray had no way of knowing who would have been the next person through that hatch. It could have been anyone. It could very easily have been Bill.

A few steps closer or a few seconds faster, and it would have been him.

His friend had nearly taken his life; he had nearly taken him away from Caroline.

That didn't sit right with him and, at the very least, he was going to find out why.

The yard was almost evacuated, and Bill couldn't miss Ray moving toward the north barracks.

He lowered his head and ran harder, trying to close the gap between them.

Ray didn't look back, didn't check over his shoulder once. As if not looking at the destruction he had caused would make it less real, less horrifying. As if guilt and shame wouldn't catch him if he refused to acknowledge them.

The anger fueled Bill even more—the anger awakened something in him. Something that he hadn't felt since his army days. He could still smell the young guard's burning flesh. He could still hear his screams.

He closed the last of the gap in a dive, driving his shoulder into Ray's back and sending them both sprawling onto the concrete of a basketball court.

Ray was first to his feet. He held a Glock pistol, probably stolen from the gun cabinet of Tower 3.

"Stay back," Ray said.

"What have you done?"

"I said stay back!"

"Why?"

Bill's voice cracked as he took a step toward the man

he had spent countless hours counseling and guiding back toward sanity.

"Back," Ray said, retreating toward the barracks.

"You tell me why!"

"I'm sorry. I'm glad you're okay."

"Glad I'm okay? I could have been killed. And what about the others you just murdered?"

"I can't. . ." Ray shook his head and turned to run.

Bill stared at him a moment, dumbfounded.

It looked like the Ray he knew. The voice was the same. The look in his eyes. But the Ray he knew would never have done something like this. Did he have the capability? Sure. Ray was a former soldier. He had killed in combat. This was different. This was the visceral act of an animal with its back to the wall. This was the final attack of a dying predator.

What could have possibly driven Ray to such a desperate, animalistic decision?

Ray had taken three big strides toward the barracks before Bill made up his mind that Ray Navarro wasn't leaving the yard.

Bill closed the distance between them in two huge strides. He threw all of his weight and momentum into a single blow. He hurled himself at Ray like a locomotive of flesh and bone. He aimed one huge punch directly at the back of Ray's head. He would hit Ray hard with one sucker punch that would instantly knock him out. The fight would be over before it began.

But Ray ducked the punch at the last second and spun around, the gun still in his hand.

Bill immediately recognized his mistake. An old drill

instructor's words floated back to him from the ether of his memory.

Go for the body. The head is too small a target that can move and shift too easily.

Bill immediately knew the consequence of not heeding that advice.

The gun flashed.

Bill saw the shock and horror in Ray's eyes.

He felt the warmth of the blood leaving the wound before actually feeling the pain of the puncture. He fell back to the concrete.

The ringing in his ears was fading away but leaving only silence in its place.

He heard the shouts of other guards telling Ray to get down. He closed his eyes. At least he had stopped Ray from escaping and hurting anyone else or himself.

Bill Singer heard the ringing. Then more shouting. Then the ringing again. And then nothing at all.

Marcus Williams kept seeing the knife plunging into the man's body. The warm redness gushing out. Blood splattering his face. Maggie screaming. The look in her eyes.

"Special Agent Williams?" the receptionist said. Her tone implied this was not her first attempt at rousing him. He must have dozed off.

"Yes, sorry," Marcus said.

"The deputy AG will see you now," she said.

He stood, and she guided him into Deputy Attorney General Trever Fagan's office. The space was cold and institutional and had a strange smell, like mint tea and cucumbers. It was free of any clutter and seemed to have been constructed with almost obsessive-compulsive attention to detail. Marcus supposed that to most people the decor and design would have appeared elegant and aesthetically pleasing. All of the elements for that were certainly in place. But those elements had been jammed in by force. It made the space seem as if it were designed by a committee or focus group rather than one person's sense of taste.

Fagan kept typing away at his computer's keyboard as they entered. He wore a blue pinstripe suit, and his hair was slicked back. It reminded Marcus of the pelt of a river otter he had seen as a kid at the Bronx Zoo.

The receptionist closed the double doors behind her. Once she was gone, Marcus tossed the file folder he had been carrying onto the immaculate surface of Fagan's desk. Marcus was sure to put a spin on the folder in such a way that its contents went spilling out onto the desk and the floor.

Fagan sighed and said in his New England accent, "How can I be of assistance, Special Agent Williams?" He still hadn't looked up from his typing.

"What the hell is this? I thought we had an understanding."

Fagan finally turned in his direction. "I told you that I understood your position, and we'd give it some thought. It was discussed and decided that, now that Ackerman can work off the substantial cost of his incarceration by cooperating with certain research endeavors from the CIA, he would be allowed to live."

"But he'll never see the light of day again."

"I'm not sure what part of all this you don't understand.

Your brother has killed a lot of people. He doesn't get a pass on that just because now you're a happy family."

"My father experimented on Ackerman's brain and put him through hell. He was forced into being what he is."

"Those facts don't dismiss the reality that he is what he is and has done what he's done."

"No, they don't. And no one is saying that Ackerman gets a completely free pass and we just drop him back into the world. But he is in the unique position to make amends, or at least attempt some semblance of that. We hunt serial killers, and we already break just about every rule in the book to achieve that end goal. Putting Ackerman to work pretty much goes right along with our SOP."

"Your brother is a dangerous man. It doesn't matter how that happened. It doesn't matter that he's been able to stop himself from murdering everyone he meets for a little while now. If I had approved your proposal, it might have been a day from now or a year from now, but he would have eventually cut the throats of you and your team and slipped off into the night."

Marcus sat down on the edge of one of Fagan's white leather chairs, so that he could look the bureaucrat in the eye. "We would have the new NSA tracking chip with the kill option embedded in his spine. If he turns on us, we put him down remotely. His experience and knowledge can save countless lives."

Fagan leaned back, steepled his fingers, and said, "I believe that the police and FBI do a wonderful job of protecting us. In extreme cases, the Shepherd Organization steps in. I see no situation extreme enough for me to ever allow Francis Ackerman Jr. back onto the street. What would you say to the families of his victims? Do you think they would approve of just leashing him up and sending him out on the trail like an old hunting dog?"

"Emily is his doctor and would be there to monitor him. She is one of his victims. And she's in favor of this."

"Emily's a unique case, and you know it."

"Yes, but she understands that Ackerman truly wants to do what's right. Aren't those victims' memories better served by having Ackerman help make sure that more families don't have to feel that same kind of pain and loss?"

Fagan stood and stepped toward his office door. Marcus remained seated. Fagan said, "The decision has been made. If you want to consult with him on a case, that's fine. But Francis Ackerman Jr. stays in a cage."

Then, without a word or gesture of a goodbye or a follow-me, Fagan just walked out of the office.

Marcus was dumbfounded for a moment, refusing to follow Fagan, refusing to give the other man the power and satisfaction that came with making Marcus chase after him.

To the empty space, Marcus said, "That's one way to end a conversation."

He sat there alone until he couldn't take it any longer, and then he ran after Fagan.

Francis Ackerman Jr. blocked a right cross meant to take his head off. Then he went low for a rabbit punch to his opponent's groin.

At this point, his imaginary opponent would have doubled over, and Ackerman would have driven the imaginary man's nose into his imaginary brain. He liked to visualize while working out, and this gave him extra time to perfect a number of killing strikes and combinations.

His knuckles were stained bloody from the pounding of his fists against the four-and-a-half-inch-thick, clear polycarbonate material. The pain was gloriously excruciating, and it sent new tendrils of agony out with every increasingly fast blow. The pain grew to a crescendo, and he slowed his pace and ferocity. Prolonging the agony. Savoring the anguish. Then he exploded with machine-gun punches until his muscles could no longer sustain the punishment his brain desired. When he felt his vision growing dim, he dropped to the floor in a heap of blood and sweat.

Ackerman had been aware of the two men observing his workout, and only now did he acknowledge their presence. He said, "Hello, brother. And Mr. Fagan. To what do I owe the pleasure?"

Fagan said, "Your brother convinced me that, before I make up my mind about what to do with you, I should come down and hear what you have to say."

Ackerman licked some of the blood from his knuckles as he regained his feet. "I always have lots to say. Give me a topic."

"How about a question?"

"Be careful, Trever. We're getting dangerously close to this turning into a game." Ackerman's grin widened. "And I'm very competitive."

"Questions or not?"

"Ask."

"Why are you punching the glass like that?"

"Mental and physical training."

"Are you going to war? You seem like you're training to kill someone."

"War and battle are funny things. They have an uncanny ability for finding warriors. So a warrior must be ever vigilant."

"And that's what you are? A warrior?"

"Since birth. My brother and I were born to walk the path of the warrior. That's the nature side of the equation. When nurture came in for me, it was in the form of a deranged father. For Marcus, it was in the form of a cop. We were born into different circumstances, but we both still possessed the warrior spirit. We turned out differently, but some things are constant. We both hunt. We both kill. Et cetera, et cetera. The thing about nature versus nurture is that in the real world, those two concepts are so intricately intertwined that they are indistinguishable from one another. Nature starts us off into a world filled with societal, economical, and philosophical differences and hardships. All those things are beyond our control and beyond the control of even our caregivers. And guess what? The sins of the father most definitely do apply to the son. And not just the sins of the father, but the father's father. Generations. Sins of the government. Sins of your race or class. All those are dumped on our heads at birth. And there's no amount of water you can sprinkle over a baby's head to wash away those transgressions. They're part of us. Part of who we are. And from birth, nature handed my brother and me a shit sandwich with a side of crazy."

Fagan checked his watch and said, "And we should just overlook all those past sins because now you're sorry? Now that you've found God, it's all better?"

"Absolutely not. But you should be enlightened enough to not hold those sins against me to the point that you won't allow me to pay penance for them."

"There is no forgiveness for the things you've done, Mr. Ackerman."

"I'm not trying to earn earthly forgiveness. I don't need it. Forgiveness is divine. And I believe that God has already given me all the forgiveness and grace I require."

"Then why worry about paying any penance or attempt to right any of your sins?"

"We're all trapped on the same life raft together, waiting for God to rescue us up to the next plane of existence. Call it Heaven. Call it whatever you like. Believe whatever you like. The point is that we're all trapped on the same life raft together, the same confined, limited existence. And it is a finite existence that we share with millions of other souls. The question is, on this life raft we all share, what kind of passenger do you want to be?"

"So what kind of passenger do you want to be, Mr. Ackerman?"

"We are all the sum of our parts. We are the collection of billions of thoughts and experiences and lessons and difficulties and sins, those from our own lifetime and those of our ancestors. That's the setup of God's plan for our lives. A plan that has led us to our own personal way of thinking and to the point in our life's journey where we find ourselves now, at this moment."

Fagan said, "You're dancing around the question I have for you with philosophy. I asked, 'What kind of passenger do you want to be?' On this life raft you described, this limited existence, why should I let a madman who has been going around throwing others off the boat for years, why should I ever let him have even a glimpse of freedom?"

"I believe that God has brought my brother and I to this point together for a reason. I believe that a divine presence, call it God, goodness, light, whatever, has given my brother and me this nature and this nurture and has led us here to use those experiences and gifts and ways of thinking in a manner beneficial to the other passengers on this big life boat we call Earth. That's how God wants me to pay my penance. By helping to protect others from men like me."

Fagan added, "And that desire has nothing to do with the fact that, to a man like you, hunting those killers and proving your superiority over them would sound like an awful lot of fun?"

Ackerman shrugged and said, "Whoever said penance can't be fun?"

Peter Spinelli already knew his face, and so Judas had decided to follow from a cautious distance. Thankfully, they were in a public place with plenty of opportunities to blend.

Peter was the technical genius who had designed the threat analysis software that made Warden Powell's new prison possible. The young tech's girlfriend had dragged him on the road to a tourist destination called Sedona, Arizona. Judas had heard someone call Sedona, with its red-rock desert landscape, one of the most beautiful destinations on the planet. It was also a haven for spiritualists and healers due to the supposed "vortexes" that were spread throughout the area.

Judas knew that Peter's girlfriend was fascinated by these vortexes. She fit the mold. Her hair was streaked in blue, and she wore combat boots with her sundress. Peter sported camo shorts and a Phish T-shirt.

Judas resented these stupid Americans and their selfish attitudes.

The gas money they used driving the hours to get here could have fed entire families in some countries. And all to pretend to feel some vortexes and purchase Native American jewelry.

Worst of all, they had forced him to make that drive as well in order to accomplish his mission.

And today was the only day this mission could have taken place. The timeline had to remain intact. If even one of the dominoes he had in place were moved, it could jeopardize the whole chain of events. Of course, he would adapt and improvise as the plan progressed, but he didn't like to improvise. He liked to have a plan. Set the script and stick to it.

Judas believed that the need for adaptation and improvisation simply meant that you had failed to see all of the angles during the planning stages. So if he had done his job correctly, every domino would fall into place on its own, naturally, inevitably. To adjust the plan was to admit failure. To admit his own fallibility. The best strategists thought at least ten steps ahead of their opponents, and he wanted his methods to be studied by historians someday. A deviation from the plan was not only an attack on him, but an attack on his legacy.

Peter's girlfriend tugged him by the hand through the crowded row of local shops selling everything from topaz southwestern jewelry to paintings and other art. The sweet aroma of cinnamon pretzels hung pleasantly in the air but was tainted by the acrid smoke of a passing car's exhaust. Honking and revving engines echoed around them as traffic flew past on Highway 89A, the drivers ever impatient to get to their next tourist destination or yoga session.

Judas looked around at the shoppers, oblivious to the danger that surrounded them, oblivious to the fact that human beings constantly teetered on the edge of death. And it was so easy to give them just a little push—they were so easy to manipulate. To use their fears and desires against them. To have the power to destroy them—or, if you were a true artist, encourage them to destroy themselves.

As he thought about this, he could feel his heart rate rising. He could feel himself losing control. He could sense the approaching storm cloud of rage. A rage not directed at the shoppers and families, but a fury directed at the person who caused all this to be necessary.

But for now, these selfish peasants would be surrogates for his wrath.

Plans were in motion, and poor, oblivious Peter Spinelli was the next domino that needed to be pushed over. And Judas had been itching to get his hands dirty again.

With a few long, quick strides, he closed the distance between himself and Peter, weaving through the crowd of shoppers. Peter was walking south along the edge of the sidewalk bordering the busy highway.

Judas slipped the coin and note into Peter's pocket, and then he tapped him on the shoulder.

Peter turned back, and his girlfriend's tugging hand slipped from his fingers. The girl didn't look to see why

Peter had released her hand. She just continued in search of her next trinket, the destination more important than the journey.

Peter didn't recognize Judas at first, but the tech genius's eyebrows furrowed with a hint of familiarity. Judas didn't blame Peter for his lack of recognition. After all, Judas was wearing prosthetics to keep anyone from turning in a description to a sketch artist.

"Hello, Peter. Enjoying your day off?" Judas said.

And there it was. A glimmer of recognition.

Peter knew his voice, as Judas had hoped. Peter's eyes lit up, and his head tilted to the side, his thought pattern likely traveling from recognition to confusion as he realized who he was looking at and wondering why the same man from work looked so different now.

It was important to Judas for Peter to know it was him. To realize who was doing this to him.

Judas could see the questions in Peter's eyes.

He shoved the slender, black blade into Peter's chest, puncturing the lung and heart, and the questions in those eyes intensified and then faded into nothingness.

Judas held on to that moment for as long as he could, and then he shoved Peter into traffic and slipped away into the crowd.

Special Agent Maggie Carlisle pulled the Camaro slowly to a stop beside the baseball field. The tires crunching and grinding gravel together reminded Maggie of the way life treated human beings, the way it had always treated her. By chewing her up and spitting her out. Despite all that, she had always been a steady optimist. She had always been a rock. But she didn't think she could keep up the facade much longer. Not after this latest news.

She bumped the tire against the concrete parking block. She put the car in first, killed the big block engine, and released the clutch. Then she dropped her head to the steering wheel and wept.

Maggie only allowed herself a few seconds of self-pity and then popped her head up and wiped at her eyes. She didn't want Marcus to ever see her like that. Vulnerable. Weak. Luckily, she never wore much makeup, and so her cheeks weren't streaked with black.

Leaning back against the leather of the headrest, she took several long, deep breaths and then stepped from the car. She slammed the door of Marcus's '69 Camaro much harder than she had intended. Something rattled and the car's frame issued a disturbing groan. She involuntarily winced and was glad Marcus wasn't with her. She wasn't in the mood for one of his lectures on the car being a piece of history and the cultural zeitgeist. Besides, she had been driving it more than Marcus had, since he had purchased his new Harley-Davidson motorcycle.

She suspected the motorcycle had something to do with looking cooler than the other dads on Dylan's team. But then again, what looked cooler than a black 1969 Camaro SS with red racing stripes? Maybe Marcus had just been watching too much of that TV show about the motorcycle club?

Dylan's baseball team was part of an outreach program designed to bring fathers and sons closer together by playing other teams made up of father-son duos. Marcus had been searching for a way to strengthen the bond between him and his son, and when he came across an article about the new program, he had seen the revival of one of his old passions as an opportunity to do just that.

But Maggie knew it would take a lot more than baseball to undo the damage done to Dylan and Marcus's relationship. Not to mention the damage done to the boy's psyche. She thought of her own issues, which stemmed from childhood trauma. And Dylan's story was much darker than hers.

In an attempt to rebuild his sick concept of family and legacy, Dylan's grandfather—Francis Ackerman Sr.—had tracked down a son Marcus hadn't even known existed and had used the boy and his mother as pawns to capture Marcus. After enduring months of torture, both psychological and physical, Marcus made it out alive. Dylan's mother hadn't been so lucky. Marcus had lost part of himself in the experience, but Dylan's mother had lost her life, which left Marcus caring for a son he'd never known and building a parental bond from scratch. Dylan had been ripped from his life, never to see his mother again, and then thrust into the care of strangers with matching DNA.

It was a good thing that the Shepherd Organization had a therapist on staff.

Maggie walked toward the bleachers but thought better of sitting on those infested boards, and so she stood beside the bleachers instead. She checked the scoreboard and discovered that the game was more than half over. Marcus and Dylan's team was down three runs.

She wasn't technically late because she hadn't planned on coming. She knew Marcus thought her reluctance to attend had something to do with Dylan but, in reality, she just didn't want to sit around with all the mothers and small children. She hadn't wanted to deal with all of that right in her face.

But this was different. She wasn't here to watch the game. She was on a mission.

The air smelled of hot dogs, popcorn, and sweat. The combination made her feel nauseous again. She had already thrown up once at the doctor's office, right after hearing the test results.

A nine-year-old boy from the opposing team threw a pitch to a counterpart from Dylan's team. Both of the boys' fathers were right there with them, helping them, personally coaching them. Then the fathers took the mound and plate and demonstrated the techniques they had been describing to their sons. It was sort of like job shadowing that allowed the dads and kids to have fun together.

Maggie enjoyed that it also reminded some of the more judgmental fathers what it was like to step up to the plate themselves and feel the anxious pressure of that moment. She liked nothing better than to watch some of those blowhard dads go down swinging.

And when Marcus was on the mound, that's what happened. Dads struck out. Even when Marcus was trying to let them hit, he still managed to fake them out somehow. Marcus had told her that he had almost gone to the minor leagues as a pitcher, but he had decided to go to the police academy instead. To hear him tell it, he knew that he wasn't good enough, and so he made the responsible choice. She knew better. Marcus never made the responsible choice.

Judging by the score, Marcus wasn't on the mound that day.

The dad at bat got a hit and loaded the bases. A high-pressure moment. Bases loaded. Down by three. Two outs.

She saw the coaches and umpires gesturing to each other and knew what was happening. It was an unwritten rule of the league that the fathers and sons would have the option to switch order if the sons didn't want to be forced into any type of high-pressure situation, in an effort to keep from crushing a boy's self-esteem when he wasn't ready.

Which meant Marcus would be up to bat next.

He wasn't quite as good a hitter as he was a pitcher. He always said that was why he was a Yankees fan, because in the American league, the designated hitter rule applied and pitchers didn't have to bat.

The other team brought in a new pitcher, and Maggie watched him warm up. He was impressive. His fastballs were fast. Breakers broke. And curves curved.

She recognized a former competitive athlete when she saw one. Perhaps even another former minor league prospect. Marcus, who was a pitcher not a hitter, was about to go head to head with another former MLB hopeful.

Maggie checked her watch. They had a few minutes to spare before their flight.

The receptionist at Sheriff Travis Hall's office was a perky little brunette, probably a cheerleader five or six years past her prime. She had big, exotic cheekbones and smelled like raspberries, because of her lip gloss, and peppermints, because of the little candies she was popping like they were made of pure cocaine.

Demon watched her with an ancient hunger as she bopped around the small waiting room.

With each step, he saw her body morph in size and shape. The flowers on her dress had come alive, hummed a couple of bars from a nursery rhyme, and gone back to being two-dimensional. People he knew weren't there kept following her around, encouraging him to tear her clothes off and rip her throat out at the same time. You need to know what her flesh tastes like. You need to know all of her.

Demon checked his watch and yawned. Damn jet lag.

It wasn't that he ignored the pleas of the Legion. He always listened to their council and heeded their advice.

Some were just disembodied voices. Not all of them encouraged violence or advised brutality. Some were even voices of reason. The demons didn't argue directly, but they often responded with opposing viewpoints.

None of the demons, however, advised mercy or kindness. None of the demons were "good." They just kept things in check with his larger goals. They helped him decide whether to kill someone right then or save them for later, or leave them alone completely if they weren't worth the time.

The perky receptionist was lucky. She wasn't worth the time. He had tasted so many others like her that he had lost count. He no longer worried about victims who weren't of the highest caliber. After so many years in the game, he had grown picky. But he had also grown patient and skilled at his craft.

The demons kept screaming in his ears, but he wasn't tempted to obey them or tell them to shut up. He had learned to be master over the Legion, not the other way around.

He was the Legion, and they were him.

Still, there was one voice which could silence all the others. One shadow who was master of them all and could take control for swift, decisive, and immediate action.

It had no name. It needed no name. The dark man was a shade. An eternal shadow, the color of a night sky.

It was always there.

Sometimes the dark man could only be seen from the corner of his eye. Sometimes it was just waiting somewhere in the background. Waiting and watching. Never speaking. Just hovering hungrily, patiently awaiting the next moment it could take control and bathe in blood.

The dark man was oblivious to the receptionist, and so Demon just sat there and waited for his appointment with the sheriff. His own assistant had phoned ahead and arranged for this meeting while he was still on the road.

The receptionist did her best not to look directly at his face, but she kept stealing glances in his direction. Her quick, curious stares didn't bother him. He was accustomed to people showing a morbid curiosity.

He could understand her position. How many times had a man wearing a ten-thousand-dollar suit with a face ravaged by scars walked through the doors of this small police station?

Demon estimated that about thirty-five percent of his face was covered with one kind of scar or another. The tissue over his left eye had been melted, but his vision hadn't been impaired. He had no eyebrows, which people always found alarming in some strange way. Knife wounds and slashes intersected most of the rest of his face, but the most prominent of the disfigurements was his Glasgow smile—a wound achieved by cutting the corners of a victim's mouth and then torturing them. When the victim screamed or moved, the wound would tear, ripping the person's face apart.

Demon's Glasgow smile stretched nearly from jawbone to jawbone. But it wasn't really straight across or even upturned like a smile. It looked more like a giant axe had cleaved the bottom of his head off at a slight angle.

His face made an impression on people, which was exactly what he didn't want. He didn't want to be noticed.

Well, some of the Legion did.

But only a small minority.

Still, he hated the fact that this perky brunette would remember him. Would probably even tell her friends about him. Would speculate on who he was and what happened to his face.

Such thoughts whipped the Legion into a frenzy. The demons chattered even more about the reasons this meeting was necessary, that this trip had been forced upon him in the first place. He knew they were right, and it was something the responsible party would answer for very soon.

Demon and the receptionist danced with their eyes for the next several minutes. Her staring, him catching her with his cold gaze, repeat and repeat. Then her phone rang, and she ushered him back to Sheriff Hall's office.

Demon had several reasons to meet with Sheriff Hall. The most important being that it was the will of the dark man.

Although the dark man never spoke to him, he could sense its will on a primal, ancient level. He could taste its hunger, its emotions, its anger.

And ever since this situation with Judas had developed, the dark man had been very angry and very hungry.

Marcus Williams took a couple of practice swings and then stepped up to the plate. He gave a tilt of his hat to Benny Stockman, the man on the pitcher's mound. Marcus had chatted with Benny once after a game and learned that Benny had played college ball but had injured his shoulder. Judging by the way he was throwing in his warm-up, that shoulder had healed up nicely.

Most of the time during these games, the dads had an unwritten rule: play at about forty percent, keep it noncompetitive. The reason they were there was the boys. It wasn't about showing off. It was about spending time with your son and leading by example.

But there was also an unwritten rule that, every once in a while, it was okay to show off a bit for your kid and make things interesting. It was just understood that you would let the other team have some warning, so that everyone knew to take their own games up a notch or two.

When the opposing team's coach had sent in Benny Stockman to relieve the starter even though they were ahead on the scoreboard, the coach had sent a very clear message—let's see the former prospects go head to head.

The coach of Dylan's team had laughed and told Dylan to let his dad bat first. Marcus had explained to the boy that the dads just wanted to see him and Benny Stockman go up against one another. He had wanted the boy to know that it wasn't that they thought he couldn't handle the pressure of the moment.

Now, standing at the plate, staring down Benny Stockman, a man who was at least five years younger than him, Marcus Williams thought of how outmatched he was in this duel.

Sure, both Benny and Marcus had once been above-average players who could have gone somewhere if fate had dealt them different hands, but what everyone seemed to be forgetting was that both Marcus and Benny were pitchers. Just because Marcus could throw one hell of a fastball didn't mean he could hit one.

Benny wound up and released the ball, and Marcus struck nothing but air. The umpire announced the strike, and Marcus felt a bit lightheaded. Probably just the adrenaline.

Then, before he really knew what was happening, another pitch was coming down the pipe. He swung and connected. He pushed through and pivoted and drove it deep but foul.

He held the aluminum bat up to his nose out of habit. As a boy, he had always loved the smell of a bat after a long foul ball, right after the lace's of the ball and the bat had rubbed together to create a little friction. The smell reminded Marcus of campfires and camping trips with his real dad.

Unfortunately, aluminum bats always smelled like dirt and metal.

Marcus stepped back out of the batter's box and gave Benny a nod of respect and a smile. He tried to maintain his macho bravado in front of everyone but, on the inside, he was feeling the weight of this moment.

He wasn't necessarily scared. It took a lot more than a baseball game to scare a man who hunted serial killers for a living.

He was just worried that he would never live up to his son's expectations or deserve his adoration. Most fathers were rewarded with that bond because they had always been there, had always been that protector and role model in their kid's life, but he'd missed out on that opportunity. And now he had to build that from scratch.

No one's life was in danger. No killer was on the loose. But Marcus felt the same rush as when he hunted a man.

He made up his mind that he couldn't fail Dylan in this moment. He needed to be the kind of father his son deserved. A man his son could be proud of.

Lately, he feared that he hadn't been doing a very good job of that. He had missed over half the practices for Dylan's team because of work. He suspected that he had missed over half of the rest of his time with Dylan during the past year as well.

It had always been a struggle to find time between his job—his calling—and his personal life, but now Dylan made the idea of finding balance a near impossibility.

Maybe this moment, this pitch, was his opportunity to gain back some ground.

He stepped up to the plate and cleared his mind. He analyzed Benny's previous pitches. He made what were probably hundreds of other small calculations and adjustments. All felt more than worked out. Variables quantified by experience and intuition.

He was ready.

The pitch came.

He swung.

He threw every ounce of grace and power in his body into that swing. He poured in all his hopes for a bond with his boy. Every dream of a family. He dumped them all in and converted them into the momentum of his bat.

He felt the weight of the ball strike the sweet spot.

Scooping up the weight and letting it ride the wave of his swing, he pivoted and drove it home.

The ball left his bat and soared over the left field wall.

Marcus rounded the bases to the cheers of the crowd and high fives of his teammates. The other team's first baseman even laughed and gave Marcus a fist bump.

But when he looked to the group of his teammates waiting to celebrate with him at home plate, he didn't see Dylan.

He scanned the faces again and then looked to the dugout. Dylan was standing inside, batting helmet cockeyed on his head, a baseball bat dangling limply from his left fist.

Marcus locked gazes with his son as he rounded third, but what he read in the boy's expression was not adoration or pride. In Dylan's eyes, Marcus saw only anger and accusation.

Demon took a seat in front of Sheriff Travis Hall's dark cherry desk. Through his eyes, the desk appeared to be made of rotting meat and writhing and pulsing with worms. There was a time in his life when he may have even asked someone what they saw, but now he had rooted himself within the real world by following social cues and considering the context of the people and things surrounding him. If it didn't make sense, then it probably wasn't real. And if it was real, then someone else in the room would notice too.

The problem came when Demon was alone, when he had nothing to occupy him, nothing to keep the Legion quiet and appeased. Those were the moments when he could never be quite sure what was real and what wasn't. Those were the moments when he couldn't maintain control and then usually the dark man would take over.

Now, however, sitting in front of the sheriff's desk, he knew that if the desk had been made of pulsing dead flesh, then the sheriff wouldn't have been working behind it. He grounded himself with the sheriff's opinion of reality and used that as an anchor.

Demon sat on the edge of the chair like a coiled snake. The scars on his face didn't seem to bother Sheriff Hall, who had the look of a man who had seen the face of death before. Hall looked him straight in the eyes and said, "So how can I help?"

Demon tried to remember what excuse his assistant would have given to set up this meeting. Probably something to do with charity; that usually worked best. The sheriff was an elected official after all. Police officers helping charities looked great in the press. Demon supposed the reason given didn't really matter. He had no plans for pleasantries or subterfuge.

He was there for one reason only, a reason Sheriff Hall was not going to like. Especially after he saw the photos held in the file folder beneath Demon's left arm.

He let an awkward and pregnant silence fall over the room. The weight of it reminded him of a storm cloud just before the first drops of rain burst forth into the world.

At this thought, rain began to fall inside of the sheriff's office. Demon hated when that happened. He hoped that it would only be rain and not thunder. It was so hard to carry on a conversation during a raging thunderstorm—a storm that only one of the people in the conversation could see and hear.

When Demon spoke, the words were warm and smooth and dripped with a deep baritone and a heavy Scottish accent. "Sheriff, I need you to put me in prison."

"What's wrong, buddy?" Dad said.

Dylan didn't look up. He didn't want his dad to see the tears that had forced their way into his eyes.

He wiped his face on his sleeve and said, "Nothing. Good hit."

Dylan couldn't really explain why he was so upset, even to himself. It wasn't his dad's fault that he was good at everything while Dylan felt like he was good at nothing. It wasn't his dad's fault that his mom had died.

But he still blamed his dad for all of those things. One day, he had a good life. Then his dad had come around and ruined it all.

Well, maybe not directly. It was really more his grandpa's fault, but it was because of his dad, and that was close enough.

Some part of him associated his dad with everything that had gone wrong. Everything in his life that was once good and now sucked.

It felt like all of that was Dad's fault.

And now, Dad had completely ruined baseball too by hitting a home run and probably winning the game for them. He already had no friends at school, and now, thanks to Dad, he was probably not going to make friends with anyone on the team either.

That was fine. He preferred to be alone anyway.

He already had to hear them talk behind his back about how awesome his dad was and how bad he sucked. They would never say anything to his face. Not after what Dylan had done to the kid who had smirked at him and asked if he was adopted.

Still, he couldn't just go around beating up every kid on the playground who gave him a funny look. And after today, and what his dad had just done, he would be the butt of even more jokes. He could almost hear them giggling.

As he took a couple of practice swings and stepped up to the plate, Dylan considered that he needed to do something big. Something to make everyone forget what his dad had done.

He could, of course, knock out a home run of his own. But Dylan knew there was about zero chance of that.

He needed to do something big. Something that would show the other boys. His dad. The coach. He would show them all.

Maggie was glad she was there to see Marcus shine, glad she was able to share in that moment with him. Marcus had always thrived under pressure, and this had been no different. He had crushed that ball and put their team up by one on the scoreboard.

She started making her way to the dugout. Marcus would have to leave the rest of the game in someone else's hands.

They had a case and were booked on the next flight out of DC.

As she wove around the cheering parents and grandparents, she kept glancing out at Marcus as he rounded the bases. He didn't smile like that very often anymore. No sarcasm. No worry. Just pure joy. It was etched onto his features.

But then she noticed his smile falter. She followed his gaze and saw the anger on Dylan's face.

The look of sorrow and rage grew even more pronounced as Dylan went to the plate. She couldn't understand that boy most of the time, and she wondered if he might have something wrong with him. Something that went even deeper than the loss of his mother. Something chemical or physical. Something that Dylan couldn't control, and they shouldn't ignore.

It was more than his reaction here at the game. He had been getting in trouble at school. His teachers called him a bully and an instigator. His artwork was dark and disturbing. And another telltale sign, he was a bed-wetter. Throw in a little animal torture, and he'd have all the signs. All the early warnings.

Maybe she was just being too hard on him.

The kid had been through a lot. Lord only knew what kind of mental landmines the boy's grandpa had laid in his brain, what the old man had done to him, said to him.

And if that wasn't bad enough, Marcus had been allowing Dylan to visit his psychotic Uncle Frank. She knew Ackerman was a master manipulator and, if it had been her call, the boy would never have had an opportunity to be infected by the madness of another sick mind.

But it wasn't her call.

Hell, if it were up to her, Ackerman would have been dead a long time ago. He deserved it. She didn't care that he was repentant or that he had helped rescue Marcus. Ackerman was a destroyer through and through, and there was no way to atone for his sins.

She watched Dylan take his first swing and not even come close to the ball. The boy had the ferocity and power down, but his timing was way off.

Dylan stepped out of the batter's box and took another practice swing. She could see the muscles in his neck and face bulging as he ground his teeth.

Glancing around the crowd to see if anyone else found Dylan's behavior disturbing, Maggie realized that she was one of the only people still watching. To everyone else, the show was already over, and now it was time to check your Facebook feed and grab a hot dog.

She glanced back at the game in time to see Dylan miss the next pitch so badly that he almost fell down from swinging so hard. Marcus ran out on the field to give Dylan some pointers and tips. The boy barely acknowledged him.

Dylan took his position for the next pitch. And then Maggie watched him swing his bat as hard as she had ever seen. The only problem was that the pitcher hadn't even started his windup, hadn't even considered throwing the ball yet.

Just as Dylan had approached the plate, the other team's catcher made some comment to Dylan. Maggie couldn't hear what had been said, but whatever it was had apparently made Dylan decide to use the catcher's head for batting practice.

The whole scene seemed to play out in slow motion.

Dylan turning to the catcher, that terrible look of rage and hatred in his young eyes. Dylan swinging the bat as a weapon. The metal connecting with catcher's facemask with a metallic ping and crunch.

She heard one of the mother's scream.

Before the umpire or coaches could even realize what had happened, Dylan had pounced on the other boy like a wild animal.

Dylan pulled off the catcher's facemask and started pounding his fists into the other boy's already bloody face.

Chaos broke out, with parents and coaches flooding the field. Marcus was the first to reach home plate, and he immediately pulled Dylan off the unconscious catcher.

Maggie remained at the fence, thinking of the way Dylan had moved. It had reminded her of the night she first met Francis Ackerman Jr. The night good old Uncle Frank had murdered a close friend of hers. Ackerman had moved with that same kind of ferocity that night. He had pounced on her just as Dylan had pounced on the catcher.

Maggie didn't even try to help. She just turned her back on the field and pulled out her cell phone. She surfed to the airline's website and dialed the 1-800 number. They were going to need to take a later flight.

Two delays and a nearly missed connecting flight later, and Maggie was on the ground at Tucson International Airport. And she was not only accompanied by Marcus, but also by the new addition of Dylan.

The boy should have been at their office and barracks back in Rose Hill, Virginia. They should have left him with

Stan. Dylan and Stan had formed an instant bond, and the boy had probably spent more time in the past year with Stan than he had his own father.

She supposed that was one of the reasons Marcus had insisted on bringing Dylan. Another was probably that he wanted to help Dylan escape the scene of the crime.

They had barely spoken on the plane ride. Maggie had been separated from Marcus and Dylan by the last minute bookings and flight changes, but she was glad for the space.

She tried to sleep but kept replaying the incident in her mind when her eyelids fell.

Dylan. The baseball bat. The gasps of the mothers. The look on the boy's face. The anger in his eyes. The brutality. Vicious and graceful. The way Dylan had moved and changed, as if a switch had been flipped from person to animal.

She found herself constantly watching the boy now, wondering what he might do next. She followed this pattern as they wordlessly moved through the airport and retrieved their luggage. Andrew was waiting outside with the rental car.

Andrew Garrison, the third field agent on their team, looked them up and down. She had overheard Marcus tell Andrew about "an incident" at Dylan's game over the phone, but she could tell by the look on Andrew's face that he had a lot of burning questions. To his credit, he knew that now wasn't the time to ask.

Andrew had another man with him, an older man with kind eyes and a big pink scar on his neck. The pair of them stood beside the open door of a gold minivan in the curbside pickup area. Passenger cars and hotel vans were pulling in and out, picking up loved ones and fares, and zooming off again. Andrew had a prime parking spot and every van driver who maneuvered around him gave him a nasty look. Some even honked. She saw a crowd of airport workers smoking nearby. The combined smell of the nicotine addicts and the exhaust from the constant caravan of cars made Maggie feel nauseous.

Marcus said to the older man, "You must be the driver."

The man said, "Yes, sir. Arthur Jones. Your friend has already explained the details to me. I'll get your luggage."

Arthur took their small go-bags—emergency travel kits containing everything they needed for quick trips.

Marcus said, "One second, Arthur. I need to speak with Maggie before you go."

Arthur flashed a sincere smile and said, "Take your time, sir. I'll just put your bags in the car. That's me down there. Third on the left. The black Lincoln."

"Thanks, Arthur," Marcus said and then motioned for her to accompany him to the side, away from Dylan.

Before he could speak, she said, "You had better not be thinking what I think you're thinking."

"It's just for—"

"Hell no."

"Let me finish," Marcus said, hands raised in surrender. "Dylan's Grandpa Cassidy has been wanting to see him. He lives in Sedona. He's on his way down to stay with Dylan for a few days. He's probably already at the hotel. The driver will wait with you, and once Dylan is set, Arthur will bring you out to the prison."

She waited a moment and said, "Are you done? Can I speak now?"

"What?"

"Is that a 'yes'?"

"Yes, please speak. Let's get it over with."

"Okay, here's my rebuttal to your proposal—hell and no. You go with your son in the town car. I shouldn't be sidelined just because your kid can't keep his bat to himself."

"I'm not sidelining you. You'll be right behind us."

"You mean that you will be right behind Andrew and I."

"Maggie," Marcus said through clenched teeth. "This is not a democracy. It's an order."

"Really? You're pulling rank on this? I told you to leave him back with Stan. That he'd just be in the way. Plus, who knows what's going on in that boy's head. He's obviously pissed off about something."

"I spoke to him about it on the plane."

"And? What was his reason for sending that other kid to the hospital. You know, you're lucky he isn't a few years older. If he was, they would have charged him with something. If it was up to that other kid's mom, I know they would have."

"You gonna let me tell it?" Marcus said, his Brooklyn accent growing more obvious as he became upset.

"Go ahead."

"The catcher from the other team—"

"The one Dylan nearly killed?"

"He told Dylan that his dad was pretty awesome, but that it was too bad that Dylan sucked so bad. Then he added that if he were Dylan's mom, he would have run away from him, too. Apparently, the kid had heard that Dylan's mom ran off with another guy, a rumor that had gotten started somehow."

Maggie took a deep breath and tried to consider her next words very carefully. "That's terrible. And cruel. But he can't go around attacking any kid that's cruel to him. You can't settle all your problems with your fists. That catcher tonight was lucky. The next one may not be. Didn't you see the way he pounced on him?"

"Yeah, I saw it. Do you think I haven't considered all this? He needs to get back in twice-a-week counseling. But Dylan's been through a lot. Things you'll never understand."

Marcus checked his watch and said, "We're already three hours late. We don't have time to argue about this now. We have jobs to do."

"That's right," she said. "And this job and kids aren't compatible. It's dangerous enough. We don't need to throw distractions into the mix. We need to be focused."

"He's my son, and he's not going anywhere."

"Just think about it. Think about what's best for Dylan."

With those words, Maggie dutifully walked over and joined Dylan and Arthur beside the black Lincoln Town Car. She didn't look back.

Marcus watched the desert landscape whip by outside the window of the rented minivan. The ground wasn't really sand but a compress of sand and rock. He knew this place started as rock and had dissolved away over the millennia. Sculpted by nature herself—Mother Nature, always refining and perfecting. Then Marcus watched the asphalt rush past. He realized that when humankind had conquered this particular ecosystem, we decided to throw out all those refining generations of nature's work and return the world to rock.

He glanced at the clock on the dash. If it was correct, then the trip to the prison had passed the halfway mark, and neither of them had said a word.

Andrew had sat there and resisted the urge to ask a single question, while Marcus had stared out the window. He almost laughed. Andrew was always the rational one, the voice of reason, the peacekeeper. Both he and Maggie could be reckless and hotheaded. But Andrew was their anchor. They were a family, not just colleagues, and this job was more than a profession or position. It was a way of life. A calling. And they were brothers and sisters in that calling.

Marcus wondered where that family would be now if it wasn't for Andrew.

He said, "I thought I told you to never rent us a minivan."

Andrew, behind the wheel, rolled his eyes and said, "It was all they had that was big enough."

"It smells like baby diapers and spilled juice boxes in here."

"It smells like a brand new car."

"Are they bringing us a replacement when it comes in?"

"I think you can deal with it on this one trip."

Marcus growled deep in his throat and looked around the vehicle's interior with disdain. He couldn't quite understand why he disliked it so much. He just knew that he did. Even the color was wrong.

Marcus killed the radio and said, "So why are we here?"

"Do you think we should conference in Maggie?" Andrew asked.

Marcus supposed that she'd appreciate the gesture, but she also wouldn't be taking his calls. He said, "You'll have to call her. She won't answer if it's me. She's in a mood."

Andrew fished out his phone, dialed Maggie, and put her on speaker. Then Andrew said, "Okay, I assume you both read the briefing on the plane, so where do you want to start?"

"Let's just break it down from the top," Marcus said. "This all started with the shooting incident yesterday."

"As far as we know."

"Any reason to think there were earlier murders?"

Andrew said, "Just saying that it's not this guy's first time."

Marcus nodded. "So we have a prison guard in the tower who opens up and kills four inmates before blowing up the tower, killing two guards in the blast, and shooting another while trying to escape."

Andrew added, "The one he shot, Bill Singer, came through. He's going to be fine. In fact, they're calling him a hero."

Marcus said, "Good." One less victim meant one less wrong he needed to right. One less family's justice that was his job to seek out.

Andrew continued, "That was yesterday. Then at about the same time, the guy who designed the prison's security software was killed. Stabbed and shoved in front of a car to cover it."

"What about this security software and the prison? What's so special about them?" Maggie said over the van's speakerphone.

Andrew said, "I don't really know all the ins and outs. I'll let Powell explain all that. But it's some kind of predictive analysis software, and the prison is pretty dependent on it. They found a typed note on the computer guy's body. It read, 'No one can stop me. No one can stop what's coming next. But call in the feds, so they can give it a shot.'"

Marcus said, "He's wanting attention. A bigger stage. A bigger opponent. He wants to prove his superiority."

Over the phone's speaker, Maggie said, "In my experience, people who actually are superior at something don't have to go around telling everyone."

Andrew added, "He's insecure. But he also isn't sloppy. He's left virtually no evidence."

"What about the shooter's family? Still no sign of them?"

"Disappeared. No trace. The boys in blue are beating the streets, but judging from the husband's demeanor, they're already dead."

"Still hasn't said a word?"

"Not one. The locals have been at him since yesterday, but he's checked out. Lights are on, but nobody's answering the door."

Marcus considered all this for a moment and then said, "The question is: Why? The person behind this obviously has a plan. Some kind of end goal in mind. He's not just doing this for his own amusement. He wants the world to know something or he wants to accomplish a specific mission."

"What does he want the world to know?"

"Hard to say. Some perceived wrong. Something he's compensating for." Marcus allowed his mind to begin the process of sliding into this killer's world, the killer's perspective. "I want to prove something. I want them to know something."

Andrew said, "What do you want to prove? And who is them?"

"I don't know yet."

"What about if he's just trying to accomplish a mission?"

"If it's a mission, then we need to look at revenge or money or some kind of ideological cause."

Andrew drummed his fingers on the wheel and said, "Okay, so it could really be any of those at this point."

"What about the Director's connection to all of this?" Marcus said. "He's been trying to get me to take some time off since what happened in Pittsburgh. And now, not only is he coming to me with a new case, but it's one with a ticking clock. I know we're not supposed to talk about it—that whole splinter cell, compartmentalization, deniability thing—but we all know that we're not the only team within the Shepherd Organization. So what's big enough to call his best team off hiatus? That means it has to be personal to him or there's something bigger at play."

Maggie started chuckling and said, "It's just like you to automatically assume that we're his best team. Maybe we were his last option. You know that's your problem. You want to assume the best. Just like with Ackerman. You—"

"Maggie, we're going into a tunnel," Marcus said as he reached over, grabbed Andrew's phone, and hung up on her.

He knew that he would pay for it later, but it sure felt good in the moment.

★★★

```
FILE #750265-6726-688
Zolotov, Dmitry - AKA The Judas Killer
State Exhibit F
Description: Diary Entry
```

My birth certificate reads Dmitry Zolotov, but I've had so many names over the years that my birth name carries little meaning for me. I initially took the name Judas because of my father, but I've come to find that it best describes who I am and the life that I've lived. From my first breath, from my first cry, what I've loved has always betrayed me.

My mother was a filthy whore.

You may think that's horrible to say about one's mother. Then you may wonder why that information even matters?

Simple. Because when future generations read and study these words and my deeds, I want them to understand the whole picture. To know who I am. To see what I've been through and what I'm about to accomplish despite the most humble of beginnings.

Some of you may not consider what I'm about to do to be any kind of an accomplishment. But to you I say, take another step back and consider all of these events.

Even though this was written prior to the first shot being fired, when you finish this diary, you will realize how perfectly all of the pieces fell into place.

Not by accident, but by my design.

Then you will see that the events that have transpired here will never be forgotten.

This is my magnum opus. My legacy. The greatest performance of my life. So for those of you studying this, to you future generations, please consider these words to be the behind-the-scenes documentary of my life. A short autobiography from one of the most infamous and fascinating men in history.

All that being said . . . back to my mother, the whore.

I don't call her that as an insult or a comment on her being promiscuous. It was her chosen profession. She sold her body and time for money. I don't fault her for that. I'm not one to judge.

So you may be asking, then why did you say "filthy whore." That seems to carry some pretty angry and negative undertones.

Here's the truth. It never really bothered me once I was old enough to know that my mother had sex with strange men for money.

But it did bother me when my father explained that I was actually her third child. And my two siblings had been aborted, just before birth.

My father also explained that my mother was not only a "shlyukha" (the Russian word for whore), but she also LIKED to get pregnant.

You would think that would hurt business for a woman in her profession but, to the contrary, there were plenty of clients willing to pay extra for a pregnant woman. Plus, she normally couldn't get much extra money from the local pornographic filmmakers. But when she was pregnant, they took notice.

That's what always bothered me about my mother. Not that she earned on her back. No, I always hated my mother because she pimped me out the moment I was conceived.

She forced me to be a whore, too.

And what I've learned is that there are some jobs that aren't just something you do. They define who you are. They infect your soul.

I've seen this most often with whores and cops.

But I didn't have a choice in that corruption. I didn't even have the option to choose death over being defiled. My mother made that choice for me.

That's why I hate her.

That's why I'm glad my father killed her and saved me the trouble.

As they pulled up to the prison gates, Marcus said, "I think you forgot to mention all this." He gestured toward a substantial crowd of protesters gathered at the prison's outermost perimeter. There were maybe thirty of them. A conglomerate of every race and age. Thirty people gathered at a perimeter gate that was barely in sight of the actual prison building. As he examined them, Marcus noticed that they seemed to be made up of at least two different groups. One group held signs touting messages of Slave Labor and Dangerous Change. Another group was more emblazoned and held signs about the ULF—ULF Killed My Son, An Eye for an Eye, and ULF Means Death.

Marcus said, "Do we have a celebrity prisoner?"

Andrew passed their IDs to the guard at the security post and then said, "I'm afraid we do. Leonard Lash."

Marcus growled in disgust. He had heard about this

on the *Daily Show* and had read an article he had seen on Twitter.

The presence of Leonard Lash raised the case's profile to the point that it would normally be something that the Shepherd Organization would shy away from. More press meant more people asking questions about their group. Their "think tank." More people digging into their cases and questioning their methods—both those that were legal and those that bent or outright broke the law.

Leonard Lash, a political activist originally from the south side of Chicago, had risen to national prominence because of his work for equal rights. But Leonard had truly become a legend when it came to public light that his group—the ULF—The Urban Liberation Front—was actually operating much like the gangs they were so opposed to. The ULF had its hands in a lot of illegal activities in order to bankroll its agendas. But the worst offense was that the ULF and Leonard himself had been calling for young men to follow the examples of terrorists and coordinate an attack on law enforcement and government buildings.

After three former gang members connected to the ULF set off a homemade bomb at a local police station, a task force of state and federal officers made it their missions to bring down the ULF. Their battle ended when Leonard Lash was given life in prison for his role in the Arizona bombing and other illegal activities.

The ULF as a whole had somehow survived the scandal and was still a thriving organization, with many claiming that Lash had been framed by the government.

All of that added up to a lot of controversy and noise and attention that the Shepherd Organization would want to avoid. And Marcus had just as many skeletons in his closet as anyone else in the group.

The guard pressed a button, and a large set of security barriers retracted into the concrete. Andrew released the brake, allowing the minivan to roll through onto a field of the same sand and gravel compress, but Marcus could see where the terrain had been flattened halfheartedly and then compressed with another layer of sand, and likely chemicals, in order to kill any attempt at plant growth. Marcus understood the reasoning. It was to create an effect. To set the mood.

The attempt and the effect were mostly successful. There was almost no plant life for at least five football fields in any direction.

The space felt harsh, inhospitable, and dangerous. Just entering the barren expanse of ground kicked off alerts within the lizard part of Marcus's brain. The lizard didn't understand all the reasons they were entering the space. The lizard just knew that to enter here was to invite death.

The lizard was all impulse driven. In this case, the lizard part of his brain wanted to turn back the way they had come—the way it knew was safe—and run.

Marcus could understand that a prisoner in the main building would want to avoid this wasteland at all costs.

It also created a strange awareness of Foxbury being somewhere beyond the reach of the rest of the world.

Andrew said, "Eerie, huh. Powell has a big thing with concentric circles of security and separation."

After being buzzed through a slightly less fortified security fence—one still equipped with razor wire and other deterrents—they came to a parking area. There was a concrete pad only large enough for a couple of prison buses and some security jeeps. Marcus saw that the small lot was well guarded. He knew that, if it were him, one of those jeeps would seem much more appealing than a stroll into the valley of death. But the extra guards at the lot seemed only precautionary, since he still could only see the main buildings of the prison over the top of a twenty-five-foot concrete wall bordered by guard towers.

He also noticed the two men waiting to meet them. One of the men was his boss, the Director of the Shepherd Organization and the man who had recruited him. The other must have been Scott Powell, the visionary behind this new prison.

Judas had killed many times over the years, but none of those killings had been quite as exhilarating and satisfying as the murder of Debra Costello. He would have given almost anything to reach that peak again. But he also realized that achieving that kind of high had its price—an especially costly one in Debra's case.

His anger made him want to get his hands dirty again and kill the engineer in her home, up close and personal.

Still, he didn't want this crime tied back to the prison. At least not yet. Which made the decision to stage the scene as a crime of passion all the more advantageous.

He parked his decoy car, an old Buick purchased for two thousand dollars cash, across the street from the engineer's home and ran down his evidentiary checklist. Untraceable shoes, untraceable generic jogging outfit, the facial prosthetics, the padding that made him look overweight. It was unlikely that he would be seen and described after the body was found, but he liked to be thorough.

He checked his watch. He would also need to be quick. He had appointments to keep.

Then he triple-checked the most important piece of his wardrobe. The knife secured to the small of his back. The knife he had used to murder Debra Costello. The one he would now use to cut off chunks of the engineer's flesh.

The Director made the introductions, describing Scott Powell as "an old friend." Then he said, "Marcus, Warden Powell is going to show you around his little . . . complex, while I have a word with Andrew. We've already heard Scott's sales pitch. We'll catch up."

Marcus followed Scott Powell through a metal gate mounted in the massive concrete wall. Powell's hair was graying, but he had a full thick head of it. His aftershave smelled vaguely of soil and freshly cut wood. Wrinkles from past and present worries blockaded Powell's eyes, but he was also in great shape and exuded a youthful vigor. Or, at least, he did in that moment, as he described his life's work.

"As you can see, the outer perimeter is all about multiple layers of security. It's my opinion that the most important duty of a good prison system is to protect the general populace from those individuals with no respect for the law." Powell spoke with a booming and authoritative Louisiana accent.

Marcus said, "I think we can all agree on that."

"But, as a society, we must go beyond that duty and

explore what other things we want our prison systems to accomplish."

They passed through the concrete wall into a large, flat inner sanctum, which contained two separate sets of buildings. One sat in front of Marcus, and he could see the other, larger set of buildings in the distance about a thousand yards up a paved road. But he was most interested in the strange building that rested directly in front of them.

It was a massive, tan-colored block-and-stone structure. The layout and profile of which made Marcus think of the way futuristic prison buildings and college campuses alike may have been imagined by an architect in the 1930s and '40s. The sprawling group of interconnected buildings was all Art Deco lines and rounded corners.

Powell must have noticed the look on Marcus's face because he said, "Pretty cool old buildings, huh?"

"That's the prison? It looks more like Willy Wonka's factory."

Powell laughed. "It does have a certain charm. But they never made chocolate here. Footwear originally and then several other products over the years. And the other half of the compound, up the road, was a mental hospital until the '80s. And now, it's our residence hall."

"So your prison is an old factory connected with a nut house?"

"Yes, that's actually a big part of my program, taking old buildings and factories and warehouses and showing that states don't have to build bigger, state-of-the-art facilities with tighter security and more manpower. We came in here and threw up some walls and fences and installed some cameras, then slapped on a coat of paint. At a tenth the cost of building a similar new facility."

The air around them smelled burnt and harsh. Marcus felt like he was on the surface of some planet not hospitable to human life. He said, "So your program takes buildings like the Buck Rogers headquarters over here and turns them into prisons?"

"No, son, my program isn't about buildings and bottom lines. It's about getting people's lives back on track. It's about helping people. And, hopefully, changing society." Powell waved to a camera beside a large set of new security doors, which had been shoved into position over the top of where the factory's original entrance might have been.

A metal latch disengaged with a clunk and a small motor whirred to life as it pulled the large metal barrier apart.

When it was three quarters open, Powell gestured for Marcus to go ahead of him. He said, "Why don't we continue this discussion in the control room, Agent Williams? Then you can see the whole picture at once."

After passing through another updated security door, they entered a large concrete chamber. Marcus guessed it was the old loading dock. He could almost hear the pounding of work boots and the grunts of the men who had once spent their days loading and unloading product out of these concrete bays. Powell led him through the loading dock, up some stairs, and down a concrete utility corridor.

Then they came to a nondescript security door with a sign that read "Control Center West." Powell used a handprint and retinal scanner to gain access and led Marcus into an auditorium-shaped space that reminded him of NASA's mission control.

The front wall was at least twenty feet tall and covered with computer screens of various sizes. They started at waist height and climbed to the ceiling.

Powell spread his arms and said, "Welcome to the prison of the future."

Judas approached her from the south. The route down the sidewalk from that direction had two advantages. He would be approaching her from behind, and even if she did turn to see him in time, she'd be looking into the sun.

The attack would be a blitzkrieg. He only needed the element of surprise and a couple seconds of action, and then she would be unconscious and safely under his control.

After that he would work quickly and efficiently with the knife, but not quickly enough to keep from savoring the moment. He would devour the pure, raw emotion of every slash, every cut. He hoped that he'd have time to cut off the breasts. That had been his favorite part with Debra.

His heart was racing now. He felt like a teenager getting ready to pick up his date for the prom.

The world seemed more vibrant, as if the colors and smells had suddenly woken up and were all vying for his attention. He noticed some creosote and sage nearby which gave off the sweet aroma of a spring rain. Maybe it was because he was so close to his own death that he was noticing such things?

These emotions were uncommon to him. He was typically cold and methodical. Sure, he had no qualms about taking life but, in the past, it had always been just part of a mission.

Just a checkbox on his list that needed to be marked off for one reason or another.

But not anymore.

Now, he killed for no one but himself. For his own enjoyment. His own glorification.

It felt wonderful.

A row of trees and shrubs hid his approach, but when he passed those, he would be in her line of sight. And he would spring into action.

As he continued forward down the sidewalk, he imagined what would come next.

His speed increases, closing the last few steps in a sprint.

He strikes her full force with the blackjack. The blow from the small club should knock her unconscious. Then he drags her inside, and he finishes up with the knife.

Simple.

He had tested police response times here in Tucson and knew that, even with police on the way, he would have a few minutes of cutting before he needed to finish her. But he hoped this body would take longer to be discovered. Still, it would work out either way. Without the other pieces, knowledge of this murder would just add to the noise.

And a few minutes would be enough time. It would have to be. Business before pleasure, and he had a schedule to maintain and many more tasks to cross off his list.

He double-checked the street and was about to make his move when he heard an engine approaching and tires rolling over concrete.

Slowing his pace, he waited for the approaching vehicle to pass.

Instead of rolling on by, a minivan the color of a ripe

plum pulled into the engineer's driveway. Three women hopped out of the car. One of them, a middle-aged Hispanic woman in jeans and a red and white flower top, held up a bottle of wine. The friends greeted each other warmly and headed for the front door.

Now he had a decision to make.

Should he try to fit the engineer in later or kill all four women now? He knew he could do it. A little fear and intimidation to control them and a few swift and brutal attacks with the knife.

He guessed he could have two of them bleeding out on the floor before the others could even react.

People were always so easy to kill. So unprepared for danger and violence.

But checking his watch, he decided against it. That would take far too long. The delay would put him behind schedule for his next appointment.

He watched the engineer shut her front door, and then he walked back to the decoy car, feeling unfulfilled.

He shut the door and tried to calm his breathing, assuring himself that he'd be back later.

A song came on the radio. One of those sappy love ballads that Debra had been so fond of.

As he thought of Debra, he heard her laughter. He heard her laughing at him. Her and her insignificant little friend.

He told himself that none of it was real, but before he knew what was happening, the knife was in his hand, and he had stabbed the radio to death in a quick attack of sparks and cracking plastic.

***

Andrew Garrison didn't like the idea of leaving Marcus alone with Powell. Marcus had an annoying compulsion toward brutal honesty, and Andrew could just imagine what Marcus would say upon seeing the prison and control room for the first time. He should have been there to make sure that his partner didn't say or do anything to position Powell as an adversary.

Instead, he stood in the middle of a parking lot with the blazing sun beating down on the back of his black suit. He walked up beside the minivan and noticed a burnt rubber smell coming from the engine compartment. If this were his personal vehicle, he'd get that checked. But perhaps that was just how cars smelled in heat like this? Andrew certainly felt like he was melting.

To the Director, he said, "What was so important? Dealing with authority figures is not one of Marcus's strong suits. Who knows what he's going to say to Powell? Besides, I'm ready to get into the AC."

The Director wore a blue and gold hat displaying the Department of Justice seal and an official-looking DOJ windbreaker of the same color. For the meeting, Andrew had chosen his standard black suit, white shirt, and black tie ensemble. He had tried to ignore Marcus's choice of clothing when he had picked the others up from the airport. Instead of a suit or even dress clothes, Marcus had chosen a black T-shirt, jeans, and a leather motorcycle jacket. Andrew was just glad that the shirt didn't display skulls or the logo of a beer company. He had learned to pick his battles with his partner.

"Don't worry about Powell," the Director said. "He used to work with me, so he can definitely handle Marcus."

"You said that earlier, but you didn't say where you two worked together."

"No, I didn't. But it's not important. What I wanted to talk about was—"

Andrew interrupted, "Was Powell a member of the Shepherd Organization?"

The Director sighed. "He was a member of my team, but that was a long time ago, and it has nothing to do with this case."

"Are you sure about that?"

"If it becomes relevant, then you'll be the first to know. But until then, Powell and my personal history is personal."

"And you can promise me that history isn't going to hamper our investigation?"

The Director took a step closer, and even in his reduced state the older man could project a sense of authority. The Director said, "You want to get into personal histories. I just received another voicemail from your ex-wife. She's worried about you. Do you want to talk about all that?"

Andrew nodded. "You made your point."

The Director said, "Good. Now, to business. How is Marcus really doing?"

"That's what you wanted to talk about?"

"After what happened in Pittsburgh, I have some questions as to whether Marcus went back to active duty too soon after his time in Kansas."

His time in Kansas?

Only the Director could take an ordeal, which lasted months and consisted of total darkness and starvation coupled with physical and psychological torture, and make it sound like Marcus had been on a family vacation.

Andrew said, "Marcus is fine."

"What about Pittsburgh?"

"He got carried away."

"I would say so. This is a high-profile case. A lot of eyes. We need to be careful and subtle. Marcus doesn't do either of those particularly well. Another incident like Pittsburgh, and Fagan will retire Marcus."

"What? He can't do that."

"Technically, he can. Fagan doesn't look at Marcus or his brother and see potential. He sees liabilities, and if we don't prove that Ackerman and Marcus can be valuable assets, then one of them will be dead and the other will be looking for a new line of work."

The large room reminded Marcus of a smaller version of NASA's mission control. Technicians typed away at keyboards and spoke into headsets, probably controlling every aspect of the prison. But all eyes faced toward the giant wall of screens. The place smelled like a coffee shop. Marcus guessed that everyone there was working overtime, in light of the recent incident, and needed the caffeine.

Powell tapped the woman working at the first terminal on the shoulder. She swiveled in her chair, and Powell said, "Spinelli, this is Special Agent Williams from the DOJ. Marcus, meet Lisa Spinelli, our resident tech guru."

Spinelli frowned at Powell briefly and then gave Marcus a fake smile. She had a gap between her two front teeth. Even with her sitting down, he could see that she was at least six feet tall and rail thin. She had a weak chin that made her seem mouse-like. She wasn't traditionally pretty, but there was something about her, a confident fire in her eyes, that made her strangely attractive.

She stuck out her hand and said, "Lisa Spinelli, Director of Technological Security."

Marcus shook her slender hand. "Pleasure to meet you. Spinelli? Like the man who was just murdered?"

She looked at the floor and said, "That's right. My brother was the one who was . . . who died. We worked as a team on this project. I created the algorithms, and he wrote the rest of the code."

Marcus said, "I'm sorry for your loss." He wanted to tell her that they'd bring justice to her brother's killer, but he fought the urge. Such promises had a way of sounding empty. Instead, he asked, "Are you sure this is where you want to be right now?"

"Our parents are handling the funeral arrangements. And I can't think of anything more worthwhile I could do for my brother than trying to protect what we built together. This software was his baby, and now it's his legacy. Since he can't be here to fight for it, I should be."

Powell said, "Lisa, would you please do a small system demo for Special Agent Williams?"

She swiveled back around to her terminal and wiped at her eyes. She said, "No problem. Let's just find a good test subject."

Marcus couldn't see what she was doing on her screen, but based on the little noises she made, he guessed she was checking to find a "good test subject."

After a few seconds, she said, "Here we go." Five of the displays on the wall switched to an overhead picture of three men in orange jumpsuits. The resolution and detail of the video was impressive, flawless. The camera angle changed to a different view. Now the picture showed the men head-on. The images were life-size. It seemed as if Spinelli had waved a magic wand and opened a portal straight to these men's location.

"Okay," Spinelli said. "These three guys are in the kitchen preparing lunch. You can see that they are all armed with knives and are chopping up vegetables. Now, let's run a little test."

She tapped a few keys and bent over to a microphone sitting beside her monitor. Marcus noticed the display around the inmates change. Now each man was followed around by a little computer menu which displayed his name and basic information. At first glance, he guessed that the system relied on facial recognition, but then he noticed the live stats showing each man's heart rate and blood pressure. Maybe they were getting the info from some other kind of monitors?

"Residents Martinez, Seville, and Ralston," Spinelli said. The three men looked up as if God himself had just spoken directly to them. Spinelli continued, "Put the knives down and stand by for a systems test."

Marcus could see the men clearly enough to see one roll his eyes as he placed his knife on the table in front of him.

Spinelli released a button on the microphone, looked back at Marcus, and said, "We do these kinds of tests on a regular basis."

Powell added, "We like to remind the residents, which is what we call the inmates, that the system is always watching. Many of them have come to call the monitoring system by the name 'Saint Nick.' Because he sees when you're sleeping, and he knows when you're awake."

Marcus said, "I get the idea, but just being monitored is not going to keep a lot of these guys from ripping each other's throats out. They didn't exactly get here based on good impulse control."

"Very true," Powell said, "but this system does a lot more than monitor and record." Powell picked up the mic from the desk and said, "Resident Ralston, this is Warden Powell." That perked up all three men, especially Ralston, the big black man in the center. "I want you, Resident Ralston, to count to fifteen and then pick up your knife. Do nothing more. Just pick it up. Nod if you understand."

Ralston nodded, and Powell said over the mic, "Start counting now."

Spinelli tapped some keys, and the displays reverted to a desktop that showed a logo which Marcus had noticed on several boxes and uniforms since arriving. She said, "I'm now in monitoring mode." She gestured toward the other technicians working at terminals inside the large, open room. "That's what most of these people are doing. Just monitoring."

When the countdown reached zero, an alert popped up onto Spinelli's screen.

The display automatically flipped back to the three men, but now the knife in Ralston's hand was flashing red.

"So what now?" Marcus asked. "You know that he picked up a knife, but what do you do about it? Guards can't make it there in time. You going to tell him to be good?"

Powell smiled and, into the mic, said, "Resident Ralston please stab Resident Seville to death."

Spinelli said, "Sir, we can't just—"

Powell silenced her with a raised hand.

Ralston also didn't seem convinced. The big black man looked from the knife to Seville and back. Then, Ralston said, "No way, man," and dropped the knife on the table.

Powell keyed the mic and said, "What would happen to you, Resident Ralston, if you did attempt to murder Resident Seville?"

Ralston said, "You'd smite me, sir."

"And what would that look like? How would you be 'smited'?"

"The jewelry around my ankles and wrists would zap me. I've been shocked once before, and I'm not playing with that fire again."

"Thank you, Resident Ralston. Please stand by," Powell said. Then to Marcus, he added, "They wear tamperproof bracelets and anklets capable of transmitting enough electricity into their bodies to incapacitate even the most agitated man or woman."

Marcus shook his head. "I still don't buy it. There's no way 'Saint Nick' here can register actions accurately enough to know when to shock them. Not every time. It's a nice thought, but it can't predict behavior. And you can't analyze current behaviors quickly or accurately enough to do anything about it."

Spinelli said, "Our system can. Our software analyzes billions of data points and conditions and can tell when one of the residents is about to break a serious rule. If it's serious and urgent enough, the system takes action on its own. Otherwise, an alert is sent, and a security technician decides if action is needed."

Powell keyed the mic and said, "Resident Ralston, I will give you one week with no work and double rations in exchange for helping with this demonstration. I want you to do your best to succeed in killing Seville. I want you to try and be faster than the system. If you succeed, you will not be held responsible. But, rest assured, you will be stopped before you can harm Seville. Surely a week of the good life is worth one shock?"

Ralston seemed to consider the offer and then said, "Two weeks of the good life. And premium channels on my box for free."

Powell laughed. "So we're negotiating now? I tell you what. I'll give you all that for trying, and I'll give you a bonus of double that if you can get that knife within two feet of him."

"Okay. Deal. When should I do it?"

"Surprise us."

Ralston was still for a moment. Then he slowly slid his hand toward the knife, paused for a few seconds, and then he snatched it up and swung the blade in a backhanded arc toward Seville. It would have been a clumsy all-in type of move in a knife fight but, under the circumstances, it would have been effective enough. The swing had the angle and force of a killing blow.

But it didn't even come close to connecting.

No sooner had Ralston started his lunge than the system had recognized the threat and delivered enough electricity to stop Ralston dead in his tracks. It looked like Ralston had run headlong into a brick wall. In the span of a millisecond, he had gone from active threat, man with a knife, to pacified threat, a man on the ground in pain.

"I still don't buy it. It just can't see everything, everywhere, every time."

Powell's face split into a crooked smile. "Since this facility opened six months ago, we have had zero successful attempts at resident on resident violence. Not one. So something sure seems to be working."

Maggie was still fuming, and Dylan was lost on his iPad in his own little world. The hotel room had double beds and a flat-screen television tucked into a dark armoire. It smelled of cinnamon and old wood, and the air conditioner was temperamental and lazy. Maggie occupied one of the beds, her feet up, back against the headboard. Dylan was in a similar position atop the other bed. The only difference being that Maggie had instantly stripped off the top two layers of the bedclothes and deposited them neatly in the corner. Then she had checked for traces of bed bugs on the mattress and, thankfully, found none. Dylan, on the other hand, was actually sitting on top of his bedspread. She wanted to explain to him that a lot of hotels never wash those top bedspreads, but she held her tongue.

Play it cool. Don't be weird.

She turned on the television. She needed a mindless distraction from all the noise in her head.

That distraction didn't come.

Instead, the television showed a handsome, young reporter over the headline, "Arizona Governor Orders Investigation."

Behind the reporter sat a security fence surrounded by protesters. She turned up the volume.

"As you can see behind me, the new experimental prison designed by Powell Prison Technologies has been a magnet to controversy since its inception. Some say that the new prison relies too heavily on technology and 'artificial intelligence.' Others have argued that it's a violation of the inmates' constitutional rights, that it's dangerous and cruel and unusual punishment, and that its true purpose is to create a slave labor force out of illegal immigrants and minorities. The controversy surrounding this prison—where inmates are given more freedom but less privacy—only increased when Leonard Lash, the former leader of the Urban Liberation Front, was selected randomly to be one of the first inmates participating in the prison's pilot program.

"And now, on the heels of the governor's decision to allow the program to move into its second phase, which would increase the number of prisoners to one thousand and incorporate the manufacturing portion of the . . ."

The reporter continued on, showing overhead views of Foxbury Correctional Treatment Facility. The strange prison she should have been investigating at that very moment.

"—the prison and the small community of Foxbury were rocked by an incident that many claim justifies all the fears and objections to this new prison concept."

"Is that why we're here?" Dylan said.

He startled her. When the boy was lost in his electronic devices, it was easy to forget he was even there.

"Yeah. Your dad's there now."

"Why aren't you there too?"

"That's a good question."

"Are you and my dad getting a divorce?"

The question jolted her like a physical blow.

"First off, your dad and I aren't married."

"But you live together and love each other? Isn't that what being married is?"

"Well, not exactly. What brought this up?"

"I don't know."

"Your dad loves you very much."

"I know."

"Why were you so angry at him during the game?"

"I wasn't. That catcher said—"

"I saw you before that. When your dad hit the home run. You were almost in tears."

Dylan ground down on his lower jaw in anger. It reminded her of a face Marcus often made.

"I wasn't crying."

"But you were upset."

"Maybe."

"Why?"

"I don't know."

"You have to have some idea."

"It's stupid."

"I'm sure it's not. Things we feel are never stupid. But we might not have any real reason to feel that way, and we need to recognize that and talk about it."

"It's just that sometimes I wish my life could go back to the way it was before I met him. Then I feel bad for thinking that."

"You shouldn't feel bad about it, but you also need to recognize that what happened to your mom isn't your dad's fault."

"I know," Dylan said but didn't sound convinced.

Maggie jumped up and dropped down beside Dylan. The

bedsprings popped and groaned as they contracted. "You want to hear a story?" she said.

"I'm too big for stories."

"That's good. Because this is a very grown-up kind of story."

Dylan's eyes perked up a bit. "What's it about?"

"It's the story of a little girl not too much older than you. And this little girl lost someone she loved, just like you."

"Is she pretty?"

"The girl?"

"Yeah."

"Sure. She's cute, but some of the other kids pick on her because she's different."

"What color hair does she have?"

"What color do you want it to be?"

"That doesn't matter. Her hair's the color that it is no matter what color I want it to be."

"I was thinking you could use your imagination and fill in some of the blanks. But let's just say that she's blonde."

Dylan narrowed his eyes and considered this. "This story is about you, when you was a girl."

"Whoa, I say 'different' and 'blonde,' and you automatically assume it's about me?"

"Is it about you?"

"No, it's some other cute blonde."

Dylan narrowed his eyes again.

She stumbled over an answer before finally conceding defeat and saying, "Okay. It's about me, Sherlock."

"What's a 'sure lock'?"

"Sorry, they probably haven't taught you much English literature yet. The point is that, when I was a couple years older than you are now, my baby brother was taken from me."

"Did he die?"

"No, Dylan, a bad man took him. Just like the way your grandfather took you from your mom."

She felt her throat tighten and her eyes water. It had been much easier thinking of it in the third person. Now that Dylan had forced her to recognize it as her story, she couldn't help but relive it.

Dylan said, "But you and Dad and Uncle Frank got me back. Did they ever get your brother back?"

"No, but a lot of people spent a lot of years trying."

"How did it happen?"

She hadn't intended to get this deep into the story, but Dylan seemed to have an ability to intuitively get to the truth of things. She had seen the same thing in Marcus.

She thought about that day. The police. Seeing her dad truly afraid for the first time. Her baby brother in the swing set. The man walking out of the shadows.

Maggie clenched her eyes shut to hold back the memories.

"Are you okay?" Dylan said.

"It was my fault that he was taken. I was supposed to be watching him. Even though I wasn't officially old enough yet, and my mom got in trouble for that later."

"Then how's it your fault?"

"Because I saw the man who took my brother, but I was too scared to say anything." She remembered him holding a finger up to his lips and looking into her soul with those hollow eyes. "I could have screamed or something. Maybe a neighbor would have heard. But even after that, I was still too scared to tell the police that I had actually seen it happen. I was so scared that he'd come back for me and my mom and dad that I told the police that I didn't see anything. Looking back on it now, I wonder if things would have turned out differently if the police had had a description of the man who took my brother. Maybe they would have gotten him back."

"But you never told them?"

"I never told anyone that. Not even your dad. The point is that I know how much I wish I had talked about things back then with my parents. So, if anything is ever bothering you, I'm always here to talk about it."

Dylan didn't ask any more questions. He just leaned his head over on Maggie's chest and wrapped his arms around her waist.

FILE #750265-6726-689
Zolotov, Dmitry - AKA The Judas Killer
State Exhibit F
Description: Diary Entry

So my mother, the filthy whore, was dead. My father—a rotund man whom I would later learn had no reservations about stealing food from the mouths of children—had murdered her and taken me. Not as a son, mind you, but as a servant. Not as another mouth to feed, but as another pair of hands and a strong young back to break.

I don't know all the details of how he killed her. The case never drew much attention. Just another dead whore in a country that didn't acknowledge such trivial things.

I'm sure her murder was clumsily executed. All knife slashes and no passion. No drama.

Besides, I'm not writing this to show you that murder is an art form. Death can certainly be beautiful, but that's not what's important. It's all about the execution. The buildup. The manipulation. The betrayal. The drama. The death isn't even all that important. It's the life.

People are so easily manipulated. They so obliviously become players in the games of others. Of their countries. Their friends. Spouses. Children.

The beauty of death wasn't found in how each puppet's strings were cut, but in the presentation—the rise and fall of the production as a whole.

My mother's death had none of that.

It wasn't beautiful.

It wasn't how I would have done it.

But that's beside the point.

My mother was dead, and I was delivered into a life of slavery.

I suppose that's why Stasi and I connected later on. Because of our shared experiences, the similar bondage of our youth.

Father had me making money for him as soon as I could follow directions. Probably before that, but I just can't remember how. I was always the dancing monkey to his organ player. Metaphorically speaking, of course.

But Father wasn't half as smart as he thought he was. He thought that he could manipulate others, but he was a fool. He couldn't predict behavior. Father thought that Stasi's death would result in a certain outcome, but he was far from correct on what that outcome would be.

But I'm getting a bit ahead of myself.

One year, Father took a job barking for a traveling carnival and sideshow.

He had worked out a deal to get time and a half pay for himself in exchange for handling all of the "shit" jobs around the place, and sometimes that term was literal. But, of course, Father wasn't the one handling the "shit." That pleasure fell to me.

And that was the first few years of my life, at least those that I can remember. My father working me like a dog and telling me that I needed to pay for my own food plus pay back rent on my miserable life up to that point.

My most vivid memories from this time in my life all involve my father's boots. Sometimes I had to clean them. But I most vividly remember them stomping down on me.

I remember my father as a giant who I knew would one day crush me and grind up my bones.

Spinelli buzzed in Andrew and the Director. Marcus really wanted to know what that not-so-discreet conversation was all about. But the more immediate question was how Powell could have achieved a perfect record of no violence.

Marcus said, "Why do you call them residents?"

Powell gave a nod to the Director and Andrew as they walked up before saying, "It's all psychological. The core concepts of this place were of my design, but there have been many researchers, correction industry experts, and psychologists who have had a hand in the mapping and execution. We call them residents to say to them that this is like no other prison. Here they are part of a community. This is the town in which they work and live. The guards are the police, and I'm the mayor."

"A mayor with his hand on the shock collar."

"That's their choice. It should be noted that the inmates in this program have been certified as having no disorder or disability that would prevent them from being able to follow the rules. These aren't mental patients. These are men who have the potential to re-enter society."

"Men like Leonard Lash?"

"Even him. I am of the firm belief that everyone deserves a second chance and sometimes third and fourth chances. And that goes back to the duties of a prison system. The goal must always be rehabilitation over incarceration. We're not just warehousing the people we don't want around. The goal of everything we do here is about preparing these men to be productive members of society."

Marcus said, "A lot of these guys can't function out in the world. That poor impulse control of theirs will kick in, and they'll do something. They'll take the easy way out of a bad situation, and they'll end up in cuffs again. Best indicator of future behavior is past behavior."

"How very pessimistic of you. So, by your logic, we should just put criminals straight to death because there is no way they could ever transcend their natures?"

Marcus immediately thought of his brother. "No," he conceded, "I do agree that everyone deserves a second chance."

Powell raised his eyebrows in surprise. "Philip!" he said to the Director. "Have you not succeeded in brainwashing this one yet?"

Marcus continued, "That second chance has to be weighed against the safety of others and society as a whole. There are no right answers there. Too many subtle levels of right and wrong. You have to find a balance between giving a second chance and allowing for restitution and making sure that criminal never hurts anyone again."

Powell said, "Exactly. Eventually, our program will contain multiple levels of re-integration. At least, that's what our roadmap calls for. Think of the idea of a halfway house. But multiple levels of that kind of gradual easing back into the world. Maybe on one level they work outside the prison. In another, perhaps they live in apartment buildings with other inmates. But the whole idea is to equip these men and women to be better. Unlike much of our current prison system, which is violent, frightening, and in some extreme instances, downright inhuman. Not to mention underfunded in the areas they need it most. Our idea of what prison should be is more likely to accelerate and perpetuate the cycle rather than break it."

"It seems like there are a lot of people who don't agree with your methods. And this shooting has only added fuel to the fire."

Powell nodded. "There are people who claim this place is dangerous, even though we've had no injuries for six months. They're irrational fools who fear change and hate anything they fear."

"What about the ones who say you're violating these men's rights?" Marcus said.

"We're preserving the rights of both the offender and potential victims. Their rights of safety, the pursuit of happiness, and to live their lives without constant fear of losing it. Think about why the justice system and the law exist in the first place. Laws are designed for the maximum benefit of your society, country, and your fellow man. When you break the law, you've caused harm to one of those things. You've shown that you can't be trusted not to interfere with the God-given rights of your fellow citizen. The first right you lose at that point is your privacy. And until those offenders can earn back that trust, then they have knowingly sacrificed their own rights."

Marcus held up a hand to stop Powell, who was becoming more fervent the longer he spoke, and said, "Don't take this the wrong way, but I actually don't care about your little experiment. I'm not here to say whether or not this place is the future of corrections or shut you down. I'm here to catch a killer. I've heard enough to know that there's more to this than murder. There seem to be a lot of forces at play. I understand that better now. I don't need to hear your whole philosophical stance or see how you handle the showers unless it relates to the case. Who stands to gain the most financially by your experiment failing?"

"That's hard to say. A competitor maybe? Probably PSI, Prison Systems International. They would be the company we would be stealing market share from. Ours is just like lots of other industries. There's one giant or a couple of giants who own the market and the customers. Everyone else is fighting for scraps. But the thing is that in almost every instance, the little guys are staying alive because of a niche they're filling. So most of the time, you're not even competing with other little guys. You're only really competing with the giants for their customer. And PSI is the largest private contractor of prisons and prison-related industries in the world," Powell said. "My company is barely a blip on their radar screen. The whole company's future is wrapped up in this prison and our predictive analysis software. And even if those succeed, we're still no threat to a giant like PSI."

"But I'm guessing that if your ideas are adopted more widely, then it would significantly cut into the bottom line at PSI."

"I suppose so, but not enough for them to kill people over it. They wouldn't have to go that far. There's probably a hundred different ways they could sabotage this project without shedding blood. They have those kinds of resources. Hell, their lawyers are slick enough they could probably shut me down legally."

"When money's involved, there's no limit to how far some people will go."

Powell shook his head. "Then why put a note into the pocket of my lead programmer and shove him into traffic?"

"Maybe to raise the profile of the case. I'm not sure yet. But don't worry. I don't make assumptions. I'll find the truth and accept it for what it is, warts and all."

Powell spread his arms. "I wouldn't have it any other way. How can I best assist with all the finding and accepting?"

Marcus thought for a moment and said, "The first thing I need to see is what your shooter saw just before he pulled the trigger."

Spinelli typed and clicked and transformed the display wall into a window into the yard and Tower 3 on the day of the shooting. The cameras seemed to be everywhere, every location covered by multiple angles.

Marcus asked, "Do you have this many camera angles all around the prison?"

"Everywhere," Spinelli said.

"Bathrooms?"

"Lots of incidents occur there," Powell said. "Privacy, remember? That's what these men have given up."

"What about meetings with their lawyers?"

"Legally, we can't watch that. In most cases anyway. But there are cameras in that room, which are active whenever it's not in use. So no inmate can try to sneak in there to avoid detection. When it is in use, we flag that room as not viewable."

Spinelli said, "Where do you want to start on the videos?"

"Tower 3 interior and then the yard," Marcus said. Then he looked to Powell and added, "Do you have files on all the shooting victims? Our briefing materials only had names."

"Absolutely. I actually assumed you would want those, but we hadn't put them together before you flew out. I wanted to make sure they were comprehensive, and so I had some of the watch commanders type up a summary of what they knew about these men. I thought that may save you some legwork and time."

"That's very helpful, but I prefer to do my own interviews," Marcus said, again wondering how Powell and the Director knew one another.

Spinelli played the video showing the interior of Tower 3. Ray Navarro climbed out from a hatch in the floor. Navarro seemed on edge. He kept shaking and running his hands through his hair. But then he seemed to go through the standard preparations of a tower guard coming on shift. Or, at least, what looked normal to Marcus.

Navarro loaded the rifle and started picking out targets.

Marcus said, "Can you back that up ten seconds and pull in closer on Navarro?"

The display changed to the specifications he had requested and resumed playing.

Marcus watched Navarro closely. He could see the sniper sight in on a target, shift to another, and another in quick succession. But without firing. A dry run. Then Navarro repeated the same movements. He lined up his shots.

Marcus imagined what Navarro was seeing through his scope and said, "Can you pause it there and bring up the corresponding time on the yard cameras?"

When the video changed to a high-definition overview of the yard, Marcus pictured himself from Navarro's point of view. He tried to imagine what Navarro was seeing. The video played out showing the yard, the men being shot, and the chaos that followed. The victims had all fallen in the areas Marcus guessed that Navarro had sighted in on during his practice movements.

"Can you show me the video of Navarro again?"

Spinelli played the video, and Marcus counted as Navarro moved. He noticed four distinct times when the sniper sighted in on something, held for a millisecond, and then moved on. Four stops. Four victims. Four pulls of a trigger. Four dead men.

On the video displays, Navarro again followed his practice movements with the real thing as he carried out the deed. Marcus noted that Navarro followed the exact series of movements on the real thing as he had on the dry run. The only difference being that he actually shot.

Four pulls of a trigger. Four dead men. But not four random men. Four targets. Four men chosen for a specific reason.

Powell led Marcus and the others, including Ms. Spinelli, out of Control Center West and through the newly renovated manufacturing plant. Marcus inspected the industrial equipment and machines and tried to act as if he had some clue as to the function of any of the metal monstrosities that filled the huge, open warehouse.

Marcus said, "License plates?"

Powell laughed. "Hardly . . . One of the companies backing my project is responsible for manufacturing everything from pipe fittings to coffee collars. When we open this industrial wing six months from now, it will make this old building the fourth-largest manufacturing facility in the state."

The tour continued forward through some hallways, which still maintained the original 1950s decor and ambiance. Then they came to an extremely sophisticated security checkpoint equipped with massive steel doors. Powell waved his fingers at the nearby camera, and the thick metal barrier crawled slowly open.

Powell said, "The old asylum building is actually a quarter mile from here. We did the math, and it was more advantageous to dig an underground tunnel between the two buildings. Plus, it also allows us to control who has access between the two. Just another level of security."

The walls and floors of the tunnel were cold concrete, but iridescent bulbs casting out a spectrum of colors had been installed every few feet. Their warm glow made the space seem more natural and less industrial. Marcus had seen the same technique used in a few airports that had built tunnels like this between separate terminals.

"This whole area," Powell said, "was once a thriving industrial zone, but most of the factories were just husks by the time we bought them up. I think the decline had something to do with the interstate being moved. In the 1970s and '80s, these two buildings were updated a bit though. The asylum owned both buildings and used the factory to make . . . plastic cups, I believe."

Andrew said, "So the asylum put its patients to work in the same way you plan to?"

"I certainly can't take credit for the idea of putting inmates to work. That's something that's been done on many occasions throughout history. Although, working conditions are quite a bit better now."

They repeated the procedure at the security door at the other end of the tunnel and followed another concrete corridor to another checkpoint which opened directly into the prison's mess hall.

From there on, Marcus felt like he had stepped back into the 1970s. The tile was pale green and speckled. The walls had once been white block but were now a dingy yellow. The place smelled just as he would have expected. Like a mildewed, musty old room holding thirty sweaty men in the summertime. The residents sat around dented metal tables, eating meatloaf and mashed potatoes. The room would have held at least five times as many diners. Marcus only saw four guards. And no overwatch towers, which meant no armed guards in range to do anything.

He also noticed that the tables were divided along racial and gang lines, just as he had seen at other prisons. "I thought your software eliminated gangs in prisons."

Powell didn't slow his pace but glanced over at the inmates. "It eliminates gang violence. I never claimed to have a cure for human nature. Birds of a feather and all that."

Once inside the actual prison complex, there was little in the way of security. Marcus said, "How many guards are typically on duty?"

"Usually twenty-five guards, plus if you count the civilian technical staff on overwatch in the two control rooms—there's a control room like the one you saw in both the manufacturing facility and the residential complex. So I guess if you count the civilians who are working video security, then we have thirty-five security people on duty at one time."

"Twenty-five guards and one hundred inmates. That's actually not as bad a ratio as I was expecting."

Powell said, "Actually, we're up to two hundred and twenty-five on the residents and are bringing in more each day as we ramp up for phase two, which will see us at a thousand strong. And at that point, we'll still have the same number of guards and staff."

"You don't think that's reckless?"

"This program is designed to run an entire prison system off of a skeleton crew. Now that we've proven the viability of the system, I'd be comfortable having ten guards. It's hard to bypass the civilian specialty workers. The doctors and barbers and maintenance and office workers and such. But you have to remember, the guards here at Foxbury are just the cleanup crew and failsafe. Saint Nick does all the real security work."

Marcus shook his head in disgust. "This whole place scares me."

"You don't trust the system? Even after seeing a demonstration and hearing our record of success?"

"I'm not a tech expert, but I do know one thing. At some point, technology always fails. Whatever can happen will happen. And to be perfectly honest, Warden Powell, I'd like to be as far away from here as possible when you learn that lesson."

Powell stopped and turned back to Marcus. "Technology most certainly does fail, Agent Williams, but not nearly as often as people."

The Director kept quiet during the walk over from Control Center West and the manufacturing facility. When he initially toured the prison, he had asked Powell several of the same questions that Marcus had been asking.

But Powell, invariably the politician, had a response for every argument. The Director had always thought Powell to be an idealist and a dreamer, and it seemed that the years had only strengthened that flaw in his old friend. Now, Powell was in for some hard lessons.

The Director's phone vibrated against his leg. He pulled it out and checked the display. The call was from Fagan.

To the group, he said, "I have to take this call. I'll catch up to you."

"We have a problem," Fagan said on the other end of the line.

"Don't we always."

"It's Ackerman."

The Director closed his eyes. "How many are dead?"

"What? Oh no, nothing like that. But I suppose it could be just as bad in the end."

"What does that mean?"

"I just got off the phone with an assistant director at the CIA. They want to get Ackerman out of their detention facility."

"I thought we had that cleared up. Ackerman helps with their R&D teams, and he gets to stay as long as we want."

"You misunderstand me, Philip. They want him out of there and working for them."

"Doing what?"

"They didn't say, but I'm guessing that they'd like him to do what he does best. They just want him to do it for them."

The Director had heard stories of the government recruiting killers to do their dirty work before. And there was no question that Ackerman had the skill set to remove any enemy of the state, foreign or domestic.

He said, "What are our options?"

"We don't have any. I was chosen to oversee this task force for a reason, Philip. When I was a DA in Boston, I screwed up the case of a man who had killed five little girls. He walked because of me. And it wasn't long before he had killed again. That was on me, and I vowed that I would never again let a killer go free. Not on my watch. The attorney general knew that story, and my experiences made him put his trust in me to be your liaison with his office. And now, I'm about to fail him and break a promise to myself."

The Director looked through the windows in the chow hall door at all of the inmates gathered there. "What if we put Ackerman to work for us instead?"

"We've been over this. I won't put a killer like Ackerman back on the streets. We have no idea what he would do."

The Director smiled. "Who said anything about putting him out on the street?"

Powell led them through the prison's long, hospital-style corridors and up to a secure checkpoint, the only one Marcus had seen since entering the residential complex. After passing through, they took an elevator up and exited into a room that was nearly identical to the other control room, with the addition of a spiral staircase leading up to another level. Powell started telling them about their rehabilitation and education programs, but Marcus wasn't really listening. His mind was on the case. And he didn't like how the pieces were fitting together.

When the Director entered, Marcus asked Powell if they could have some privacy.

The warden led them up to a small conference area connected to Control Center East. A dark, boardroom-style table occupied the center of the room, which smelled of fresh paint. Marcus leaned against the edge of the table and waited for Powell to leave.

Once they were alone, Marcus said, "I don't think we should get involved with this case. This whole thing is a powder keg for controversy and spectacle. Fagan has lectured me countless times about avoiding both those things. We're not supposed to draw any attention to ourselves or the SO."

The Director said, "Already handled."

"Care to share?"

"I'm bringing in an FBI agent who worked with Powell and me back in the days of old. And before you even ask, the answer is yes. Powell knows who we are. He was a part of my team when I was you. He's the Andrew to your me."

"You and I are nothing alike."

"I don't think you believe that, but Powell and Andrew are very different as well. Andrew maintains the peace diplomatically. Powell shoves it down your throat."

"He seems to have some good ideas. Even though they'll never work or be accepted by the mainstream."

"He's a fool. He always has been."

Marcus started to speak, but the Director cut him off. "Before you even ask, there's no drama there between Powell and me. Not all of our lives are quite so complicated as yours."

Marcus wasn't convinced but said, "It doesn't matter as long as it doesn't get in my way. But even with an FBI buffer, we're letting it all hang out here. If this thing blows up as big as I think it will, there's a real potential for some reporter to want to dig deep into our lives. And I mean going beyond the fake backgrounds we all have. Beyond our fabricated, glossy cover stories."

"You're saying this because the victims weren't just chosen at random? I already saw that on the video. What does that really change? We know that Navarro's hand was forced. And the real killer outed himself with that note."

"But if your only goal here is to kill and create a spectacle, then why kill those specific victims? Why wind Navarro up and point him at those men?"

The Director shrugged. "Because they pissed him off in some way only he understands. That's something for us to figure out. I still don't see how that makes this case any higher profile than our others. What did you see on that tape?"

"I didn't just notice that Navarro was carefully choosing his targets. I noticed who his targets were on the food chain. Each target was at the center of a cluster of men. Black, brown, yellow—this guy didn't discriminate. He told Navarro to kill the top gang leaders."

"How could you tell that from seeing them in the yard?"

"Because each of those men was the center of attention in their group. If they weren't the alpha, then they were a major up and comer."

Marcus could tell the Director was starting to get the picture. Marcus leaned in close and said, "It's nothing definitive. But why take out a player in each group?"

The Director nodded and said, "Because you want to take over. But still, what's the point in here? There's no black market or drug business to take over. You know what. That doesn't matter right now. I'm saying that I get it. This goes big and deep and has the potential to wrap us up. But we are handling this for Powell. He's a friend of the organization. I'll take care of the public relations end of things. You just get in this guy's head and catch him. That's your concern. Plus, I think I know a way to make taking on this particular case just as personal for you as it is for Powell."

"How's that?"

"I just got off the phone with Fagan. Your big brother is going to be giving us a hand on this one."

"What? I thought Fagan—"

"Ackerman is being prepped for transport as we speak."

"I'm not exactly happy about this," Fagan said.

Ackerman laughed. "Trever, please. You really must stop trying to play the role of the idealist. It doesn't suit you. I don't care what mistake from your past it is you're trying to cover. At your core, you're an ambitious realist. You want to be attorney general some day. Maybe even more. But men who rise to those heights always have one thing in common. Think of every great leader in history. Disregard beliefs and whether or not they are perceived as good or evil. All that is irrelevant. All those leaders who were legendary for their leadership skills, those who set the minds and hearts of a populace on fire. All of them did one thing very well."

Fagan rolled his eyes. "Oh, please do enlighten me."

Ackerman had been secured to a metal gurney that had been tilted up, but he was still inside the cube of four-and-a-half-inch-thick, clear polycarbonate material that had served as his home over the past year. The cage that he had allowed to temporarily contain him.

"All of those leaders—the most powerful, the most cunning, the most remembered. All of them used the resources they had on hand wisely and inventively in order to achieve their goals. They thought outside the box. That's what you're doing here with me."

"I'm only doing this to satisfy a curiosity and because

you will be undercover inside a prison and still in custody. But have no illusions. The option to simply have you put down like a rabid dog is still very much on the table."

The corners of Ackerman's mouth and eyes curled up into a malicious grin. "Trever, do you still believe that I'm actually your prisoner?"

"Says the man strapped to a table in an impenetrable glass box that sits inside a secure CIA black-site facility. Who is monitored by three personal guards around the clock. Not to mention that you would have to escape the outer room, which requires handprint analysis and an eight-digit code. The handprint analysis also checks that the person is alive and not under duress. There's no escaping your cage. If I wanted you to rot here forever, then that's what would happen. But don't worry, this experimental prison you're going to seems to be every bit as secure."

A large set of steel doors opened up in front of them. They were the kind of doors designed to hold King Kong and could only be opened from the other side. They were used for prisoner transport.

When the doors parted, five guards wheeled in a lightproof box a bit larger than a casket. The guards all eyed him warily. As it should be. He had been called a lot of names by law enforcement over the years—the Experiment, the Boogeyman, Frankenstein, the Monster—but out of those many nicknames and stories, Ackerman most enjoyed the one the guards here had come to call him , , , The Man with No Fear. It had a nice ring to it.

He said, "I'm sure I could find a way to escape from this new prison as easily as I did this room."

Fagan said, "There's no escaping this room unless someone like me says so."

Ackerman closed his eyes and pictured the escape that could have been. Then he said, "The toilet and shower here in my little apartment clog quite easily. Bit of a design flaw. Say that toilet should become clogged up by something, like it did eight months and three days ago. The guards would have me stick my arms out a slot in the back wall of my cube. Once I'm sitting on the floor, arms behind me and secured outside the cell, maintenance would enter and fix the toilet. One guard remains behind me, watching my hands, so I can't work a way out of my restraints. Another guard is in the cube with me. He monitors me from this side as the maintenance person does their work. The third guard is on overwatch from the catwalk holding a shotgun chambered with Taser XREP shells."

Fagan said, "Sounds pretty damn secure to me."

"Oh, it is. They try hard here. But imagine if I were to break both my thumbs before they even start any of this. I'm already wet from the clog. It makes it easier to rip my hands directly out of the restraints. I'd probably lose some patches of skin on my hands and forearms, but I can't say that I wouldn't actually enjoy that part. From there, I kick out the guard inside the cube's feet and disable him. He's armed with a single shot Taser. I take that and use it on the next guard. The plumber's of no concern."

"But the guard on the catwalk would drop you."

"On some days perhaps. But if it's a day when the blond guard with the beard is working, then he'll be down here with me. He's always down here with me when he's on shift. Maybe he's their toughest man. Best in hand-to-hand.

Either way, his presence is important because he keeps a knife in his boot, which I suspect is against the rulebook. I can take that knife from him and throw it into the flesh of the catwalk guard, throat or thigh depending on my mood. Then I parkour up the corner of the room—parkour is a type of free-running martial art, in case you aren't versed in such things—and I reach the catwalk."

"And you're still trapped in this room. We gear up an assault team and take you down at our leisure."

"Or I could just open the door and walk out."

Fagan said, "Sure. Right past the latest in biometric analysis and an eight-digit code that you couldn't possibly know."

"In *The Art of War*, Sun Tzu teaches to pretend inferiority and encourage the arrogance of your opponent. I've never been good at the pretending inferiority part. For the biometrics, I would cut off one of their palms. Just the top few layers of skin and muscle. Then I would wear their flesh like a glove."

"You promised your brother that you wouldn't kill anyone. At least, not without permission."

"The guard would survive. The skin would grow back nicely. I'll even take it from his non-dominant hand. That way he can still wipe his ass without difficulty."

"How thoughtful of you. But there's still the code. And there is no way that you could know what that is."

The blond, bearded guard walked up and said, "We're prepped for transport, sir."

Fagan turned to the man. "Do you have a knife in your boot?"

"Sir?"

"If you do, it had better not be there tomorrow. Now, get Mr. Ackerman out of my sight."

The guards went to work securing Ackerman. They lifted the black box on its edge, covering him with shotguns while they wheeled him out of one box to the other.

As they were about to close the coffin's lid and wrap him in darkness, Ackerman said, "22537626."

The look on Fagan's face was priceless. Ackerman took a mental snapshot.

Fagan said, "I won't confirm or deny that you're correct, but out of pure curiosity, why would you guess that specific code?"

Ackerman smiled. "Don't worry about it, Trever. Daddy will tell you all about it when he gets home from work."

Powell had requested that Officer Navarro remain in custody at the prison to aid in the investigation. The local sheriff had agreed. So there they sat. Inside a secure conference room with brown-paneled walls, maybe the same one lawyers used to confer privately with their clients. A dead zone. Marcus had made sure of that.

The metal chair creaked under his weight as Marcus sat down opposite the man who twenty-four hours prior had shot four inmates and blown up two of his coworkers. Ray Navarro still smelled strongly of smoke and blood, and his odor filled the whole room.

"How's your day going?" Marcus said.

Navarro's eyes didn't waver from the floor. He hadn't spoken a word since his capture.

"I hope today's going better than yesterday at least.

Yesterday was probably the worst day of your life. So were you involved, an accomplice, or were you forced to murder those men?"

Marcus laid a few file folders on the table in front of Navarro. He opened them up. Fanned out the pictures inside. They were family photos of the two guards who had died in the explosion.

"I had to request these photos from the families of your victims."

Navarro wrestled his eyes up to the images, human nature and curiosity cutting through his grief. His eyes were bloodshot from crying.

Marcus said, "When I return these photos, should I tell them that the person responsible has been brought to justice, or is that person still out there?"

Navarro said nothing, but his facial expressions showed that he was understanding. He wasn't completely catatonic.

Marcus said, "Did you kill your family?"

Tears ran down Ray Navarro's cheeks. Marcus could almost feel Navarro's thoughts. The man was thinking that he might as well have.

Marcus leaned back in his chair and said, "I had a similar experience a while back. But mine lasted for months. I was thrown into a dark hole and tortured and forced to do a lot of things I'm not proud of. But you know one thing that kept me going was the thought of making sure that something similar didn't happen to someone else. If you don't talk to me, Ray, then other families are going to suffer and die. Other kids will go to bed without a parent. You may feel that you didn't have a choice up to this point. You may have been trapped. But that's not true anymore. Now, you have a choice. I don't judge you for what happened, but I will judge you if you don't make a choice right now, a conscious choice, to help me make sure this doesn't happen to anyone else."

Navarro said nothing, but he did look up.

Marcus said, "How about I run it down from the beginning and you fill in the blanks? Just nod if that's all you feel you can do."

But Navarro did more than nod. His voice sounded like dried leaves crumbling as he said, "Why aren't there pictures of Bill's family in there? You didn't mention him."

"They didn't tell you? Bill Singer is doing okay. Well, he has one too many holes in him, but he'll live."

Ray started weeping. He raised his head to the ceiling in what seemed to be a silent thank you. Marcus imagined they were the kind of tears a father would shed after a child pulled through a dangerous surgery. They were tears of joy, of relief.

"Your coworkers say that you and Bill were close."

"Why past tense? I thought you just said he's okay. Did I imagine that? Was that in my head?" With each word, Navarro would rub his throat as if he was in pain from speaking so much.

"Stay with me, Ray. I was referring to your friendship in the past tense. I'm sure you shooting him put bit of a strain on the relationship."

"I'm just not sure what's real anymore."

"I've been there. But this man who started the ball rolling, he's real. Here's how I figure it so far. Some guy busts in and takes you and your family hostage. He knows that you were a Marine sniper. He knows you're a man who has killed before. Killed for something you cared about. For the right reasons. Killed for your country. He knows that it's a short shove, just a little push, to get you to kill again in order to protect something you love. Hell, all the targets are convicts, nasty ones. You're practically doing the world a favor. What I don't understand is why your family hasn't turned up one way or another. Dead or alive. They've just vanished without a trace."

"They're dead," Ray said in a hoarse whisper.

"That's something else I don't understand. You haven't even asked about them. If you didn't kill them and you didn't watch them die, then why are you so sure they're gone?"

"I figured he was going to kill them either way, but with what I did, they're dead for sure."

"What did you do?"

"I didn't follow the plan. My mother-in-law has been staying with us. She was taken as well. He killed her just to make a point. Just to show how serious he was. He was very clear. He told me in detail what he would do if I didn't follow the plan to the letter."

"You only saw one man? You sure?"

"Positive. He had us in a dark room with hoods over our heads, but he left us alone a few times. Anyone who had a partner would have kept a guard on us. I never heard any other voices."

"The partner could have been on another mission or this guy could have been one member of a larger group."

"I suppose, but I didn't get that feeling."

"What part of the plan didn't you follow?"

"It doesn't matter. Nothing matters anymore."

"Ray, I think your family may still be alive."

"The other cop said the same thing. But you weren't there. You didn't look in his eyes."

"This killer isn't a sadist. He doesn't kill just for the joy of killing. He's mission-oriented. He killed your mother-in-law to prove a point. He had you kill those inmates because they fit into his plan somehow. He wants attention. It's not about the killing. It's about proving his superiority. Over you, Powell, law enforcement. Killing your family doesn't prove he's superior to them."

"He wouldn't just let them go. I knew a guy like him in the corps. People might as well be flies or ants. The lives of other people mean nothing to men like that."

"What was the plan? What went wrong?"

Ray teared up again.

"What were you supposed to do?"

"I knew he was going to kill them either way. I had to do something. I had to try. But Bill stopped me. He got in the way."

"What did you try?"

"To get away. I was supposed to kill myself with the bomb. None of the other guards were supposed to get hurt. I chose my family over them. I thought maybe I could sneak back and . . . I don't know what I was thinking."

"You were making impossible choices and doing the best you could with an unthinkable situation. If he wanted you dead, that means you know something that can hurt him."

"I don't know anything. He wore a mask and disguised his voice electronically."

"Where did you get the bomb? How did you get it through security?"

"I didn't. The bomb was already here waiting for me."

Marcus stared out the enormous window and surveyed the prison complex. Powell's office was a sort of watchtower itself. It sat above all the others, built upon one of the prison's many interconnected buildings, some of which looked as if they were about to—or already had—fallen in on themselves. The office rested in a twenty-five-by-twenty-five-foot space sitting at the very top of the tower. Each of the four walls had large viewing windows. Sunlight bathed every corner of the room, and the scent of boiling peppermint oil hung heavy in the air. The office took up a whole floor of its own that could only be accessed via the spiral metal staircase Marcus had noticed in Control Center East.

Powell walked up and handed Marcus a cup of coffee. Marcus looked down at it like it was a breath of air to a drowning man. He hadn't had any caffeine all day. How was he supposed to catch bad guys while suffering from withdrawal?

Powell said, "They call this office the Ivory Tower. It was designed by one of my more grandiose and arrogant predecessors. I hate it. Makes me feel like I'm lording over these men."

"Aren't you?"

"Perhaps. In a sense. But I like to think of the relationship more as that of a father to a child. One of love, but also of discipline."

"So you think of yourself more as a god to these men rather than their king."

Powell seemed to consider his next words carefully. "Special Agent Williams, Marcus if I may, do you take particular issue with me or what I'm doing here?"

Marcus took a long sip of his coffee. Normally, he would have dropped a sarcastic remark or smart-ass comment, but he wanted Powell to open up and tell him the truth about something and, sometimes, the easiest way to get someone to let his or her guard down was to let down your own.

"I'm sorry," Marcus said. "I sometimes get so wrapped up in the case that some of my natural tendencies shine through."

"I've been there. What you do isn't easy."

"I hear you know from firsthand experience."

"Yes, but that was a lifetime ago."

"Why'd you quit?"

"The past is the past, son. I think your boss and I would both like to keep it there."

He thought of his boss. The Director. What kind of a guy goes by a codename and doesn't give out his real name to the people he works with? It was only because of Ackerman that he knew the Director's real name was Philip. On any information of a personal nature, the Director was more than just a closed book. He was a book that didn't want to be read.

Philip had left for the airport in order to greet Ackerman's private plane at the hangar. Marcus had wanted to be there himself, but his boss had insisted on briefing Ackerman while he updated the local sheriff and prison leadership.

The Director had finally convinced Marcus by suggesting that he could pick up Maggie on the way, and maybe try to cool her down a bit. Marcus wasn't expecting great results from that plan, but it was worth a shot.

They were still waiting for Powell's public relations manager. He checked the time on his modified Apple watch. If the PR guy wasn't there in five minutes, the briefing would begin without him.

Marcus said, "I need to know why you quit."

"It has no bearing on the case."

"I didn't say that it did. I noticed the pictures here in your office. Your daughter is definitely old enough to have been around when you were part of the organization."

Powell nodded in understanding. "I heard you have a son. You'd like to know if I quit because of my daughter? Well, it's more complicated than that."

"It always is."

"I will tell you this. I love my daughter, and we have a strong bond. A bond that would not have been possible if I had been working at the SO."

Marcus was about to probe deeper, but Powell's secretary called out from across the office, "Excuse me, Mr. Powell. I just got word that Mr. Reese is on his way up. Are you ready to start the briefing?"

While Marcus had been interrogating Navarro, Andrew had decided to speak with some of the guards about the incident and the prison in general. As people started to gather around the conference table in Powell's office, Andrew was surprised to see one of the men he had questioned earlier at length. A young guard who had been present at the time of the shooting.

Andrew walked up and shook the man's hand and said, "Hello again, Jerry."

Jerry Dunn answered with a smile and a nod as he limped past Andrew toward the marble conference table filling one side of Powell's office. Andrew had learned that Jerry had only started working in corrections a few months ago. Based on his lack of seniority, it seemed strange for Jerry to have been invited to this meeting. The others he could understand—the assistant warden, Major Ingram, Spinelli, Sheriff Hall, Powell's PR rep, and Powell's secretary—but Jerry Dunn seemed out of place.

"I didn't expect to see you here," Andrew said.

Jerry Dunn paused his shuffling gait and said, "I requested to help."

"Do you mind if I ask why?"

Dunn had a strange way of vomiting up his words. He didn't exactly stutter. He just seemed to have a hard time getting started. Like the words were thick and sticky and got caught in his throat.

Dunn said with effort, "Sergeant Singer is my friend. And if I wasn't the way that I am, I think I could have got there in time to keep him from getting shot. I asked Major Ingram if I could be a kind of liaison between the guards and the investigation. I think I can help."

Andrew nodded and put on a mask of sympathy, thinking in the back of his mind that some killers liked to insert themselves into the investigation.

From across the room, Marcus said, "Let's get started."

The gathered group took their seats at the conference

table. Marcus stood on one side, next to Powell. Andrew had purposely chosen a seat far away from Marcus on the opposite side of the oblong table. As Marcus conducted the briefing, Andrew would watch the reactions of the people in the room.

Marcus said to the group, "Let's start with what we know so far. At a quarter past four yesterday, Officer Ray Navarro opened fire on the yard and killed four inmates with a 30-06 rifle, and then took out two correctional officers with an improvised explosive device. But there's more to it than just what's on the surface. If you saw this on TV, you would instantly think disgruntled employee. We don't believe that's the case. We believe that our real perpetrator abducted Navarro's family and forced him to execute the four prisoners. They weren't random targets. They were men marked for death. The obvious question is: Why those four men? One thing they had in common was that they were all high-ranking gang leaders. Major Ingram, any other connection you can think of between the victims?"

Ingram was a large black man with a bald head and a gray goatee. He shook his head and, with a voice like a bear's growl, said, "No, sir. There's no connection we've found between them. And despite the gang connection, I can't see how anyone would benefit by killing them."

"Another question. Why was a man who helped design your software, Peter Spinelli, murdered at the same time as the shooting?"

At the mention of her brother, Lisa Spinelli said, "We're going over the system with a fine-tooth comb. So far we've found nothing. And my brother would never sell the software, if that's what you were thinking."

"I'm not making any assumptions. Just keep digging and keep thinking. There must be a reason he was targeted beyond just sending a message to bring in the feds. Which is another question. Why does our killer want more attention and more people trying to catch him? What is he planning that he needs a big audience for? Sheriff Hall, are there any groups around—militia, cult, extremists, glory hounds—who might do something like this? Anyone we should be looking at from a local angle? Sheriff?"

Sheriff Hall was in his late thirties, and Andrew pegged the man for a former Boy Scout turned military turned cop. It was all there in the man's high and tight haircut, the precise way he wore his uniform, and the erect posture he had maintained since entering the room. But now, Sheriff Hall wasn't playing the role of the good soldier. He was staring off into space. Hall's eyes seemed distant, but they were moving rapidly from side to side as if he were scanning a newspaper from left to right. Hall didn't acknowledge Marcus. Major Ingram tapped the sheriff on the shoulder and said, "Sir, Special Agent Williams is asking you a question."

Hall looked at Marcus and apologized. Then Marcus repeated his question, Hall gave an answer that shed no light on the investigation, and the briefing moved on. Andrew was proud of Marcus for how he had handled Hall. He had come a long way with utilizing local resources and working with a team. Andrew wished the Director was there to see Marcus conducting the briefing. Maybe that would have assuaged some of the old man's concerns about Marcus's stability in the field.

Marcus said, "What about the Navarro family?"

"Still no sign of them," Sheriff Hall said. "No evidence. No trace. But finding them has been our top priority from the beginning."

"I'm going to be helping with that search personally. As for the rest of you, consider yourselves all part of the Foxbury Investigation Task Force. If I were an Old West marshal, I would say that you've all been deputized. And I have specific jobs for each of you."

Marcus ran down a list of action items for each person, mostly information gathering, and then he sent them all of on their individual assignments.

After the briefing, as the dispersing group gathered papers and moved with purpose toward their new objectives, Andrew approached Marcus and said, "Nice job with the briefing."

Marcus replied, "I hate working with people. We need to get more cases where I can sit in a dark room alone with nothing but the evidence and the killer's mind."

"That sounds both depressing and disturbing."

"What did you learn?"

Andrew referred to his notes and said, "Bradley Reese, Powell's public relations guy, is a bit of a narcissist, but I suppose that goes with the territory in his profession. The sheriff's obviously worried and distracted about something."

"Yeah, could just be the pressure of such a high-profile investigation falling in his lap, but we'll definitely have Stan dig into him too."

"Then there's the guard who was sitting beside Ingram—"

"The one who was present at the shooting."

"Right. He requested to be here. To help the investigation."

Marcus nodded. "Have Stan take an extra long look at him."

Andrew said, "We're going to have to research every guard and every staff member. Any of them could have planted the bomb for Navarro to find."

"I don't know. I think it would have taken a certain level of access."

Andrew added, "But I thought of something even more important during your briefing. Navarro told you that he was supposed to kill himself with the bomb and then the guy said he would let his family go. I initially thought that having Navarro kill himself was to lead the investigation down the wrong path. To throw us off his scent."

Marcus finished Andrew's thought and said, "But if that were the case, then why call attention to himself with the note at the same time."

"Right. Because he's not trying to throw us off. He just wanted Navarro dead for some reason."

Marcus hefted some of the file folders into his arms, but then he checked the name on each and laid them all back down. Andrew realized that Marcus had decided he didn't need the files. He must have already scanned and committed them to memory. A couple of years prior, Andrew would have doubted Marcus's eidetic abilities, but now he knew better. If Marcus had scanned them, then he would be able to recall them if the need should arise. Marcus had explained his memory like a never-ending reel of microfiche, the kind that old newspapers were stored on. Marcus didn't remember the words on the pages, he remembered the images, the frames of the film.

Marcus laid the files back on the conference table and

said, "I already had the guards on Navarro doubled and told Spinelli to keep an eye on him."

Andrew said, "Okay, good. No one's getting close to Navarro, but why does our puppet master want Navarro dead in the first place?"

"My guess? Navarro knows something. He may not even know that he knows. But I'm betting that there is some detail, some clue, that Navarro has locked away inside him. Maybe he knows something that leads to our killer. Maybe he knows something that points us back to the location of his family. Either way, we have to figure out what that detail is."

"So how are we going to get him to remember it? All that trauma is too fresh in his mind."

Marcus cracked his neck. "Yeah, I'm afraid we're going to have to go old school to get it out of him. I have a couple of ideas."

"He's been through a lot. He's a victim in this too."

"I know. But if our roles were reversed and that was me in his spot, I would want the investigators to do whatever it took to find my family and the man responsible for this mess. I would endure whatever it took. Navarro and the info locked away inside him is the key to everything."

Ackerman had been hooded and gagged, and so he couldn't see the world around him. But his other senses were more than capable of filling in the gaps about his surroundings and situation. He felt the change in pressure and the landing gear hitting the runway. He heard the flight crew hooking up hoses, hydraulics whirring, the engines cooling, the metal creaking, breathing. He smelled the diesel of refueling trucks. His coffin-like transport container tilted and started moving. Ackerman gauged the distance they had traveled, catalogued the sounds of all the surfaces, and tucked away every voice and background noise alike. He could never know for sure when one of those details would give him an edge over an opponent or an opportunity to gain the upper hand.

They arrived inside a hangar, and he was left in the same position for several minutes. To fill the time, Ackerman imagined different scenarios of him escaping in that moment. He imagined himself killing the owners of all those outside voices. He imagined their blood on his hands, in his mouth.

Sometimes just playing out the scenarios in his mind was enough to sate the beast's appetite. But other times, the urge to kill was too strong to be satisfied by a mental killing spree.

Kill them and the pain will stop, his father's voice in his head told him. The voice urged him to kill the first person he saw when he opened his eyes. And the next. And the next. And to never stop until someone stopped him.

Ackerman ignored the voice. He intellectually rejected it. He isolated and analyzed the urge to kill and shoved it back down into the depths of his soul.

But the longer he went without drinking in someone's pain and fear, the louder his father's voice became. The stronger that urge, that instinct, that wolf inside him became. He would never have admitted it to anyone, least of all his brother, but Francis Ackerman could almost feel himself losing his grip on the darkness inside himself. They called him the Man with No Fear, but if there was anything that had ever come close to truly frightening him, it was the monster within. The thing he became when he lost control.

"That's how we're transporting him?" said a voice from outside his box, a voice Ackerman recognized.

The Director added, "It looks like we're sending Dracula through UPS."

After another few moments, Ackerman was free from darkness and being wheeled across an aircraft hangar where the Director and Maggie waited for him.

He smiled at Maggie and said, "Hello, little sister."

She looked like she wanted to gouge his eyes out. "Stop calling me that. You and I are not related. Not by blood or marriage."

"I hope that doesn't mean that you and my brother are having troubles. I could recommend a good counselor."

"Dr. Phil?"

"Actually, I was thinking about me. I can be quite insightful."

The Director interrupted and said, "Okay, enough pleasantries."

Ackerman had noticed Philip's gradual withering. But his aging seemed to have accelerated somehow, like all the cold of winter hitting a flower at once. The withering man went on to explain the ins and outs of Foxbury and its software and what had happened so far with the case. Ackerman listened patiently. Information was a tool, a weapon. And Ackerman liked to be well armed.

His only question was, "Where do they get the data for the analysis software?"

The Director said, "It comes from tamperproof bands

on both wrists and ankles. I assume that it pumps back all kinds of vital signs to their software."

Ackerman tried to nod, but his head was still secured to the transport gurney. He said, "Blood pressure, heart rate, spikes in adrenaline, and other chemicals. All biological and involuntary signs that choreograph what that person will do in the next millisecond. The software just has to be faster in seeing those signs coming than that man's body can complete the internal processes and take violent action. Sounds like a challenge."

Maggie stepped forward. The look on her face reminded Ackerman of a lioness protecting her cubs. She said, "Before you start getting any ideas about rising to meet that challenge, remember that this is your last chance. If you screw things up here, Marcus will no longer be able to protect you."

Ackerman laughed. "Why are all of you under the impression that I'm here for any other reason besides that I've chosen to be here? I've allowed you to cage me and poke and prod me and experiment on me like a lab rat. To be honest, the whole experience makes me feel nostalgic about my childhood."

The Director said, "We've never doubted your abilities, Ackerman. We just question your motives. You're not here to test the prison's security or prove that you're the most frightening killer on the cell block. You want to be part of the team? You want to prove that you're an asset? That you can be trusted? Here's your chance. But being part of the team means following orders. Can you do that?"

"I'm yours to command, my liege. I would bend a knee in fealty but, unfortunately, I'm still restrained."

"Can you follow orders?"

"I promise. I'll be a good boy. Well, maybe not 'good,' but at least moderately helpful. When it suits me."

The Director shook his head. "At least you're honest. Here's what we need you to do: find out everything you can about the inmates who were killed, this ULF leader who's one of the other inmates, and keep your ear to the ground. Find out if there is any chatter among the population. Anything that seems strange. Gather intelligence and report back. That's it. Stay under the radar."

"Got it. Murder the leader of the ULF and lead an uprising." Ackerman gave Maggie a wink.

The Director said, "If you try to murder or even touch anyone, you'll be surfing a wave of a thousand volts before you can blink."

"I was just kidding. If we're going to be working together, the two of you have to lighten up. Also, I thought you said that this place is filled with cameras. Why can't they just monitor what the inmates have going on?"

"Technically, I think they can. Problem is that they don't have the staff to listen to every word by every inmate. The software can flag keywords and has a whole lot of other algorithms I'll never understand for identifying potential threats and anger and escapes, but the bottom line is that you're there to get a boots-on-the-ground feel for the inmates and whether anyone on the inside is connected to the killings."

Maggie said, "Only a few people will know that you're working for us. Everyone else will believe you're just another new prisoner. Don't draw attention to yourself."

"What am I in for?"

"Tax evasion," Maggie said.

"You're joking."

"There's a folder of fake background info you'll need to study before the prison transport arrives," the Director said. "The important thing is that you keep a low profile. You're a spy, not a conquering warrior. And, most important, no one is to ever learn your real identity. Fagan, me, Marcus, and even your new friends at the CIA are all in agreement on that. If anyone finds out who you really are, it risks exposing us."

Ackerman smiled. "How exciting. I always wanted to be a secret agent."

Ray Navarro stared at the piece of white paper and the black ballpoint pen resting in front of him. The paper was the kind used in copier machines—no lines, not designed for writing by hand. As he gazed at the white and line-less paper, he felt like he was drowning in a mar de blanco. The sea of white smothered him. He had so much to say but no idea what to write. It was difficult to sum up your entire life and your hopes and dreams in a few words. But he knew that the time he had to share those words was running out.

The interrogation room had no clock, and so he had no idea how much time had truly passed. It felt like it had been days. But in regard to time, relativity made it difficult to judge such things.

He kept thinking of his family. The man who had abducted them had told Ray that if he played his part then his family would be released unharmed. The man had explained the plan to Ray and had made him believe it. Their tormentor had said all the right things to assure him that there would be no reason to hurt Renata and Ian as long as the instructions were followed.

Ray had been a good soldier. He could follow orders.

And so far, Ray had done everything exactly as the man had directed.

He had eliminated the targets, placed the bomb, attempted escape, and had kept silent until questioned by federal investigators. Then he told the investigator exactly what he had been instructed to say.

The kidnapper had always stressed that killing Ray's family did not advance his larger plans. They hadn't seen his face. He had no reason to kill them.

Ray kept repeating that to himself. Replaying the man's words of assurance.

If he completed his mission, his family would not be harmed.

He had to believe it. He had no other choice but to believe. The alternatives were unthinkable.

Still, he had doubts. He had started to second-guess himself and question if he could have done something differently or stopped this from happening.

He thought of the thing that man had made him swallow. He rubbed his throat. The thought of ingesting that thing reminded him that his time could be short.

He looked again at the paper.

What to say?

When his superiors had sent him overseas to kill, and die if necessary, he had gone gladly because he believed in what being a soldier meant. He believed in protecting his country, his home, and his family. And he would have laid down his life for those beliefs.

In his mind, that was a death with meaning.

Nothing had changed since then. He would have still sacrificed himself for the ones he loved and for what he believed. And that's what he was doing.

But how could he express that in words his young son and his wife could understand?

He put pen to paper and started to write. His hand shook, and the words came out as big letters that would have taken up two or three whole ruled lines, if this paper had been made with lines.

Renata, I love you. You and Ian are my world. Explain to him.

Ray Navarro read the words, folded the paper, and placed the pen back on the table.

Then he closed his eyes and waited to die.

He hoped it would be quick. Even though he knew that he didn't deserve that mercy.

The interrogation room holding Navarro was on the second floor of the main building. If Powell had followed Marcus's directions then five men would be guarding Navarro, two in the room with him and three patrolling the surrounding corridors, which would be off-limits to prisoners. Marcus hoped that Powell had understood the importance of those instructions.

His intuition told him that all roads led back to Navarro. The shooter was the key, but Marcus also couldn't shake the feeling that they were being led. Was he following clues and investigating or was he simply following a path designed by some unseen puppet master?

Designed to prove what?

It's all about superiority.

As he and Andrew walked through the corridors of the prison or hospital or whatever Powell wanted to call it, Marcus couldn't help but remember *One Flew Over the Cuckoo's Nest*. The hallways of the makeshift prison were dry and institutional. They had fresh new paint, but the grime of the past still showed through. And new paint couldn't cover the feeling of the place, an aura reminiscent of laboratories and shock therapy. What it did do was add to the smell, combining that new-house smell with Pine-Sol and mildew and sweat.

Prisoners passed them several times. The inmates or residents, as Powell called them, were allowed to go about their business freely. After all, Saint Nick was always watching and reaching down with the miracles of wirelessly powered and wirelessly controlled shock bracelets and anklets.

Marcus glanced into some of the rooms. They looked more like tiny apartments than prison cells. Some even had amenities like refrigerators and televisions. Powell had explained that the reward system functioned much like real society. Good behavior meant increased rewards and privileges. It also gave them things to take away from those lifers who often had nothing to lose. For those who would be re-entering society soon, it gave a more realistic view of the world.

Marcus didn't necessarily like the idea of murderers getting any kind of reward system, but he understood that there had to be a balance between punishment and rehabilitation.

Major Ingram, the highest-ranking correctional officer at Foxbury, had volunteered to lead them back down to the interrogation room, in order to discuss security measures. The thickly muscled Major marched military-straight in front of them, explaining the security chokepoints and how he had maximized guard patrols for response times. But Marcus noted that everything still revolved around the cameras and security software.

Marcus soaked in the words coming from Major Ingram, but he also absorbed information that "normal" people would have disregarded as background noise.

He tried to focus in on only the relevant bits of data. He supposed normal people did this with ease, but for him there were always a million different distractions, all vying for his attention, demanding to be heard, seen, felt, and analyzed.

Over the years, he had learned to focus on only what was important, but he couldn't help but catalog all the other sights and sounds as well. And sometimes, even after years of mental training, he still caught his mind wandering off like it did when he was a kid in Brooklyn.

And as they walked the corridors, every once in a while, his mind would go on a little journey. His brain would travel down the hall to locate the sound of a leaky faucet. His mind would open the bathroom door, break down the faucet to its base components, and identify the faulty component. Probably just a rubber o-ring that a maintenance guy could pick up at a hardware store for ninety-nine cents.

Marcus snapped back to reality when he heard the distant

sound of running footsteps followed by the not-so-distant clanging of alarm bells.

All the surrounding guards were converging on the interrogation room holding Navarro. Over a radio on Ingram's belt, Marcus heard Spinelli saying that Navarro was "down." The guards swooped in on Navarro's location like moths to the flame. And Marcus was drawn to the fire as well, although he already knew what they would find.

He had been stupid. He knew their mastermind had wanted Navarro dead. He should have done more to protect him. A part of Marcus wondered if he had used Navarro as bait. If he had just let Navarro dangle out there, so the mastermind would kill him and give the investigation another clue to follow.

But that's something his brother would have done. Not him.

He shoved past Ingram, past the other guards in the hallway. His shoes squeaked against the speckled green tile as he navigated his way inside the interrogation room itself.

Navarro was sprawled over on the table, face down, unmoving.

Jerry Dunn stood behind Navarro, a hand on the dead man's neck. Dunn said, "He's dead."

Marcus shoved Dunn back from the body. He screamed, "What the hell are you doing in here?"

The dark-haired young man stammered out some unintelligible reply as he stumbled backward.

Marcus said, "Did you kill him and then try to act like you found him this way?"

He stepped toward Dunn again, but Andrew held him back.

"Whoa," Andrew said. "Let's watch the recording and see what actually happened before we make any accusations."

Marcus pulled himself under control.

"Right," he said. To Major Ingram, he added, "I want Officer Dunn taken into custody until we watch that recording."

Marcus then moved back to Navarro's lifeless form and personally checked for a pulse or any signs of life.

His findings matched Jerry's earlier assessment.

Ray Navarro, the only man who had any firsthand information on the case, had just died. In a locked room, while under constant surveillance.

```
FILE #750265-6726-690
Zolotov, Dmitry - AKA The Judas Killer
State Exhibit F
Description: Diary Entry
```

My father was fat and lazy, but he wasn't stupid. He knew that a con man, even a small-time con man like himself, needed to go where the money was. And the money and the biggest marks alike were most plentiful in the United States. So before my tenth birthday, we had conned and robbed our way into the good ol' US of A, fake documents and all.

What Father didn't count on was the fact that a lot of the old cons he got away with on the streets of Moscow didn't work in America, either because of cultural differences or the greater diligence of law enforcement. Either way, a man with my father's skill set, who also wanted to only work a few hours a week and be blackout drunk the rest of the time, was limited in his opportunities for employment. Which forced Father to be inventive.

I was eleven years old when he created the first iteration of The Judas Game.

We were working the midway at a traveling carnival. The kind which moves from town to town, county to county, leaching onto community events and local festivals. Most people didn't realize, but the different games at the midway weren't operated by the carnival itself. The big carnival company handled the rides and the bookings and setting up the events, but the actual slots and spaces for games on the midway were rented. Someone with a game that they thought would be popular could rent the "privilege" to run it there in the midway.

So next time you're walking through the carnival, take notice of the man running the duck pond and the balloon game and the water guns. In some cases, that game is that man's business and all he owns in the world. That little booth is his means of putting food on the table. Respect that.

My father was like that for a while. He had purchased an old wheel of chance game from one place or another and had weaseled his way onto the circuit as part of Mr. Mackey's Magical Midways, touring over half the country. Which wouldn't have been a bad life for me. It was at least better than starving on the streets of

Moscow. But there were times when we had to pay as much as $1,600 for the "privilege" at some of the bigger fairs. Add that up with the cost of the little trinkets we gave away, and we were barely making enough money to keep father drunk and me from starving.

As I said, Father wasn't stupid. In fact, when circumstances demanded it, he was quite shrewd. He knew that we needed to adapt. Father loved the theater and had once dreamed of being a stage actor. Unfortunately, he was ugly and had no talent. A note to historians—you can take my word on this as a statement of fact. I fully believe that any other sources you could unearth about my father will corroborate my assessments.

So Father decided to incorporate a bit of theater into the midway.

He left the old "Wheel of Chance" game in my capable hands—with him still making all of the profit, of course—and he rented out another space right beside me. That meant twice the "privilege" payment. And Father had no extra money to buy a game or build one of his own. Plus, most of the cheap and easy options were taken. The duck pond, ring toss, ball toss, and the like. The only way to stand out among the other established and time-tested games was to do something that cost money. Games that required air-driven BB guns and water spraying equipment.

But that was where Father got inventive and pulled back to his roots in the theater.

He set out to design a game with no start-up cost that could also be the top-grossing "attraction" on the midway. And my father was not a humble man. Not a reserved man. He bragged about what he was going to accomplish before he even had the slightest clue of how he would attain it.

Father believed that the selfish nature of man informed all of our decisions. He firmly felt that when faced with a choice, every person will always choose the option that would benefit him or her the most.

I disagree with Father. People aren't that black and white and clear cut. But he was right in thinking that it wouldn't take a lot of money being on the line for a person to sell out a friend.

So Father started out to design a theatrical game involving betrayal, a concept he felt to be the one thing shared by all humanity. It didn't take long for the title of "The Judas Game" to be born.

Episode 2

Andrew Held his tongue until they were alone and running back toward Control Center East. The CCE occupied the floor beneath Powell's office. Ingram had mentioned earlier that the entire Ivory Tower could be closed off and was one of the only areas of the prison that residents were never allowed to enter.

Andrew said, "It's time we talk about what's going on with you."

Marcus said, "I know."

No challenge. No smartass comment. Andrew wasn't sure if that was a good sign or not.

He said, "Let's start with Pittsburgh."

Marcus paused long enough for Andrew to think further prompting was required, but then Marcus said, "Now's not the time. The killer is here. We have him, and I'm not letting him slip away."

Marcus seemed to have increased his pace to illustrate the point. He pulled ahead in the empty corridor, and Andrew kicked his legs into the next gear to catch up. Residents watched them from every room. Earlier, the metal doors of each cell had been open, allowing the inmates to roam freely and go about their daily business, the goal being a simulated society. Andrew guessed that the alarm had triggered a command for all of the residents to return to their apartments. He had noticed that the left bracelet on each prisoner's wrist contained what looked to be a small speaker. Maybe the alert had triggered a command that was then transmitted out to the bracelets. He certainly hadn't heard such an announcement over any kind of prison PA system.

Either way, the residents were back in their cells and secured. That fact made Andrew feel much safer, despite Powell's assurances about his security and software.

As Andrew came up beside Marcus, he said, "There's never a good time, just the time we have."

"You get that from a fortune cookie?"

"Are you not in good enough shape to talk and run?"

"I can still run circles around you."

Marcus sped up again. Andrew matched him and said between breaths, "The Director said that after Pittsburgh, Fagan is ready to pounce if you screw up."

"Fagan's a bureaucrat. He's all bark."

"The Director doesn't think so. He says Fagan is ready to retire you and put Ackerman in the ground."

Marcus said nothing.

"Is it just rage? You having trouble controlling it?"

"I don't know what it is. Sometimes I wonder if a piece of me died down in Thomas White's dungeon."

Andrew, barely finding the breath to form words, said, "I can't imagine what you've been through."

"Sure you can. We all have our scars."

They reached the security checkpoint leading up to the Ivory Tower, and Andrew was glad for the chance to catch his breath. The guard, sitting inside a small room behind what was probably three inches of bullet-resistant glass, allowed them access to the secure elevator.

Once inside, Marcus stood straight up and down, looking anxious and ready to strike but not at all fatigued by the run from the murder scene.

Andrew bent over and placed his hands on his knees. He said, "You're not alone."

"I know."

"You can talk to me."

"I know. I appreciate it."

He grabbed Marcus by the arm. "I mean it. Sometimes, I understand that doing this job means that you have to let the demon out. And that's fine. Use that. But don't give it too much space in your head. Don't let the demon start calling the shots."

The elevator bounced and dipped at their arrival. The doors parted. Marcus started to walk through them, but then he turned back and said, "But what if the demon is the only part I have left?"

Marcus paced back and forth in front of the wall of monitors, balling his fists and cracking his neck. He could see the last frame of Ray Navarro's life still hanging in suspended animation on the interconnected network of seamless screens. He said, "Are you sure no one touched him?"

"Positive," Spinelli said. "I've checked back through hours of video and the software has an interaction search that can display every physical exchange."

"You need to check every frame manually."

"I have people on it."

Marcus turned to Andrew and said, "Could he have been poisoned before the shooting?"

Andrew tapped his fingernails against his front teeth as he considered the idea. Marcus hated when Andrew did that, but he was also certain that his own annoying habits outweighed a bit of tooth tapping, so he kept his mouth shut about it.

After five taps, Andrew said, "It's certainly possible, but I would have expected Navarro to be showing more physical symptoms leading up to his death, if that was the case." Andrew said to Spinelli, "Can you play it back again? Right before he slumped over?"

The wall of screens showed Navarro, still alive, secured to the table. There was a guard in the corner of the room. Marcus didn't recognize him. It wasn't Jerry Dunn. Officer Dunn had only shown up afterward. He hadn't visited Navarro before the alarm.

Still, something about Jerry Dunn rubbed Marcus the wrong way.

He tried to ignore the feeling. He had a habit of instantly analyzing a person and deciding whether he liked them within about two seconds of meeting them. The problem was that his intuition wasn't always correct. People did surprise him. And even if he did like the person, that didn't correlate with them being worthy of his trust. He had often liked and loved the people who had hurt him the most. And just because he didn't like someone as a person, that didn't make them the person he was hunting.

Spinelli clicked her touchpad to play the video again. Marcus watched as Navarro glanced around the storage room. Navarro seemed to be waiting for something, anticipating something. Ray would adjust the position of his arms, look to his wrist as if to check a watch, look to the guard as if to ask for the time. Marcus sensed the building anticipation even from the recorded event. Navarro looked like a man awaiting his execution, wanting to do something to influence what was happening and what was coming but being powerless to change the outcome.

Navarro was deep in concentration, eyes darting back and forth, and then the man just went blank. All the anticipation. All the worry. Everything that Ray Navarro was and was becoming was gone.

Eyes still open but vacant, Navarro slowly slumped forward and sprawled across the gray metal table.

Andrew said, "See that. That looks more like a fast-acting poison to me rather than something that would take hours."

Marcus stopped pacing, cracked his neck, and said, "Unless he wasn't really poisoned."

"But what else could have had that kind of effect?" Powell said from somewhere behind him.

The words seemed to shake Marcus from a stupor. He supposed that a part of him had registered Powell and a few of his people enter the control room, but he had been so singularly focused on the case and what clue to follow next that he had subconsciously chosen to ignore them.

He looked Powell straight in the eyes and said, "We need to shut down the whole thing. Evacuate the prison. Send your residents somewhere else."

Powell laughed. "That's very helpful. Thank you. Rather than finding whoever is trying to sabotage my company and my project, let's just give them what they want. Let's shut it down!"

"You could reopen once we catch this guy."

"If we shut down, we never reopen."

Marcus rubbed at the spot on his chest where his old cross necklace had once hung. It had been a gift from his mother. His father had taken it from him the previous year, right before tossing him into a dark hole. The necklace had never been recovered, and Marcus decided to have a cross necklace tattooed into that spot instead of replacing his old one. That way no one could ever take that away from him. The flesh surrounding the tattoo was still a little sore. He pressed his fingers against the spot and imagined the necklace that had once hung there. It helped him think, helped him to find the right path.

He had known Powell would refuse to kill his pet program even before he spoke the words.

People were going to die here.

Maybe a lot of people.

And maybe he could stop it.

He could get in contact with the Arizona governor. Pull some strings to get Powell shut down.

But that would seal the fate of Powell's experiment for sure, and Marcus didn't want to do that if he could avoid it. Plus, the Director and Fagan would probably side with Powell.

He told himself there was nothing he could do—and maybe there wasn't—but he couldn't shake the feeling that he wouldn't go over Powell's head and shut this place down because he wanted to catch this guy, because some dark traveler inside him wanted to hunt.

He said, "I can't tell you exactly what's coming, Powell. I don't know why this guy is doing this. Not for sure. But I know enough to be sure that it will end bloody. Maybe you should take a moment and consider whether or not this place, this idea, is worth people's lives."

Powell stepped down a small set of stairs and said, "Don't force me into that kind of choice, Agent Williams. Philip says that you and your team are his best and brightest. Catch this man for me. Outsmart him and stop whatever 'bloody' event is coming."

Marcus ran a hand through his hair and looked back to the screen. The image was frozen on the lifeless form of Ray Navarro. He turned to Andrew and said, "Think you can still remember how to perform an autopsy?"

Ackerman stretched his arms and legs as they finally released him from his chains. There were two guards from the CIA black-site facility still tagging along. They were joined by four others who must have been from the local sheriff's department. Ackerman noticed the state on the uniform's insignia. Arizona. He knew it well. He had spent a lot of time on the run in the southwest. He liked the wide-open spaces. More places to hide—less people to hear screams.

The Director received a call and excused himself. Maggie hovered around the open airport hangar like a falcon with a full stomach, not yet ready to pounce but always lining up its next meal.

The guards instructed him to strip and change into the orange jumpsuit of an Arizona Department of Corrections inmate. One of the sheriff's deputies gasped at seeing his scars. Ackerman guessed that his jumpsuit would have long sleeves to hide his father's handiwork from the world, but he found that he had only been half right. The jumpsuit was short sleeve. But someone had the foresight to add a long-sleeve white thermal as an undershirt.

Maggie frowned at him as he pushed the sleeves of the thermal halfway up his forearms.

She said, "What's with the box?"

She kicked her sneakers against a metal transport container with his initials on it.

"My books."

"They didn't let you have any possessions at the black site. Hell, the only thing you own is that bowie knife you talked Marcus into letting you keep."

"I love that knife. Are you taking good care of her?"

"Sure, we walk it every night. What's with the box?"

"I told you. My books. They wouldn't allow me any possessions, but they did set up twenty stands on the outside of the glass. I could see the books there, any I wanted to read or read again, and then the guards would flip the pages for me once an hour. It was part of the deal we made with the CIA in exchange for me cooperating in their tests. I requested to bring them along, so that I could finish them more quickly if I have any down time on this mission."

Maggie unstrapped and opened the container. As she picked up each book and set it aside, she read the titles aloud. "*The Art of War* by Sun Tzu, *The Rostov Ripper: The Story of Serial Killer Andrei Chikatilo*, *The Bible*, *A Brief History of Time by* Stephen Hawking, *The Pawn* by Steven James, Some big medical book, Max Lucado, *The Five Love Languages*?"

She looked up at him and cocked her head. Her expression was half disdain and half question.

He said, "What? In order to manipulate people, you first need to understand them."

Maggie tossed the books back into the box and closed it up.

He said, "It's good to be working with you again, little sister."

She didn't respond. She just checked her watch and went back to hovering.

Ackerman pulled the crate over and sat down within the circle of armed guards. He closed his eyes and imagined himself on a battlefield with soldiers dying and crying out all around him. Then he got bored with that and switched to the Middle Ages at the time of the Black Death. He imagined the piles of burning bodies. He drank in the aroma.

He lived in that time for fifteen minutes until the prison transport bus arrived. It was long and earth toned, and its engine growled and snorted like an overweight rhino. The windows were barred. The perfect tour bus for his kind of celebrity.

The guards worked in tandem to get him secured and loaded aboard the bus. Maggie didn't even say goodbye or wish him good luck. But that was okay. He forgave her.

As he boarded the bus, he saw that either he had this entire transport as his personal limousine or he was the first pickup. Either way, it made him feel special.

And Words of Affirmation was one of the five love languages.

The guards placed him in a random seat in the middle of the bus. Then they departed and a moment passed before the hydraulics whirred and the bus took off. Almost an hour later, the bus made a second stop and loaded on ten more men in matching orange. They seemed to be using the local sheriff's department and its parking lot as a bus depot for unloading from one bus to another. It made sense, he supposed. A police station was by definition a secure location, or at least as secure as anywhere could be.

Philip had mentioned that the experimental prison was ramping up to capacity and making regular drop-offs of new prisoners as they pressed the prison's population up to the projected second-tier capacity. Ackerman saw two more buses pull into the lot. Each had the name of a different prison stenciled on its side. Guards unloaded about twenty inmates from one of the buses and loaded them onto his bus.

None of the convicts spoke. They had been told not to, and there really wasn't anything to say.

They loaded a young Hispanic man to his left. The kid looked street smart but anxious, like a wannabe gangster always looking for different angles.

But Ackerman forgot all about the kid when the guards seated an interesting new arrival into the spot in front of him.

He waited to speak until the prisoners were all secured and the bus was rolling toward its final destination, but then he leaned forward and said, "I love the scar. Did you actually get that Glasgow smile in Glasgow?"

With a thick Scottish accent, the man said, "I'd be happy to demonstrate the technique for you, friend."

Ackerman laughed. "So it is a genuine Glasgow! I ask because I've always wanted to do that to someone. Snip the corners of their mouth and make them scream. The reaction. The pain. The inner conflict as they fight against the animal desire to acknowledge the pain. It all sounds so fascinating."

The dark-haired man looked over his shoulder at Ackerman, and then he settled back into his seat. "I've been on both the giving and receiving ends, and I'd much rather be the one doing the cutting."

And there it was again.

Ackerman felt it like a shiver, a pulse of information only received on some primal level. It felt like a small beacon announcing another predator in his midst. It was electric and exciting.

Ackerman said, "So what are you in for, friend?"

"Killing someone who asked too many questions."

Ackerman laughed. "Oh, come on. You can do better than that."

The man with the Glasgow smile said, "I'm not here to make friends or enemies. I'm just doing my time in solitude, so mind your own—"

"Keep it shut, ladies!" a big guard in a brown uniform yelled from the opposite side of a security fence.

Ackerman leaned back and imagined himself in the Middle Ages again. There would be ample time later for making new friends and enemies alike.

Andrew popped his knuckles and picked up the scalpel. It had been a long time since he had performed an autopsy, but he hoped that cutting people open would be the medical equivalent of riding a bike. Foxbury's morgue was small and cold and clean, but Navarro's body had filled the whole room with the smell of smoke and evacuated bowels. The prison's doctor, a white-haired man with kind but serious eyes hovered over the opposite side of the table. The old doc said, "Back when I was an Army medic, we had to be ready for anything. But even back then, we weren't ready for crap like this. This is becoming a whole new level of FUBAR."

Andrew gave a noncommittal grunt, knowing he had seen much worse than this, and this was just getting started.

He focused his mind on the task at hand.

They'd already given the body its external examination. Checking for any clues to the cause of death. Taking samples of the hair and nails. Then he took the scalpel and created a y-incision in Navarro's chest. With the old doctor's help, he peeled back the skin and muscle. And, exchanging the scalpel for the rib separators, he cracked apart the skeletal barriers keeping him from accessing Ray's organs. He had been taught the Rokitansky, the Virchow, and a few other methods for autopsy and dissection he couldn't remember the names of. But, if his memory served, today's procedure mostly called for Virchow.

The difference between Andrew's days as a medical examiner and today's autopsy was that he now had the flexibility to go off-book. The old prison doctor and one of his nurses could weigh the organs and run down the checklists. He already had a theory that could save some time.

He had watched the tape of Marcus's talk with Ray Navarro before his death. The young man's voice had seemed overly hoarse during the discussion. As if his throat had been wounded somehow. Andrew had assumed, at first, that the injuries had come from a blow Navarro incurred during the shooting incident. But after seeing the way that

Navarro died, he realized that Navarro's throat could have been damaged because he was forced to swallow a foreign object prior to coming to work on the day of the shooting.

Andrew went straight for Navarro's stomach. He spilled and examined the contents. And there, among the expected juices and partially digested food, he saw two things that didn't belong.

One was an old coin.

The other was the object responsible for Ray Navarro's death.

Marcus had called the Director and updated them on the drive back from the airport. Maggie was happy about that. It meant that she may not have to hear Marcus's voice at all when they reached the prison.

Maggie entered the room marked as Control Center East and didn't even acknowledge him. The Director introduced her to Powell, who flirtatiously described his grand plans for Foxbury.

Maggie took it all in. She asked questions about security, and Powell had just offered a demonstration when Andrew rushed into the CCE.

He announced, "Things are getting weirder," as he deposited two evidence bags onto the desk beside Spinelli's workstation. He displayed the contents and said, "This is what I found in Navarro's stomach."

One of the items was a coin. An old coin. The more Maggie looked at it, the more she guessed it was probably an ancient coin.

The other object was pill shaped but much larger than

any pill she'd ever seen. It was the size of a loaded Swiss Army knife, and it looked about as complex as one. There was an LED display in its center. The whole thing appeared watertight. The two ends looked like they unscrewed. One was clear and empty; the other end was just a metal tip like that of a missile.

Marcus was the first to say what most of them were thinking. "What the hell is that?"

Andrew said, "Best I can figure it, the device is designed to lodge in the victim's stomach. It has a timer. The clear end held what I assume was some kind of fast-acting poison. When the timer ran out, it released the poison, killing Navarro."

Maggie leaned in close. "Poor guy had to swallow this. It looks custom fabricated."

Marcus said, "What about the coin?"

Andrew replied, "That was also in his stomach. I snapped a picture of it and sent it to Stan to have him give us a work up on what it is and what it could represent. Then I think we should have the sheriff rush the actual coin in for metallurgic testing and also put a rush on finding out what type of poison was used."

Marcus nodded. "Good thinking. We may be able to trace either of those back to a source. Have Stan keep in touch with the locals on it."

Andrew then used a pair of latex gloves to pick up the pill-shaped device. He said, "But that's not everything this little guy was designed for." He unscrewed the cap from the metal end of the device and held it up for all of them to see. It was a USB dongle, like a thumb drive.

Marcus closed his eyes and cracked his neck. Maggie

always noticed him doing that when he was preparing for a fight.

He said, "What do you want to bet that's a message from our killer?"

After intake processing, they fitted Ackerman with new accessories for his wrists and ankles. A big, ginger-haired guard explained the security system and rules to all of the new prisoners. Ackerman had already heard this information, and he noticed that his new friend from the bus, the dark-haired gentleman with the Glasgow smile, also seemed disinterested.

Then they shuffled all the new arrivals to their cells—or, apartments as the guards called them—and released them to go on their way. The guard explained they would receive their jobs in the morning, but right now they had some time to familiarize themselves with the facility. It was the fastest intake process Ackerman had ever seen. Even to him, the whole prison seemed rushed together, as if the man who designed it didn't have the time or money to do it right and so he did the best he could with what was available at that moment.

Three minutes later, Ackerman was standing in the prison yard, unrestrained and anxious to hunt. He analyzed the small clumps of convicts scattered around the paved areas and gravel running track. As he quantified and weighed each group of his fellow inmates, he was reminded of the film *Jurassic Park*.

He had never actually seen the film. He had merely noticed it playing on a television once in an electronics store, right before his father had ordered him to murder the shop owner and his wife. The scene from *Jurassic Park*, which Ackerman had glimpsed, showed one of the scientists arriving at the park and seeing the dinosaurs for the first time. The scientist commented on the dinosaurs moving in herds.

Ackerman felt like that scientist as he surveyed each group of prisoners and made a mental checklist of how he would ferret out the truth from this place. He didn't expect it to take long.

He thought of those old prison clichés. Like establishing dominance by picking out the toughest guy in the yard and provoking a fight. In his experience, such public spectacles were rarely necessary or effective. Groups of men like this tended to fall into a natural food chain regardless of such displays. It was a primal thing, the lizard brain's survival instincts at their most pure. Maybe it was the smell of fear or something hormonal. Ackerman wasn't sure. He made a mental note to look up the biological reasons. He was sure that someone out there had studied, quantified, and devoted their life to acquiring such knowledge. But regardless of the biological motivations, as he walked among the prisoners, he could sense it. Some of the convicts gave off the scent of gazelle. Some smelled like tigers. Some lions. And others had the aroma of lion tamers, the heads of gangs, the leaders of packs of dangerous animals.

Ackerman knew that he had always given off a unique primal aura. He was different in a way that naturally frightened others. And the lizard parts of their brains told his fellow convicts to steer clear of what was different and therefore frightening. He supposed that was why prison populations so naturally formed into herds along racial lines. They did so out of fear. And he supposed that was also why he didn't conform to many social standards, seeing as he lacked that fear.

On some instinctive level, the other convicts knew to stay out of his way

He rarely needed to prove that to anyone.

But there always seemed to be that one guy.

That one convict whose instincts weren't very in tune with reality. The gazelle who was curious about the lion.

And, from the cocky look in his eyes, the man now walking toward Ackerman was that guy.

Marcus told Spinelli to pull up whatever was on the drive, but she refused, explaining, "Our system is completely offline to avoid any intrusion. A closed system. That drive could contain a virus designed to overwrite code and take down our whole grid. Anything. We need to have it tested."

From the back of the group, Powell's PR rep, Bradley Reese, said, "I have my personal MacBook here. It's not connected to the system, and it's brand new. Could we use that?"

Marcus opened his hands to Spinelli and said, "Would that work?"

Her expression told Marcus that she didn't like it, but she said, "Bring me the thing." Then she crawled under the desk and came back out with a video cable. She took the laptop from Reese, booted it up, and attached the cable using an adapter. The portion of the monitor wall previously occupied by Spinelli's system changed to an Apple logo and then Reese's virtual desktop. Spinelli then brought up a terminal window and started typing commands. She said nothing, but Marcus guessed that she was doing something to make Reese's system more secure.

As Spinelli's fingers flew over the keys of the laptop, Marcus's gaze strayed to the other four sections of the display wall. The other headset-wearing techs in the room were also typing away, and each section of the wall showed cameras zooming in on certain inmates as the software threw out alerts and the techs monitored for potential infractions.

"Ms. Spinelli," one of the techs said.

Spinelli looked up and said, "Not now, Rachel."

The young blonde tech said, "Mr. Spivey is about to antagonize the new intakes again. Do you want me to stop him?"

Spinelli growled. "That guy really gets on my nerves. Mr. Powell, should we give him another verbal warning?"

Marcus said, "What's going on?"

Spinelli continued to type on Reese's laptop but said, "Spivey, that robust African-American gentleman on her screen, thinks it's hilarious to provoke the new arrivals. About every fourth guy gets ticked off, forgets about the restraints, and tries to take a swing at Spivey."

"In which case, they get shocked for trying to harm another inmate," Marcus said as he watched Spivey moving with purpose across the yard.

But then Marcus saw where Spivey was headed. Straight toward his big brother, Francis Ackerman Jr.

Spinelli started to give further directions to the other technician, but the Director interrupted by saying, "Let it happen. I want to see how that new arrival handles a little provocation."

Marcus opened his mouth to argue but stopped himself. He was also curious as to how Ackerman would react. Of course, he supposed that he was wanting to see Ackerman handle it well, while the Director likely expected Ackerman to lash out and receive the shock.

He watched as the tech zoomed in on Ackerman. His brother cocked his head at the big black man approaching him. The gesture reminded Marcus of the look of a curious puppy. Then Ackerman bent over and picked up a handful of the dry sandy soil covering that portion of the yard. Ackerman let the sand and tiny gravel slip through his fingers and be dispersed by the wind. Then he grabbed up two big fistfuls of the sand and stood back up, arms at his sides, waiting for Spivey to arrive.

Marcus rubbed at the cross tattoo on his neck and prayed that his brother wasn't about to do something really stupid.

Ackerman held the handfuls of sand and dirt at his sides. He supposed it made him look tense, fists balled up, ready for a fight. But he also supposed that a guy who couldn't read the giant neon sign saying danger that hung over Ackerman probably wouldn't register any other nonverbal cues.

Ackerman said, "How can I help you, gentlemen?"

There were three of them. Ackerman ignored the convicts on the right and left. He focused in on the one in the center: the large black man in the white tank top and black bandanna. He was clearly the leader. He even walked a step ahead of the others, the trio naturally falling into a V-formation, like a tiny flock of geese.

The big man's voice rumbled deeply as he said, "Hey, Fish, I'm Spider."

Ackerman said, "I'm sure you are."

"And you're going to be my new dessert."

"That sounds nice."

"I'm going to eat you up every night from here on out. You're gonna be like a little white mint on my pillow. You know what I'm saying, Fish?"

The smaller man beside Spider chuckled. Ackerman cocked his head at them and said, "Is that it? Is that your whole thing?"

Spider leaned forward, puffed out his chest, and started to speak. Ackerman stopped him. "Yeah, you're done."

Spider looked like he wanted to take a swing but was just smart enough to know better.

Ackerman continued, "I thought that maybe we could have a little fun with this exchange, but after that display, I realize that you're not even taking this seriously. And you're wasting my time. You calling me Fish was mildly amusing, but the whole sexual innuendo thing, that was weak and boring. I don't tolerate boring very well."

Spider's lips curled back into a snarl, and he said, "Listen here, Fish—"

Ackerman said, "You're just going to make it worse."

Spider's muscles coiled up. He looked like he was preparing to pounce, but he kept stopping himself.

Ackerman laughed. "The funny thing about this is that you came over here with the intention of provoking me into attacking you. And now, with very little effort on my part, I have you tugging against your own leash instead."

Spider ground his jaw together and tensed his muscles.

Ackerman would have guessed, after hearing the prison's description, that such reactions would have garnered an electric shock. He supposed that the big black man was still too far away. The software's algorithms must factor proximity. He filed that data away in his mental storehouse. Spider had proved to be a better test subject than he had expected.

But now it was time to take the experiment to the next level.

The tech had switched the audio to the control room's speakers, and Marcus and the others listened to the exchange between Ackerman and Mr. Spivey or Spider, as he referred to himself. Marcus thought they might have reached a stalemate with both men knowing that a violent move would be futile, but then Ackerman proved him wrong.

Nothing in Ackerman's expression or behavior betrayed what he was about to do. The blur of movement from Ackerman was so quick and unexpected that it caught Marcus by surprise.

Ackerman tossed the two handfuls of sand into the air, lunged forward through the cloud of particles, and with his fingertips, struck Spider in the Adam's apple.

Ackerman immediately fell back as the fail-safe system shocked him into submission. But he wasn't the only one on the ground. Spider was writhing on the ground also, clutching his throat.

Marcus leaned forward over the dark-gray surface of the desk. He held himself up on his fists and took a deep breath.

Ackerman had been there for only a few hours and

already he had perpetrated the first incident of inmate on inmate violence in the prison's history and possibly killed a man.

Marcus wondered what the hell he had been thinking by campaigning for Ackerman to be allowed to work cases. His brother was just too far gone.

Marcus's sweep of emotions went from disappointment to anger as he realized how much Ackerman's little display was distracting him from the case at hand. There was a mother and her little boy missing. People were dying, and instead of focusing his energies on that, he was going to have to answer for his brother's actions.

The room was silent.

The prison's tactical team arrived and carried Ackerman off in chains. Another group checked on Spivey.

Spinelli was on her feet now. She had taken the other tech's headset and pressed it to her ear. After a moment, she announced, "Spivey's fine. Just got the wind knocked out of him."

Powell looked like he was about to fall over. His voice shook as he said, "Who the hell is that resident?"

Spinelli started typing, pushing the other blonde tech out of the way and usurping her system.

The Director said, "Don't bother. He's one of ours."

Powell said, "That's the agent you put on the inside? He's sure not keeping a low profile. What was that all about?"

The Director shrugged. "Consider it a favor. He's just pointing out a mis-calibration in your system. Nothing that can't be adjusted, I'm sure."

Powell looked as if he was about to throw up. "Absolutely. Just a little recalibration. After all, the system did shock him before he could actually hurt the other man." Powell laughed, but Marcus could almost see the dreams dying in the older man's eyes. First the shooting, and now this. Nails in the coffin of his life's work. Both Powell and Marcus and probably half the other people in the room knew that if Ackerman had had a knife, as in Powell's earlier demonstration, he could have slit Spivey's throat.

Marcus felt sorry for Powell, but this was no time to mourn dreams. He placed a hand on Spinelli's shoulder and said softly, "The thumb drive."

"Of course," she said and shifted back to the laptop. "It's a video file."

"Play it," he said.

FILE #750265-6726-691
Zolotov, Dmitry - AKA The Judas Killer
State Exhibit F
Description: Diary Entry

It didn't take long before Father's game was the biggest money-maker on the Midway.

But The Judas Game started out as just an idea involving betrayal with no startup costs. I remember the night he worked out the details to his golden goose. He had just spent the last of our money on paying our way into one of the biggest fairs in the Midwest. And not just for our normal spot, but TWO rented spaces, TWO privilege payments—one for the wheel, and one for "The Judas Game." Which at that point in time was just a title for a game about betrayal.

I take back what I said earlier, now that I think of it. Father did not spend the last of our money on the two privilege payments. He spent the last of our money on two bottles of Russian vodka.

Father paced back and forth outside our camper, drunk, at three in the morning the night before the fair, using me as a sounding board for his ideas. I always hated when he did that. Not the drunk part. Or the pacing. I hated when Father spoke to me. A conversation with him, for me at least, was a game in itself.

You see the ideas he was sharing in situations like this were what would keep me from going hungry. I genuinely wanted him to succeed. I wanted to give good advice. And tell him when he was out of his mind.

But he didn't really want my opinion. He just wanted to talk "at" me, not "with" me. And I had to be careful to walk the line of helpful but not critical.

"It needs be something like a guessing game. But something so different and intriguing that people won't need prizes or care about any fancy displays. Guess my age but with chance betray someone," Father said. His Russian accent always grew stronger when he was drinking, but he had insisted that we both speak English at all times, for practice. Russian was only to be used if we were being secretive for some reason, which did come up now and again. To his credit, he never even broke that rule when he was slobbering drunk.

I replied with something like, "But there will already be three other guessing games at the fair tomorrow."

And Father said, "How about I put this cigarette out in your eye?"

Luckily, inspiration struck him quickly. I remember the first words he spoke after the lightbulb turned on in his head. "What if we set up a mouse race but with people who don't even know they're the mice?"

I had no idea what he was talking about, but I didn't want a cigarette in my eye, so I remained silent.

Father went on to explain his idea. A game with six players. We had a small PA system that had come with the wheel game. Father liked to use his "acting" skills to draw in the customers. A six-person game gave him the opportunity to draw in people using lines like, "We only need one more person to play!" It was easier to get someone to stop and play when they saw that five other idiots had already signed up. Father described it as social currency. The people who were already signed up were giving a silent testimonial to those walking by.

So Father brings in six players, and he has each one of them pick one of six (or however many are remaining) cards. The card represented their player number. They would then whisper a "sin" or a "secret" in Father's ear. Once he had all the answers, he would betray all of the players and reveal each of the sins or secrets and what player had given that answer. It was all part of the game because the people who had the cards would now walk up and place them on the table in an area designated with six numbers, one for each of the players. Father would instruct the players to use their cards as a vote for the best, or worst, sin or secret.

Father liked the idea of giving people a chance to hear some gossip and have someone else's sin exposed. Of course, it was just for fun and the "sins" and "secrets" typically ranged from "I have three nipples" to "I really don't like Mom's mashed potatoes." Father would, of course, sensor everything for inappropriate content, but he was sure to let some crude humor sneak in.

And the most appealing part of the game from the player's standpoint was that you could win the money of the other players. You won the game by being the player whose secret received the most votes and your prize depended on how many votes you received.

If you were good at the game and came up with the best or worst secret, you could get all of the other players to vote for you and multiply your initial entry by five. You, of course, couldn't vote for yourself, which meant that for every game played, the house always made at least the price of one entry. But most of the time, we would bring in about three entry fees per game and pay out three. We had initially started out asking for a one-dollar entry fee. That soon became three dollars and then five dollars. And then we purchased another booth space so we could run both higher and lower stakes games.

People ate it up. We were attracting lines and crowds of people who just wanted to watch.

There were always jokesters who would come up with hilarious sins and secrets and lots of good-natured fun was had by all. But the moments Father loved, the moments he had envisioned from The Judas Game's inception were those when people realized the potential for betrayal. When people playing the game figured out they had been given a rich environment to win money through collusion and cheating.

People would form alliances and cheat ten bucks

out of a few people with no risk of losing any money themselves. People would reveal horrible secrets in order to piss off a family member and get their vote and their money. My personal favorite was the time a young junky played with his mother, father, and three siblings. He revealed something that I can't recall, but I do remember that his secret made his mother cry. He received all of the votes at a five-dollar entry fee and walked away with twenty-five dollars that he could shoot into his arm.

As the game grew, Father changed things up and introduced bigger and grander set pieces. He incorporated numbered silver coins as the "thirty pieces of silver" and had me hanging from a rope and a fake tree at the back of the booth. I would hang there for hours, jerking or gasping every once in a while for theatrical effect. And Father insisted that my eyes remain open. No sleeping on the job, even if your job is just hanging there like a dead person.

Fortunately, he quickly figured out that a dummy worked just as well for our Judas, and I could be doing something that would make him more money.

Father was running the players through like cattle as quickly as he could at some of the busiest fairs in the country. I would guess that he was averaging twenty to twenty-five games an hour at a five-dollar entry fee times six players. The rake depended on the votes cast, but we were bringing in probably two hundred and fifty dollars an hour clear money from The Judas Game.

Life was as good as it had ever been for Father and I.

It was also around that time that I committed my first murder.

★ ★ ★

As Spinelli started the video, Marcus felt like he was playing Russian roulette. At this point, he had no idea what to expect from this killer. It could have been instructions on where to find their bodies. It could have been ransom demands. It could have been the slow deaths of Renata and Ian Navarro.

It turned out to be none of those things.

The killer's movie started with the image of a woman. She was bound at her wrists and ankles with white nylon rope. A white hood covered her head. Blood had soaked through the hood. Besides the hood and the rope, she was nude. That was, of course, if you didn't count the blood as clothing. Even though that's how it clung to her small, pale body, like a coat of crimson.

Despite the blood and the hood, he could tell the woman was not Renata Navarro. Her shape was different. Her arms. Her complexion. But he could have been wrong. They'd send it to Stan for digital analysis to be sure.

Marcus said, "Anyone who doesn't want to see this in his or her dreams should leave this room immediately."

The camera angled, zoomed, and moved slowly down the woman's body. It was meant to show off every small cut, every second of torture. The filmmaker had spent a disproportionate amount of time inflicting pain on her pubic area and breasts.

Marcus felt others quickly leaving the control room or gasping, but his focus didn't waver from the show. It was his job to watch. To experience it as the killer would. Marcus had no choice but to study every detail.

At first, he didn't see much that would be useful.

She had a tattoo, but it wasn't the type they could track. It was more like something a teenage girl would get on spring break from some guy at a party. It was a butterfly.

The video was excruciatingly slow. The woman was shivering. The longer he stared at the screen, the colder he felt and the more his surroundings faded away, and then Marcus was inside that torture chamber with her, feeling what she was feeling.

Then he saw the scar. Right across her bicep. A big pink X on the side of her left arm.

It seemed familiar; a fresh memory. He felt like he had just bumped against a mental tripwire.

He glanced around the room to see who had left and who had stayed. All of his team had stayed, of course. Spinelli had stayed but was only stealing glances and listening. Powell had stayed but was looking away from the screen. Major Ingram was trying to be a good soldier, but it seemed as if he might throw up at any moment. Reese and Dunn had both left the room, along with all the other technicians.

The movie zoomed back out far enough to show that the woman was inside a large, glass-walled enclosure. Nothing happened for a moment, but then sand started sprinkling down on the woman from the enclosure's ceiling. The sand fell all around her, but it was a very slow seeping. The video faded to black, apparently to show the passage of time because when the enclosure reappeared, it was one quarter filled with sand. The picture faded to black again, and the sand was halfway up on the enclosure's sides.

The woman was clawing and punching, but the sand kept coming.

The picture faded to black and reappeared again, and this time the woman was gone. The enclosure was filled with sand from top to bottom.

The camera's angle held on the shot of the massive enclosure, and a man in a black robe walked into view. He pulled a metal chair along with him. The chair's legs scraped and squeaked against a metal floor. It looked like they were inside a shipping container or storage unit of some kind. The robed man sat down in the chair very slowly and carefully. It was all a big production. Marcus wondered how many times the bastard had practiced this routine.

The robed man raised his face to the camera, but his identity was concealed beneath a white theater mask. It was the tragedy mask. One half of the pair of masks often associated with stage productions and acting troops. The mask displayed the guise of a frowning man. In the killer's version, black tears ran down both of the mask's white cheeks.

When the man on the video spoke, his voice was deep and distorted, obviously employing some kind of electronic voice-altering software. He said, "You may call me Judas. What you have seen on this video was merely a demonstration of what will happen to Renata Navarro and her son. If you don't stop me, that is. And by the time you see this video, the sand will already be falling."

A group of numbers appeared on the screen. Marcus immediately recognized the numbers as latitude and longitude.

Judas said, "Go to these coordinates, and you will find a clue to their whereabouts. If you're quick, maybe you can save them before the sand takes them away. You'll find an old shipping container there. Only two may enter the container. The agent in charge of this investigation and Warden Scott Powell. The two will enter and retrieve the clue. Only those two. And they are not to bring any communication devices into the container. They enter the container alone. Completely alone. If my instructions are not followed to the letter, Renata and Ian Navarro will be buried alive."

Ackerman had been imagining mass graves being covered over with dirt when the lights came on in his administrative segregation, or Ad Seg, cell. He sat in the middle of the room on the floor, legs crossed. He squinted through the light until his eyes adjusted, and he saw his brother on the opposite side of the glass.

Marcus said, "That little stunt may cost your life. Fagan is probably going to have you transferred back to DC and put to death."

Ackerman laughed. "Executed for following orders? Hardly. You worry too much, baby brother."

"Following orders? Your mission was never to try and beat this prison. All you had to do was gather some intelligence from inside the prison system. Ask some questions. Keep a low profile. But instead, you immediately start trying to prove how smart and fast you are. And you nearly kill a man."

"I just gave him a little love tap. Believe me, brother, when I want someone dead, the person in question does not merely get a little choked up and piss their pants. They die."

Marcus rubbed at his temples. "I don't have time for this.

Our bad guy has a woman and a little boy chained up in a box somewhere. I have better things to do. I just wanted to tell you in person to get used to solitary confinement. You're not leaving that cell."

Ackerman pushed himself to his feet and approached the bars. "You asked me to help you find this killer. That's all I was doing. By all accounts, things are escalating. He's getting bolder. Time is not on our side. What I did out there established instant credibility. It also helps to prove that I'm not a plant or a spy. Now, after what I just did, maybe my questions will be answered. Under normal circumstances, I could have administered a bit of calculated torture and extracted anything you needed from anyone here. But working inside the confines of this unnatural environment of anti-violence, my task became a lot more complicated. I needed to go big."

"You never have a problem with that."

"If you're going to be a bear, be a grizzly."

Marcus closed his eyes and cracked his neck. He checked his watch and said, "The tactical team from the sheriff's office is sweeping an area about twenty minutes from here. I need to be ready to go in when they're done. We'll talk when I get back."

"Brother," Ackerman said, "you need to get out in front of this train or it's going to run you over."

"Thanks for the update. You haven't been any help with that so far."

"Listen, I'm sorry about making a spectacle of myself. Maybe it wasn't the optimum choice. But you have to understand that I have trouble processing the difference between the most direct path to an objective and the socially appropriate one. When the concept of fear eludes you, it makes such distinctions seem so abstract."

"It's not complicated. The Golden Rule. Do unto others as you would have them do unto you."

"But I enjoy pain, so that would mean—"

"Seriously? Throw me a bone here. Give me some sign that you understand me."

"I'll never be normal. You know that, don't you?"

Marcus ran a hand through his hair and said, "I know. And I know that's not your fault, but I also know that you can do better. You can blend in. You've done it before."

"I'll try harder."

Marcus held his gaze a moment and then said, "Don't make me regret this."

Sheriff Hall's tactical team had already scouted the coordinates that Judas had provided and found the old intermodal shipping container, the kind normally found on a cargo ship or a train or the back of a truck, sitting in the middle of nowhere, nothing around it but cactus and scrub brush for miles. Marcus instructed them to hold back to a perimeter of a few hundred yards and not to approach the container itself. Judas had been very specific about no one but him and Powell entering the container, and they had also been instructed to bring in no communication devices of any kind. Marcus didn't like the idea of going in blind with no backup, but they had little choice. The lives of a young mother and her son hung in the balance.

Powell drove a big, off-white Chrysler SUV and now sat behind the wheel, following the flashing lights of a police escort. Powell had stuck his phone in a car cradle mounted to the dash. Apparently, he had turned it off at some point, because he held the button to activate the device and then swore at the sight of a voicemail notification that appeared on the screen. Powell said, "Damn it! I missed another one."

"Another what?"

"A call from my daughter. She's on a month-long mission trip to India. So time zones are obviously an issue, and reception is spotty. And me having to deal with all this mess. She's called and left me messages several times, but I haven't actually spoken with her for two weeks now. I know she's okay. She says so in the messages, but it's still so frustrating not to be able to hear her voice and know that she's okay. You'll understand one day when your son is older."

My son.

Marcus felt a hot stabbing of guilt. He hadn't even thought about Dylan since they had arrived at the prison.

What kind of father was he? What kind of father should he be?

He said, "I heard that your daughter is engaged to your PR guy, Bradley Reese."

"Yes. Bit of a whirlwind romance, I'm afraid. But he seems like a good kid. Sharp. I've kind of taken him under my wing. He makes her happy. That's the important thing, I suppose. But it's hard for a father to let go."

"Did you run a check on him?"

Powell laughed. "Of course. Everything seems to be in place with him. No more than a speeding ticket. And he's an orphan, so there are no in-laws to contend with. Still, she's my baby girl. I worry."

Marcus said nothing.

Powell added, "But you shouldn't worry, kid. At least not about what you're worrying about. You'll never have it all figured out when it comes to raising children. If you do your best, you'll be fine. You'll make a lot of mistakes. But making mistakes isn't the thing to focus on. Turn your eyes to how you can correct those mistakes. Be a wiser man tomorrow than you are today."

"But what if I screw him up? I hunt these men. Men who once upon a time I would have called evil. But now I would call them disturbed or sick."

"You don't believe in evil? I'm not sure I'd go that far. I've seen a lot of evil in my life."

Marcus said, "I believe in evil. I just don't believe that people are evil. I think that men carry out evil deeds because they've been corrupted in one way or another, by lots of unseen forces. Things they had no control over. Society, family, mental illness, the devil."

"So you feel sorry for men like Judas? You don't think it's his fault? That we should blame the culture?"

"I don't think we should blame anyone or anything. Unless you believe in the devil, I suppose. But maybe even he's really just another lost soul. Blame isn't important. It's like you said. What do we do about it? That's where we come in. These men hurt others and corrupt others. Someone has to stop that cycle. And that's what we do. It's what we have to do. Think about it. People fall into one of three groups in regard to that cycle. Those who perpetuate the pattern of violence and pain. Those who bury their heads in the sand. And those who do their best to break the cycle and make the world a better place, one person at a time."

"And that's also why I believe in Foxbury."

"The point is that most of these men that I hunt have been harmed the most by the men and women who should have protected them and raised them to be the kind of people who break that cycle in one way or another. Instead, by either neglect or a darkness of their own, the parents of the men I hunt almost always contributed to putting their kids on the road to Crazy Town."

Powell said, "And you think that somehow your parenting is going to cause your son to be mayor of Crazy Town?"

Marcus wanted to say that Dylan had it in his genes, but he wasn't sure how much Powell knew about his heritage. Instead, he said, "I suppose it's just natural to think that way. To worry about the job you're doing as a parent."

Powell nodded. "I think every good parent asks themselves that question at some point. Am I doing something wrong? Am I screwing up my kid? That's normal. The best advice I can give you is to make sure that he knows you love him and you're proud of him. If you do those two things, then he'll be fine."

"But what if I'm just not cut out to be a father? What if I don't have those loving, nurturing instincts?"

"I've noticed that you're very focused in on your cases. You get very wrapped up in them emotionally. You worry a lot about stopping these men and saving the victims. You get inside the heads of these killers. You get so intense about accomplishing that task that you forget about everything else."

"Maybe. What's your point?"

"Just a warning not to forget about your son being part of that mission. You want to be one of the people who breaks the cycle? He's one of your best chances to do that. Put as much focus into being a good father as you put into catching bad guys, and I promise you that Dylan will turn out to be a great man."

The cop car ahead of them pulled off the highway onto a path of nothing but sand and gravel. Five minutes later, they were at Sheriff Hall's perimeter. Marcus stepped from Powell's Chrysler and looked down at the intermodal shipping container in the center of a small valley below.

Maggie was the first to approach them. She wore a black DOJ windbreaker over her bullet-resistant vest and tactical gear. Her blonde hair was pulled back in a ponytail.

"About time," she said.

Marcus couldn't see her eyes through her dark aviator sunglasses. He said, "Don't start."

"Had to go visit your big brother, huh?"

"I said, don't start. It was a two-minute conversation, and the tactical team needed to secure the scene anyway. Now's not the time."

"You're right," she said. "But I don't like this, Marcus."

"What's to like?"

"This guy's playing with us. We can't go by his rules."

"Oh, I guarantee whatever it is he's cooked up is all designed to prove his superiority to us. That's why he wants us here. We need to get ahead of him."

She said, "That's what I was thinking. I think I should go check out the training academy for the guards. Ask around about everyone who works at Foxbury. See if anyone has had any problems. Anything strange during training. There could be a clue there."

"It's worth a shot. Take Major Ingram with you. And

now that I think about, take that Dunn kid with you as well."

"Why?"

"To see if you can get a feel for him. He's as much a suspect as anyone else, plus he inserted himself into the investigation."

"But he was at the prison when the shooting occurred? He couldn't have killed the software designer."

"No, but that assumes that this Judas is a one-man operation. Never assume."

"If I go to the academy, I'll be asking questions about Jerry Dunn while he's in the room."

"Exactly. See how he handles that. I think that will tell us more than what's in the file."

"Okay, I'll pick them up and head over to the academy. I checked with Ingram earlier, and it's only about an hour's drive from here. Maybe I'll see if the Director wants to tag along as well."

"The Director went to pick up his FBI friend, Special Agent Derus, from the airport in Phoenix. Apparently, he would actually get here quicker by flying in there and driving than flying to Tucson. Because of the flight schedules. The Director figured he could save time by briefing Derus on the way, and he has an interview scheduled with the competitor that Powell mentioned. But I think you'll be okay on your own."

"I always am."

"Just keep someone from the team updated on what you find."

Maggie looked at him like she wanted to say more, but she ultimately just turned and walked over to the rented minivan she had driven to the scene.

Sheriff Hall walked up and handed Marcus a pair of binoculars as his men fitted Powell with a Kevlar vest. Marcus had already slipped his body armor on in the car. Judas had said no communication devices. He didn't say anything about protective gear. And who knew what they would face inside that container.

Marcus looked down the rise to the corrugated metal container. It was forty feet long, eight foot high by eight foot wide. Dull red in color but showing signs of several years of wear, its surface was marred by the kind of scratches and scrapes it would have acquired during a few hundred loadings and unloadings. But it wasn't worn to the point that it looked like it had been sitting out here in the desert for very long. More like someone had purchased a used container and transported it out here recently.

Sheriff Hall said, "There are no wires or cables we've discovered leading up to it, but there are a pair of solar panels on the back side. So it probably has power inside."

"Who owns the land?"

"Old farmer. Lived here for about forty years. He never comes out this far."

Marcus handed Sheriff Hall his cell phone. Hall said, "If you have any problems in there, you give a shout, and we'll come running. I have my men listening with parabolic microphones. Backup is only a few seconds away."

Marcus nodded. "Thank you." Then to Powell, he said, "You ready for this?"

Powell gave a little laugh. "I don't miss this kind of work at all. But yes, let's go break that cycle."

★★★

Andrew listened over the radio in the control room as Marcus and Powell prepared to enter the container. He hated that he wasn't there with Marcus. But there wasn't anything he could do to help, and Marcus had asked him to stay behind and quarterback Ackerman and the other avenues of the investigation.

His phone vibrated with a message from Stan, which he hoped pertained to one of those other avenues. It read, *Video me. Have some info.*

To Spinelli, he said, "Can you do Skype on your system?" She tore herself from the keyboard of the main terminal and picked up the laptop Reese had left for them. She plugged it back in and, after setting up the program and asking for Stan's username, she brought a picture of their team's tech guru up on the screen.

The big New Englander sat behind his desk back at their headquarters in Rose Hill, VA. If you didn't count the tattoos—several of which displayed old video game characters—then Stan was nude from the waist up. At least that's all they could see of him.

"Clothes, Stan. We've talked about this."

"I'm a nudist."

"You're not a nudist."

"Don't tell me how to live my life."

"There are ladies present."

Spinelli leaned forward into the frame of the laptop's webcam and waved. She smiled as she said, "I don't mind."

Stan said, "Well, hello, pretty lady. You like what you see? Here's my newest tatt." Stan flexed his pectoral muscles and made a tattoo of Q*bert jump up and down. Spinelli laughed. Andrew wondered how Stan kept getting tattoos when he was agoraphobic. Did tattoo artists make house calls?

Andrew said, "What did you find?"

"The coin you pulled out of the dude's stomach was a Tyrian shekel. Or an excellent replica. And it matches the coin found on Peter Spinelli. I did some research on it, which I've sent to all of your phones. But the highlight is that the original Judas is believed to have been paid with Tyrian shekels. They were the Biblical pieces of silver."

"That makes sense. He's using the coin as a calling card."

"Also, based on your search criteria, I've narrowed your list of suspect guards down to a list of six. And I've sent that info to all of your phones as well."

"Anything unusual in the backgrounds?"

"All of these guys had been vetted already, so they look shiny and clean. But our guy definitely has the skills to falsify a background. I'm digging deeper on all of them."

"Dig as deep as you need to, by whatever means necessary."

"Always do."

"What about the analysis on Judas's video?"

Stan said, "Marcus was right. It's not Renata Navarro in the video. The woman is most likely in her late twenties, early thirties. Caucasian. And about that classified file Marcus told me to check regarding her scar . . . He was right on that too. How is he going to play that whole deal for now?"

"You know Marcus. He's going to keep his cards close to his chest for as long as he can. Until we know for sure, we're not going wide with that info."

Spinelli said, "What are you guys talking about? What info? What lead?"

Stan said, "Drew, can I say it?"

"Say what?"

Ignoring Andrew's question, Stan said, "That's classified, pretty lady. Stan out!" He then exaggerated the motion of pressing a key on his keyboard to end the call's transmission.

Spinelli stared at the screen a moment and then said, "He's cute. But you bunch aren't at all how I would imagine federal agents."

Andrew's mind wrestled for a response. He suspected that Ackerman would respond here with a quote from some famous historical figure while Marcus might make some witty but slightly snotty remark. But Andrew was usually the one they were responding to, and he had come to find that those responses annoyed the hell out of him. Still, he knew his response wouldn't be any less agitating to Spinelli.

With a bobbing of his head, he replied, "We're a special task force," as if that explained everything.

Then he said, "Do we have a video feed from the site of the cargo container yet?" Spinelli frowned in response. For some reason, Andrew always noticed his Boston accent becoming more pronounced when he lied or changed the subject.

The yard at Foxbury was an octagon filled with basketball courts and free weights and running tracks. A set of bleachers rested against one end of the basketball courts. Leonard Lash sat in the middle of the bleachers with a sea of dark faces surrounding him. The others had him boxed in and watched the yard like a group of Secret Service agents.

Ackerman wondered why Lash was worried about having bodyguards when no one in the prison could touch him. Unless he knew there was more going on here, and he was being cautious.

Ackerman looked up to where Tower 3 had once been. In the briefing, Maggie and the Director had explained the attack and who the victims were. They explained Marcus's suspicion that the men weren't targeted randomly. As usual, his brother's instincts were impeccable. Too bad he didn't fully trust them more often. They would work on that together.

He walked along the edge of the basketball courts. The men playing stopped mid-game and started whispering. He knew they were talking about him. The first man to successfully strike another. The first convict to beat the system. They would remember his name. Too bad that name wasn't his own, but merely some concocted alias.

He ignored them and made his way over to the bleachers. As he approached, two behemoths rose from their positions beside Lash and stepped in front of him. Ackerman smiled and said, "What are you going to do? Hit me?"

The behemoth on his right said, "You have no business here. And yes, if need be, we will stop you from getting anywhere close to Mr. Lash. Whatever it takes."

"I admire your dedication," Ackerman said, "but I just want to have a chat with your imperious leader."

"Call his office and make an appointment."

"Funny. Let him know that the man who put Spider on the ground would like a word."

"Okay, I'll tell him." The big black man didn't move or turn back toward Lash. After a few seconds, he said, "I checked. He's not impressed or interested in chatting. Now step off."

Ackerman moved closer. The behemoth didn't budge but said, "What? Does that make you angry? What are you going to do?"

"Getting angry releases an enzyme called tryptophan hydroxylase that temporarily reduces intelligence. I don't get angry and neither should you. At your level of brain power, a little bit of anger probably brings you down to the IQ of a giant Mr. Potatohead."

The big man showed no reaction.

"I'm going to call you . . . Bozo, because you remind me of one those old children's punching bags," Ackerman said. "Now, Bozo, please step aside so that I may speak with Mr. Lash."

"Not gonna happen."

"Fine. I'll let you have a free pass for now, but you tell him that I'm going to keep coming back here to him and drawing attention every half hour until his busy schedule frees up. I may even try to fight my way past you goons and draw even more attention. I don't think he wants that. I don't think he went to all the trouble of killing those men in order for a fly in the ointment like myself to ruin all of his well-laid plans."

Ackerman started to turn around, but Lash gave a nod to a different sentry who tapped Bozo on the shoulder. Bozo said, "Mr. Lash will see you now," and stepped aside.

Ackerman walked up the bleachers and dropped down beside Lash. The supreme leader of the ULF was movie-star handsome. He reminded Ackerman of a prominent African-American actor he had seen on the Academy Awards once. Ackerman had just killed the couple watching the show. He had gotten them both without even knocking over their TV dinners. He supposed it was a bit sad that all of his cultural interactions involved murder in some fashion. He would have to work on making better memories. Regarding Lash, he supposed that good looks and charm didn't hurt one bit when trying to form a Nazi-like hate group that called for uprising and murder against anyone with a different skin color.

Lash said, "What can I do for you, Mr. Alexei? Mr. Frank Alexei."

Ackerman had almost forgotten his alias for this mission. He guessed that Maggie had chosen that name for him. A reminder of some friend of hers he had killed. Ackerman knew better than to tell her this, but he could barely even remember gutting the baker. He definitely didn't remember the man's face or his last words. He did, however, remember the smells of freshly baked rolls and the way the flour mixed with his blood. Memory was a funny thing.

Lash must have mistaken his musing over old memories for concern because the ULF leader said, "That's right. I may be in here same as you. But we're not the same. I have resources beyond your imagining. You think you can't be touched because of the cameras and all this metal jewelry. If someone gets on my bad side, there's nothing that stops me. No prison. No guard. No fancy tech. You stand against me, you fall."

Ackerman blinked several times and said, "I'm sorry. My mind started to wander about halfway through that. Did you make a point in there somewhere, or may I tell you why I wanted to speak with you?"

Lash laughed, but the reaction was superficial. It didn't reach his eyes. "You're a funny guy. I hate funny guys who try to act tough around me. It shows me that they're either too stupid to know who they're dealing with or too crazy to care. Either way, it doesn't sit well. What do you want?"

"I just want to be on the winning team. So I'm offering you my services."

"I have no idea what you're talking about. I don't play games, and I'm not hiring."

"True, while the invisible fences are up, you have ten times the muscle you need. But when the defenses go down. You may find me useful."

"Again, I don't know what you're talking about."

"Let me break it down for you. Someone forced a guard to target high-ranking members of every other major faction in this place. Every team in the game lost a player, except for you. Why might that be? It seems to me that you were establishing your dominance. And why establish dominance and make such an aggressive move when you're under constant surveillance? It's not like there's an illegal underground or drug business to take over. You don't need to send a message like that unless the walls are about to start crumbling down. And when they do, you want to make sure that you emerge from those ashes as the new king of Foxbury."

Lash said, "Your file says that you're in here for federal tax evasion. I have good accountants. I don't need another."

"Al Capone went to prison for tax-related offenses. That doesn't mean that it defined his entire skill set."

"And what skill set might you have that I would find useful?"

Ackerman shrugged. "A little of this. A little of that. What was it you said . . . 'You stand against me, you fall?' It's something like that. Plus, I want out of here. I think we can help each other."

"Comments like that will get this conversation flagged. They monitor everything." Lash pointed toward one of the many cameras mounted around the yard and added, "Saint Nick's always watching. And you've got a big mouth. You remind me of this kid I knew back in the old neighborhood. Good kid, hell of a ball player. Loyal. His name was Deandre. He always talked too much, which is something I hate, but he was family. A member of my crew. I loved him like a brother. See he had this girlfriend who used to get him all drugged up and sexed up and get him talking. After all, he loved to talk. We didn't know this at the time, but he would tell her everything. Even about jobs he did for me and our fledgling organization. Everything. And then she would run down to a local detective in narco and sell him that info in order to get her next fix."

Ackerman said, "Loose lips sink ships."

"Exactly. We found out about all that and, unfortunately, we had to remove Deandre from the organization. Even though he didn't betray us on purpose. He just never knew when to keep his mouth shut, and that wouldn't change. Point is that I loved him like a brother, and I don't even know you. He was what you call a known quantity. He was a friend. You, on the other hand, are an unknown quantity. Which means I don't have any past behavior to predict your future behavior. You are an undefined variable in our little equation. And I hate surprises."

Ackerman said, "Surprises are the spice of life, my friend. Every surprise is a good surprise. Every new challenge is a new opportunity. When Jesus was tested in the wilderness, he didn't complain about the surprise, that extra complication to his plight. No, he used those tests to display his strength and the path of righteousness. Surprises are good or bad depending on how we respond to them. Surprises are inevitabilities. You just need to choose to use that surprise in a way that furthers your ultimate goals. So, as I said, I'm here offering my services. That may have been an unexpected development. I may be an unknown quantity. But that's not important now. Right now, you need to ask yourself how best to use that unknown quantity to accelerate you toward your destination."

Ackerman stood and stepped down the bleachers. When he reached the ground, he looked back and said, "Think about it. Meet me in the laundry room or send one of your guys in an hour or so. Just have him give me a thumbs up if you want me on your team. Then, when the time is right, I'll know who to fight for."

Demon had been observing Frank Alexei since their arrival. Mr. Alexei was an enigma. A puzzle. And Demon liked puzzles. First, Alexei made a show of beating the security system on his first day. Then he was thrown into Ad Seg. When he was released from Ad Seg, he instantly provoked Lash. The man had either no fear or no damn sense at all.

But then there was the matter of Alexei's scars. They had

been mostly covered when he had arrived, but Alexei had come out of Ad Seg in a jumpsuit only with no thermal beneath it. This put his forearms on display. They were completely covered with scars. And those scars seemed familiar to Demon in some strange way that he had yet to explain.

Many of the Legion had been begging him to attack Alexei, but they were the same creatures who begged him to attack everyone in sight. He ignored them. If need be, he would deal with Alexei later. For now, he would stick with the plan and wait for the right moment to step in.

The horrific creatures he had been ignoring started to become angry. They called him names. They threatened him. They said horrible things to him. But he had dealt with similar outbursts from the Legion all of his life. Their desperate machinations and manipulations really didn't bother him much anymore. Most of the time anyway. There were those days when the Legion struck a nerve, and all he wanted to do was die. He had gone as far as writing out the suicide notes. But then the next day, he would look back and realize what a fool he had been. Why would a man with such freedom and power commit suicide? Maybe it was a chemical thing. Maybe even some chemical thing related to his other conditions.

Still, he refused to submit to medications. All any drug did was take away from who you really were. And he was the Legion, and the Legion was he.

Demon watched as Alexei made a show of his confrontation with Lash, and then the strange, fearless man headed back toward the main residence hall.

Out of the corner of Demon's eye, the dark man shot

forward as a wisp of smoke and shadow and took up step behind Mr. Alexei. Demon didn't ask questions. He followed and caught up to Alexei just as he was approaching the brick facade of the main building and the brown metal doors leading inside.

Demon called out, "Hey, you! Frank Alexei!"

The scarred man turned around and said, "I don't remember giving you my name."

"I asked around about you. You've been after drawing a lot of attention to yourself since you arrived. And now you've went way the hell out of your way to provoke the richest and most powerful man in Foxbury."

Alexei cocked his head and said, "All statements of fact. Is there a point?"

The dark man took another step toward Alexei, and Demon mirrored the movements. He was the dark man, and the dark man was he.

Demon said, "What's your game, Alexei?"

The scarred man laughed. Demon wasn't used to hearing laughter in his presence. He scared most people. Something about the intensity in his eyes. And a face ravaged by scar tissue. But this Frank Alexei seemed to have no fear of him at all.

Alexei said, "I do enjoy a good game. But I don't remember asking you to play, Mr? What was your name again?"

"Demon."

"Mr. Demon. Well, this has been fun. But I have to run. I have some preparations to make, but I would love to get a rain check on the story of how you received that Glasgow smile. Maybe get some pointers from you on that."

"What you're doing doesn't make any sense, mate? You don't smell like a cop. Yet, you seem to be messing about with matters which don't pertain to you."

"So where do you fit in then, Mr. Demon? How do such matters pertain to you?"

"I'm just offering some friendly advice. Lash is going to come for you."

"I'm counting on it."

"And that's what I'm talking about. The moves you're making don't make any sense."

"I suppose you just have to see and know the bigger picture to understand. I work in mysterious ways. Now, if you'll excuse me."

Demon said, "Tell me about the second time you took a person's life. I don't need the police report. Just tell me how it made you feel."

Alexei smiled and said, "When I was a boy, I never formed memories of carnivals or amusement parks. But to put it into a bit of a parable which could be better understood by someone with more typical memories and social correlations. For me, my second murder made me feel like a little boy who had just got to ride the rollercoaster for the second time in a row with no lines. I could hardly believe that I had a second opportunity to ride again. To experience that rush, that feeling of being alive and free, again. I'm an opportunist, Mr. Demon. And right now, I see an opportunity to serve my own needs by harnessing the power of the storm brewing here at Foxbury."

The dark man accepted that answer. At least for now.

The shadowy form of the dark man now stood beside Alexei, no longer in complete control of Demon's body and actions. Demon found this Alexei to be more and more interesting and perplexing by the moment.

And Demon would have some positions on his own management team opening up soon . . .

Demon said, "I won't keep you any longer then. But we'll speak again shortly. I'll have my people call your people."

The door of the intermodal container groaned and screeched in protest as Marcus pulled it open. Something on the inside of the container clicked, and fluorescent lighting hummed to life and filled the space with a pale glow. The interior was lined with black padded material that resembled flipped over egg cartons. Soundproofing. Which meant the sheriff wouldn't come running if they screamed for help.

A voice from inside said, "Close the door."

Marcus recognized the same distorted voice from the video.

The voice added, "And have a seat."

The cargo container had been divided in half by a partition of what appeared to be some type of polycarbonate. It looked like glass but was thicker and had the shine of the materials often used as partitions in police cruisers. There was a door made of the same material mounted in the righthand section of the dividing wall. On each side of the barrier, metal chair had been welded in place. Sitting beside each chair was a set of small metal tables. There appeared to be a few panels recently welded onto the container's ceiling, but there was nowhere else a living, breathing person could hide.

Judas said, "Mr. Powell, please take the chair on the opposite side of the barrier. The door is unlocked."

Marcus guessed that Judas was speaking to them through a live cellular connection or something of the like. He nodded to Powell, knowing they had little choice but to play along. He checked the metal chair closest to him. There didn't appear to be any tricks to the seat itself. No wires or places for bombs or hidden blades. No restraints ready to clamp down. He sat in the chair and looked through the glass at Powell, who had taken his place on the opposite side of the clear barrier.

"Put on the jewelry sitting atop each of your tables. You may recognize them."

Marcus had noticed the devices sitting beside the chairs. A pair of the same restraints used on inmates at Foxbury. The kind designed to monitor vitals and issue electric shocks.

He picked up the restraints and examined them. They were about what he expected; some kind of tempered aluminum or other lightweight metal. A small speaker on one wrist. A few LED lights. Silver contacts running along the inside of the bands.

He clicked the anklets in place but simply clicked the bracelets together and set them aside.

"If you're testing a theory, I can see you, Agent Williams. But it was worth a shot. Put on the bracelets as well."

Marcus picked up the bracelets and clicked them into place around his wrists. He motioned for Powell to do the same, and then he tugged against the device a bit to adjust the fit. He felt a mild electric tingle from the bracelet as he started tugging. He remembered Powell referring to the restraints as "tamperproof." But they couldn't have been functioning as designed inside the container. The restraints would only work properly when coupled with the prison's software and monitoring systems. Still, even here, the experimental restraints from Foxbury appeared to detect tampering.

Powell looked like he was scared but managing it well, as Marcus would have expected from a former member of a Shepherd team. Marcus wanted to feel bad for allowing Powell to be put in this position, but it wasn't like he hadn't tried to warn him. Maybe Powell was starting to realize that Foxbury wasn't a dream worth sacrificing anyone's life over.

"Where are Renata and Ian?" Marcus asked.

"I'll give the stage directions on this production, Agent Williams."

Marcus listened for further instructions, but Judas seemed to be making them wait for dramatic effect. Marcus guessed the killer had some acting or stage background. Maybe even someone who just worked on the crew at a playhouse. He listened for any other noises within the container. Any other surprises. There seemed to be a slight buzzing beneath the hum of the fluorescent lighting, but that was all. Maybe that was the sound of the solar panels or batteries.

Marcus wondered where Judas gained the knowledge and resources required to set something like this up. It all seemed overly sophisticated. Too high tech for Judas to be some simple disgruntled employee or former prisoner Powell had wronged somehow. Judas had specialized resources and knowledge way beyond the reach of a normal person. As if he did this kind of thing on a regular basis. Perhaps even for a living. A private or government-trained assassin?

"Agent Williams, there is a black bag on the table beside you. Please retrieve the contents."

He did as he was told and pulled a syringe from the bag.

Judas said, "That is a shot of epinephrine. I doubt that Mr. Powell has informed you of this, Agent Williams, but he's highly allergic to the venom of stinging insects like bees and wasps."

He looked across at Powell, whose eyes went wide as he scanned the container for bees.

"He's so allergic that he has to carry a shot around with him in case he's ever stung." As if to illustrate the point, Powell pulled out the syringe from his pocket and readied it. Judas continued, "Unfortunately, I've replaced his shot with saline solution. The one in your hand, Agent Williams, is the real epinephrine shot."

Powell looked at the syringe in his hand and then to Marcus, and then he opened his hand and let the EpiPen fall to the floor.

"What do you want?" Marcus said.

"I find that the people and things we love most are the ones most likely to betray us."

"So who betrayed you?" Marcus said to the disembodied voice. "Did Powell betray you?"

"Life is betrayal, Agent Williams. To trust is to be betrayed. And now Mr. Powell will know what that feels like. You see, he will be betrayed by the thing he loves the most. His own prison. His precious predictive software. In a moment, Mr. Powell will need the contents of your syringe injected into his blood stream, or he will die."

Powell's gaze shifted around the container, searching for the threat.

"But the problem is that you won't be able to inject him. You won't even be able to get close to him with that deadly weapon. The software will recognize you as a threat, and since you are attempting bodily harm on another person, you will be subdued. Your friends outside won't be able to hear your screams for help. And Mr. Powell will die."

Marcus glanced at the syringe in his hand. It made sense that the large needle would be viewed as a weapon if they were within the walls of Foxbury. But how could the software do anything when they weren't at the prison? Unless Judas had his own copy of the software or very high-level access to it. The implications of that were staggering.

Marcus stood up and said, "Powell, get out of there now."

Powell rushed to the clear door, but when he yanked against it, the hinged piece of polycarbonate material wouldn't budge. Marcus pulled and pushed against the door himself. He said, "Stand back," and then started kicking.

A buzz and a click startled them both.

They looked toward the origin of the sound, and Marcus watched helplessly as a trapdoor built into the corrugated metal of the ceiling opened up and a massive hornet's nest fell to the metal floor.

The hornet's nest shattered like it was made of glass and spilled out a black cloud of angry stinging insects. Marcus had no idea how hornets identified their targets. Maybe they just flew around and stung everything in sight. Whatever the case, a squadron of them had zeroed in on Powell. The warden ran to the back corner of the container, slapping at the hornets and trying to escape their wrath.

Marcus yanked against the door with even more force. Putting his feet up on the clear barrier and throwing all his weight into it, he screamed as he pulled.

He heard the sound of low, distorted laughter from the speakers. Then he heard a buzz and a click come from the door he was tugging on. It flew open, now moving easily with the lock disengaged. Marcus, caught halfway into his pull, fell backward onto the corrugated metal floor.

Scrambling to his feet, he lunged through the doorway, hoping to avoid any further surprises.

The hornets immediately attacked. Swarming around him like a pissed-off sandstorm. He swatted them away and ignored their stings. Luckily, most of their attacks were ineffective because of his body armor.

He slapped and pushed his way through the swarm to reach Powell.

The warden was already on the ground and gasping for breath in the container's back corner. Marcus wasn't sure how long it normally took for the effects of a hornet's sting to reach critical levels, but he knew that Powell's system was flooded with venom and more was being injected by the second.

Marcus reached for Powell's neck to check his vitals, but the closer he came to the man, the more intense the electric shocks grew from his wrists and ankles. Powell hadn't explained that there was a kind of warning system built in that increased the electrical output as you grew increasingly closer to a violation.

He swore and pulled his hand back. He looked to the syringe that he held in his left hand. Judas had already told him that he would never get close to Powell with the dangerous weapon, but Marcus had to at least try. He refused to believe that Judas would ever tell him the truth, or at least the whole truth.

With as slow and nonthreatening movements he could manage, he reached his left hand toward Powell. The electric tingle started before he had even stretched out his arm to its full length. By the time he had closed to within two feet of Powell, the shocks were so strong that he could no longer stand, his muscles quivering and losing control.

He dropped to his knees and rolled away, and the shocks subsided. His muscles felt like he'd just run five miles, and the hornets were still on the offensive. He slapped at them with his right arm as he thought of a different tactic. Maybe he could throw the syringe into Powell like a dart? Then Powell could press the plunger himself. He looked at the needle. In terms of a dart or throwing knife, it was a flimsy substitute. It would never stick, even if he threw it perfectly.

Marcus dropped to the floor and rolled as close to Powell as he could before the invisible fence kicked in. Powell had started to convulse and his eyes were closed. Marcus said, "Powell! You need to take this syringe from me. I'm going to roll it to you. You have to inject yourself or you're going to die!"

Powell's eyes fluttered open. His stare was glassy, but he nodded in understanding.

Marcus placed the syringe on the metal floor. The injector was completely round, like a toilet paper roll, the kind that an allergy sufferer carried in their pocket. It would roll easily. He gave it a little push toward Powell, and the warden shakily fumbled his fingers around it.

Powell raised the syringe with great effort. He brought it up to a position directly above his thigh, and then he allowed gravity to pull his arm down, driving the needle into his leg.

He pressed in the inset plunger and closed his eyes. The hornets had also, thankfully, lightened up on their attacks, but Marcus hoped that it wasn't all too little too late.

Powell kept gasping and shaking. His breathing seemed to be growing more shallow and forced. Something was wrong. The shot wasn't working.

The distorted voice of Judas said, "You know, I may have gotten a bit mixed up. Maybe the saline solution was in the syringe I gave to you, and Powell's original EpiPen did contain the epinephrine."

Marcus gritted his teeth but said nothing. There was no point in wasting time complaining or cursing at Judas. His laser focus was on the task at hand.

He replayed the scene from earlier in his mind. Powell pulling out the syringe. Judas saying he had replaced the contents. Powell letting the syringe fall from his right hand. The syringe hitting the floor and rolling.

He scanned the floor where it should have been, but there were chunks of the nest scattered everywhere. He rushed over and scanned the debris. The hornet attacks grew more ferocious and coordinated the closer he came to what was left of the hive. He could feel himself starting to succumb to the venom of the stings, even though he wasn't the least bit allergic.

Beside a chunk of papery nest, he spotted the syringe. The

words EpiPen were stenciled on this one's side. He slapped away at his attackers and snatched up the emergency injector.

Then he returned to Powell and repeated the procedure. Lying on the ground, rolling the syringe.

This time, Powell barely had the strength to lift his arm, but he feebly completed the maneuver and managed to inject himself.

Marcus didn't have time to decide whether the medicine was working or if Judas had betrayed them again before light flooded the container and the tactical team entered in a swarm of their own.

Foxbury's laundry room was a large open space with twelve-foot ceilings and green tile. Steel cages filled one end where the clean clothes were stacked and handed out through a window that opened into the connecting corridor. Right now, the windows were shut and secured, and all was quiet. The workday had ended, and the worker bees had returned to the nest.

Ackerman had chosen this spot because it was the perfect place to test a theory.

He waited in the dark for Lash's men to arrive.

He considered where he should visit in his mind.

The prison setting prompted the memory of the infamous Khmer Rouge regime that ruled Cambodia from 1975 to 1979. The maniac at the heart of the regime was named Pol Pot. He tried to return the country to the Middle Ages. After declaring that the year, in their country at least, would return to "Year Zero" and abolishing money, private property, and religion, the Khmer Rouge started murdering anyone who could have been considered intelligent, going as far as executing people for wearing glasses or speaking a foreign language.

That was where Pol Pot lost Ackerman. He could understand the isolation and Marxist views, at least in theory and principle. Pol Pot was trying to start anew, to make his vision of a perfect society a reality by any means necessary.

Ackerman could respect that. Pol Pot wasn't just sitting on his butt complaining about what was wrong with society. He was out there doing something to change it.

Pol Pot was also deeply disturbed, and his ideas ludicrous, but Ackerman could at least see where the man was going up to a point.

But executing people for wearing glasses, that was a level of insanity that had abandoned all rationality. Pol Pot should have at least kept the intelligent people around for breeding.

Ackerman imagined himself inside one of the most notorious and bloody facilities where such executions took place. The S-21 jail. He wondered what it would have been like to be a convict at that prison. Diseased, starved, exhausted from back-breaking labor, in constant fear of death.

He wondered if Powell was making a similar mistake with Foxbury as Pol Pot had made with his society. Powell was forcing people into roles that they were not meant to play, in which they didn't fit, and wielding over them godlike power.

The light in the laundry room clicked on, and the warming and humming of fluorescent bulbs filled the space. Before Ackerman opened his eyes, he analyzed the sound of their footsteps. He dissected the footfalls and guessed that there were five different men entering the room.

He opened his eyes and saw that he was wrong. There were six of them. Lash and five other strapping young men in tight, white thermal tank tops.

Ackerman said, "I didn't expect you to come down yourself just to give me a thumbs up, Mr. Lash. To what do I owe the honor?"

Lash placed a small, black electronic device on a table along one wall of the laundry room. He pressed a button on top of the device, and then he gave a head nod to one of his men, who closed and barricaded the laundry room door.

Ackerman pushed his way off the metal table and said, "That seems like something that would trigger an alert. It has obvious implications that you're planning bodily harm on another resident. I'm sure you just sounded an alarm. Unless that device you activated is some type of jamming or camouflaging gear. Something that makes this room invisible to the eyes of the prison's predictive analysis software. If that's the case, then you could do or say whatever you wanted while inside this room."

Lash started clapping softly. "Wonderful analysis, Professor. Now, tell me why we're here."

"The presence of such a device confirms most of my suspicions about you. Your use of it now implies one of two possibilities. The first is that you considered my gracious offer and have made the wise decision of accepting my allegiance. Then you would use such a device to inform me of the details of your escape plan."

Lash said, "Not so much. What's the alternative possibility?"

"That you decided that me being an unknown quantity is a threat to your plans. So you and your associates are here to kill me."

"Ding ding. We have a winner."

"But you'd have to have a way to dispose of me without alerting the prison when you turn off your device."

Lash said, "Don't worry, Professor. We have our bases covered. So I'm here to respectfully decline the offer of your services."

"I have to admit that I like you, Lash. You should have taken the offer. But you see, either way, you've confirmed for me that you are indeed planning something. The walls are about to crumble. And now, I have to decide how to best use that information."

"You won't be deciding anything. You'll be dead."

"Many have tried. Many have failed."

The five members of Lash's goon squad reached into their pants and removed finely crafted prison shanks. They held them up. The blades looked sharp and menacing. Beautiful, to Ackerman's eyes.

"I like our odds," Lash said.

"Do you ever watch National Geographic, Mr. Lash?"

"Not much of a TV watcher."

"Neither am I, but I've always had a special place in my heart for nature programs. The brutality. The elegance. My father only allowed me to view graphic educational programs when I was a boy, and I developed a lasting affinity for them. I recently saw a program detailing a battle between the Japanese hornet and the European honeybee."

As he was speaking, the five members of the goon squad fanned out and took up positions surrounding him.

Ackerman continued, seemingly oblivious to his attackers, "I have to admit that watching those hornets attack the bees was one of the most brutal things I've ever seen. And I've seen a hell of a lot. The hornets' goal is to gorge themselves on the honey and kidnap the children of the honeybees as food for their own offspring. So the hornets fly in and start using their mandibles to bite off the heads of the bees. They go about it methodically. They exterminate the bees. The much smaller honeybees may kill a few of their attackers, but their stings are mostly ineffective against the ferocity of the hornets. It's not really a battle. It's a massacre. Thirty of these hornets can kill thirty thousand bees in a matter of a few hours and, when they're done, the ground is covered with the severed heads and dismembered bodies of the fallen warriors. Many of them still twitching, hanging on to the last threads of life, of existence, refusing to give up the ghost. Maybe still thinking they can claw their way back up and rescue their offspring. It was so beautiful. So fascinating."

Lash laughed and said, "Okay, Professor, before you die, I'll bite. What's the point of that big story?"

"The point is that you've made one very serious tactical error."

"And that is?"

"You assumed that you and your men are the hornet in this battle."

The goon squad was closing in from all sides, and they had him outnumbered five to one. Ackerman only counted the five ULF enforcers as attackers because he knew that Lash didn't intend to lift a finger.

Leonard Lash stood beside the entranceway to the laundry room, hands in his pockets, and a sadistic gleam in his eye. Ackerman made a mental note: Lash likes to watch. The ULF leader didn't drag over a seat and pull out a bag of popcorn, but for all his body language telegraphed, he may as well have.

Ackerman glanced around at his attackers with a circular motion, as if his gaze was the rhythmic ticking of the second hand of a clock. He analyzed each man, his eyes scanning for weaknesses, vulnerabilities. As he spun, he catalogued and quantified each man. Which foot did they lead with? Right or left-handed? Physical attributes. Big, small. Wiry, muscle-bound. How did they handle the knife? What was their skill level? Did they truly possess the killer instinct or were they just faking it?

Not all of the men were thugs, covered in tattoos and mouths filled full of golden teeth. There was only one of them who fit that mold. Two of the five could have been former military. They were precisely dressed with high and tight haircuts. Another had the look of a former college football player with NFL aspirations. The diversity made sense. The ULF and Lash attracted all types of young black men who felt marginalized by society.

With one rotation lasting only two seconds, Ackerman knew exactly how the coming conflict would play out. He knew which one of the five men would attack first. He knew which would hang back. He knew the order in which he would dispatch them.

He laughed to himself at the multitude of tactical errors Lash had made while dealing with him. How had Lash ever risen to such prominence? Ackerman supposed it was all good looks and charm rather than brains and common sense, as it was with many politicians and cult leaders.

First of all, Lash should have known that it was always a mistake to let your opponent see the attack coming. If your opponent was skilled, that gave him or her a chance to analyze, adapt, and overcome. Surprise was key. Ackerman's father had always drilled that into his head. A shocking, blitzkrieg-style attack was always more effective.

Of course, Ackerman couldn't judge Lash too harshly. After all, he himself seldom followed that particular rule. Something was lost in a surprise attack. He missed the fear on the face of his adversary. The anticipation. The regret. The doubt. Humanity at its best and worst. In a furious stealth strike, the attacker only received a second of that. That had always seemed a terrible waste to Ackerman. He enjoyed the foreplay almost more than the payoff.

Lash said, "Are you aware that you're talking out loud? And in the third person?"

Ackerman shrugged. "Apologies. When I get bored with a situation, I sometimes do a sort of voice narration in my head. Anyway, I already surmised that you had a way of deactivating the security system here at the prison. How else would you plan an uprising?"

Lash said, "What uprising? How would you know anything about any kind of uprising?"

"The one that's supposed to cover your escape."

Lash narrowed his eyes. "Who are you?"

Ackerman continued, "If you couldn't speak freely, then you couldn't work out your escape plan with even your most trusted lieutenants. And to pull off something like this, you would need some help on the inside. You have the money and resources. You could hire someone with the skills to get you out. Someone who could infiltrate a facility like this. You've obviously been planning this since you first had the opportunity to come to Foxbury. Maybe you even arranged for you and your men to be some of the ones chosen to become part of Powell's experiment. And I would also surmise that you have contingencies in place to cover not only your escape from Foxbury but from the country as well."

Lash just smiled as he said, "You can kill him now, please."

Ackerman raised the extension cord and the pair of scissors above his head. He held them up like a talisman. Like Moses poised to turn his staff into a snake.

Ackerman had expected this outcome and knew that he needed a way of triggering an alarm. The most direct way he could think of to trigger an alarm was so simple that thousands of toddlers managed it every year. But his tools and options were restricted by the prison's behavior analysis software. Still, it hadn't been too difficult to make plugging in an extension cord and using a pair of small scissors seem non-threatening under the guise of the laundry room. He had simply pretended to be a convict mending a shirt.

Ackerman paused and looked at the floor. Was he thinking all that or had he said it all out loud? He supposed it didn't really matter either way.

He held the wires up high and made sure Lash understood what they were before he said, "I set this up so that I could jam these scissors into the end of this extension cord. By doing this, I will succeed in kicking a breaker in this room. Now, ask yourself why would I want to kick a breaker?"

Lash's lip curled up as if he wanted to snarl at Ackerman rather than speak. Lash said, "Because kicking a breaker could mean that a resident is trying to disable the cameras, or lots of other things they wouldn't want happening. A kicked breaker in a room like this, where no one is working, would probably trigger a full-on alarm."

"And send the guards and the tactical team running. I think they might find it interesting that you were about to kill me, but their security system didn't notice."

"You don't know for sure that kicking a breaker will trigger an alert and send the guards," Lash said.

As he spoke, Lash gave a signal with his eyes to one of the men behind Ackerman. Lash was clumsily trying to distract him and trigger an attack.

The whole thing insulted Ackerman a bit. Did Lash really think that he was the kind of man who wouldn't notice something like that? Did Lash still underestimate him? Did his adversary still not respect him? That injustice needed to be rectified.

Normally, in a situation like this, Ackerman would have killed all of the attackers, but he had promised his brother not to murder anyone. That promise, however, did not cover maiming or paralyzing.

Ackerman jammed the scissors into the end of the extension cord, right into the slots where the prongs would normally fit. Then he twisted until the lights went out. As darkness fell, he spun on the large black man who had been trying to sneak up on him. The one with the look of an NFL linebacker. Ackerman ducked under the man's clumsy attack and brought the heel of his shoe down on the outside the man's knee. The leg cracked and gave way under his substantial weight. The linebacker dropped to the ground, screaming.

Ackerman rushed forward a few feet, rolled onto one of the sorting tables, and stood on it to analyze his surroundings. He watched the vague shadows of his attackers get their bearings in the dark, let their eyes adjust, and then he watched them scanning for him.

The thug in the group reached him first. Thug jumped up onto the metal sorting table beside Ackerman and then came at him low and hard, as if he intended to tackle him. Ackerman dropped all the way to the table's surface and spun on his axis in a sweeping kick that dragged the thug's feet out from beneath him. The man slipped off the side of the sturdy, metal sorting table, his upper torso rotating around and his head cracking off the table's surface.

Ackerman dropped and rolled to the ground and moved back to where he had originally been standing. He had kept hold of the tiny scissors, not that they would do much damage.

As he moved, he was very careful where he stepped.

The next contender was one of the former military men. This one had some training and skill. He had kept hold of his shank and held it out with confidence. He swiped at Ackerman with fluid and controlled movements. Ackerman was impressed. The man clearly had skill with a blade.

But Ackerman also had skill with a blade. And brains enough to cheat. He held out the small scissors as if they were a bowie knife and gestured for the military man to bring it on. The big former soldier laughed and then lunged forward. He closed up the distance between himself and Ackerman in one big step.

Unfortunately for him, he stepped right onto the spot where Ackerman had intentionally spilled fabric softener in preparation for this very encounter. The military man fell and cracked his head on a metal post.

Ackerman hoped the man didn't die from that blow. If he was going to break the promise he had made to his brother, he at least wanted to savor it and put in some quality time with a knife. He definitely didn't want to break his promise by having some clumsy oaf break his own skull open.

The football player was still screaming on the tile floor. Ackerman scooped up the homemade knife that the linebacker had dropped and turned back on the final attacker, who was closing in for one last-ditch effort with his own crudely fashioned weapon, a lead pipe. The final member of the goon squad was a huge bodybuilder type of man, and although his muscles gave this last opponent a lot of power, they hindered the grace of his movements.

The bodybuilder came at Ackerman in much the same way a gorilla with a lead pipe would approach a poacher. Ackerman spun like a flamenco dancer, slashing his newly acquired blade across the bodybuilder's abdomen. He made sure not to push too far—just enough pressure and depth to make a painful but superficial incision. In the past, he would have spilled the man's guts. Not doing so now felt like such a missed opportunity.

The bodybuilder grabbed his stomach and dropped the pipe. Ackerman reversed the motion of his arm and drove his elbow into the bodybuilder's spine, sending the big man stumbling forward. Ackerman then kicked out the bodybuilder's legs, dropping him fully to the floor. The big man caught himself against one of the sorting tables. He was regaining his balance with relative ease.

Ackerman was proud of him, but he also needed the bodybuilder out of commission, and so Ackerman drove the prison-made shank straight through the center of the man's hand, embedding it in the surface of the table.

By this time, Lash had apparently decided to take a more active role.

He came at Ackerman like a man with knowledge of a blade, like someone who had killed with one in the past and had enjoyed it. But it was also clear that those skills hadn't been put to use in some time. The knowledge was there and, in most cases, that would have been enough. But to try to take out Ackerman, Lash would have needed daily practice for years. The mind and the body would have needed to work in perfect unison.

The sloppy maneuvering and desperate attack from the aging ULF leader really was the last straw of disrespect for Ackerman. He felt that he had more than adequately demonstrated that he was both intelligent and formidable to this man, but still Leonard Lash treated him like a common criminal. Did he think he was just some nosy thug who needed to be eliminated like a losing investment from a stock portfolio?

Ackerman caught Lash by the wrist as the older man lunged with his shank. Then Ackerman drove his own forearm into Lash's and wrenched back on the man's wrist with the opposite hand. The forearm snapped, and Lash screamed in agony, dropping to his knees and clutching his damaged wrist.

Ackerman pounced on Lash, driving his knees into the man's chest and toppling him back onto the tile floor. He dug his fingertips into the flesh of Lash's neck. He thought of how easily he could rip out the contents of this powerful man's throat. To hear the crunch, feel the warm gush around his fingers, hear the gurgling as Leonard Lash's lungs filled with blood.

Tactical flashlights lit the room as guards pushed their way inside. They screamed for Ackerman to release his hold and get on the ground. But all Ackerman could think about was drinking Lash's blood and watching the life fade from his eyes.

He was glad that the guards at Foxbury were all armed with handheld Tasers. If they hadn't been, he wasn't sure if he would have been able to resist tearing out Lash's throat.

But, thankfully, he felt the sweet pain of the spikes penetrating his body and the cool rush of an electrical jolt coursing through his muscles.

In every other prison at which he had been a guest, guards weren't allowed to carry weapons of any kind, but here at Foxbury, the guards played by different rules. It showed the level of confidence Powell had in his system. A system which Ackerman knew was about to fail. And all the electrical shocks in the world were not going to stop that from happening.

```
FILE #750265-6726-692
Zolotov, Dmitry - AKA The Judas Killer
State Exhibit F
Description: Diary Entry
```

The first "person" I killed was a little boy about my age. I think I was eleven at the time. It's hard for me to place events by my age because we never celebrated my birthday as a child. The only memory that ever came close was once when Father tossed me a McDonald's bag loaded down by a half-eaten quarter pounder with cheese. He said, "Happy birthday. I think you're double digits now." That was at the beginning of November, and so I estimate my age based on the time before or after that event.

But I don't consider that other little boy to be my first kill. My first kill was the dog.

We were working a local homecoming festival just a bit outside Boise, Idaho, when I decided to take things to the next level. I never really did much in the animal experimentation phase, torturing alley cats and such. I was usually too busy working for Father. But with the windfall of cash coming in, we had hired some other guys and had started branching out. Father started easing up the leash and allowing me a bit more freedom and free time.

Well, I suppose the devil makes work for idle hands.

I had been skimming money off the top of Father's operation since we started on the midway. At the beginning, that didn't amount to much, and I spent it all on food. Now with the success of The Judas Game, Father actually had something I could steal.

I used some of that money to buy a ridiculously large knife from one of the small tent vendors who followed the fair circuit. He smelled like baby oil and had hungry eyes, but he also had all kinds of cool stuff. Imitation

Oakleys. Airsoft guns. Toys. But the items in his inventory that interested me the most were the knives.

I had been having this recurring daydream about killing an animal with a knife. I don't think I knew what kind of animal it was. The dream was more about the feelings of the act. And I remember fantasizing about it and feeling great power. So I wanted to see if that experience in real life would live up to my imaginings.

I planned the event in great detail. I went out one night after Father passed out and wandered the neighborhood of the small town we had stayed the night in. I knew we'd be there for at least one more night. So I went on a recon mission that first night. I wandered the barely lit back streets of the town. I moved with the shadows, staying out of sight. I felt like a knight going on a quest. Hell, the knife I was carrying was practically a sword compared to my small frame at the time.

It took a bit of walking, but I found my dragon. He was some ugly, malnourished mutt. Brown and white and looking like some pit bull and Rottweiler mix. I found him lying in the dirt beside an old clapboard dog house. I could see the spots in the yard where he'd run out and barked his head off at some encroaching enemy. He was guarding his double-wide trailer kingdom.

During my recon mission, I walked up close enough to get the dragon to charge. I looked in his eyes. The ferocity and animal purity I saw there was beautiful.

Killing him would be like slaying a dragon. It would be a feat of courage and strength.

I sat down in his yard just beyond his reach. He didn't let up. He was going to tear my throat out if it took pulling against that chain for a thousand years. I sat there and watched him until I heard his owner coming to shut him up. Then I ran home and started my preparations.

The next day was long and tedious, but I finally reached the evening. Father had passed out on the toilet, and I donned my knight's armor and went out to slay my dragon.

When I reached the enemy's kingdom, I crept as close as I could and then I charged. I think he was taken aback. This dragon had probably never been challenged like this. But its confusion and shock lasted only a split second, and then anger and ferocity took over. From that point on, it was biting and blood and slashing and stabbing. Just a blur of well-planned but poorly executed attacks. What I remember most is standing over the body of the dragon, its head nearly severed, my left arm and shoulder dripping blood where the creature's teeth had torn into me.

Standing over that beast, having defeated it in combat, proving that I was more than just a slave. I felt like a gladiator winning his freedom. I felt more powerful and free than I ever had before.

The sign at the entrance was brown and red and yellow and in the shape of the state of Arizona. The top third resembled a sunset and displayed the words Arizona Department of Corrections. The bottom two-thirds was the color of wet sand and announced the name of the facility itself: Correctional Officer Training Academy.

COTA, as Major Ingram had been calling it, sat on

forty acres in the western foothills bordering Tucson. The buildings were made of light-red and brown brick. As they pulled through the gate, Maggie wondered what the place looked like from a satellite's view. Other than a few areas of fake grass and concrete, the facility probably blended right into the desert landscape.

Commander Emery, the head of the academy, greeted them at the front door and, after a bit of friendly catching up between him and Major Ingram, led them past classrooms and training areas to a conference room adjoining his office. The whole place smelled of lemon-scented cleaner and reminded Maggie of a community college. Two men and one woman in brown and tan uniforms waited for them inside. Emery took a seat and said, "These are three of my best instructors. They have direct contact with all of the recruits. What do you need from us?"

Maggie slid six manila file folders across the dark cherry table. "The man behind this isn't just some normal guy who snapped. He has resources and skills beyond what we would expect from a person like that. This guy's a professional. He's doing this for a reason. Probably money or some kind of cause. So it's unlikely that any veteran guards would have committed this crime. We believe that someone who graduated from the academy within the past year would be most likely. Luckily, Foxbury doesn't have as many guards as a normal prison, and they've all been vetted for behavior and psychiatric problems. They're all clean."

Commander Emery said, "If all the guards are clean, then what do you need to speak with us about? Any incidents of note would have been in the files."

"Yes, but we want to get an impression of these men. Out

of the thirty officers at Foxbury, we've narrowed the list to these six men." Maggie read off the names, saving the best one for last. She kept her eyes on Jerry Dunn as she said the last name. His dark hair looked greasy. His tan shirt was slightly too large, but she could still see that there was muscle beneath it. Dunn wasn't necessarily small. It was more that he presented himself as being small. As if he sucked in the space around him and shrank in perception only.

Maggie had done some friendly questioning of Dunn on the ride from Foxbury to the training academy. She had kept it light and personal, just getting a feel for some things he should have had genuine reactions to.

She had asked Ingram to drive, and she rode in the back, studying Dunn and his every twitch, his every stutter, every movement of his head, eyes, his posture, and his breathing. Having warned Ingram about her intentions, she had asked some friendly yet deeply personal questions. Unfortunately, none of Jerry's reactions had indicated anything strange. It either meant Jerry was who he claimed to be, or he was exceptionally skilled at pretending to be someone else.

She dropped the last file on the table and said, "And Jerry Dunn."

Jerry looked up at his name, but he didn't seem surprised. Instead, he gave a quick double nod and stuttered out, "I figured you would want to check me out too. And hey, whatever helps stop the guy who hurt Bill. I have nothing to hide. And the quicker you can eliminate me as a suspect, the quicker you can zero in on the real bad guy."

She didn't acknowledge his addition to the conversation. She just said, "So what can you tell us about these men?" She resisted the urge to look down at Dunn again. He had answered reasonably and appropriately, but his anticipation of this coming up displayed some deep forethought. She still hadn't decided if Jerry was their guy—was he a professional killer playing a part? Judas did wear a theater mask—or was Jerry Dunn just a good kid wanting justice for his friend, who had treated him like a son by all accounts?

She could definitely relate to wanting justice for a family member. But there was something that still didn't sit right about Jerry. Like he had another level. Like there were strong currents in the waters beneath the calm surface that was Jerry Dunn.

The instructors and the commander flipped through each file, refreshing themselves with former graduates. Commander Emery said, "I don't remember any incidents or problems with any of these men."

Two of the instructors, the two men, both quickly agreed with the commander. The female instructor—a dark-skinned, middle-aged woman with black, curly hair pulled back in a low-hanging ponytail—seemed conflicted. Maggie had noted that the instructor's features tensed up a bit more after each file was discarded, and she had shaken her head as she set the last file aside.

Maggie said, "There was nothing dark or strange or even over-zealous about any of these men? Don't just think of negative things. This guy might be working toward something, but he's definitely disturbed. And he has a deep desire to prove his superiority. Even if he was playing a part, it's unlikely that he would have been able to hide that part of himself completely." She looked down at Jerry. He was just listening thoughtfully, displaying no reaction one way or another.

Commander Emery thought a moment but said, "Nothing that I can remember." He looked to his instructors. The men just nodded, but the female instructor seemed like she had finally made up her mind to say something.

Maggie glanced at the instructor's name tag. It read Sergeant J. Usher.

Sergeant Usher said, "I'm sorry, but I have to volunteer something."

"Of course," Maggie said, "anything you think can help us, we want to hear it."

"He's not in your stack of files, but there's a former graduate who I believe could have done something like this. In fact, when I saw the news about the shooting on TV, I made a bet with my husband that it was Clarence O'Neal who had done the crime. I had heard that O'Neal had volunteered to work at Foxbury."

The other two instructors seemed to consider this and then gave nods of approval. Commander Emery said, "Clarence O'Neal graduated almost three years ago."

Maggie leaned forward and gently moved all the files aside. She said, "All of you remember Clarence O'Neal that vividly? What was wrong with him?"

"A lot, I think," Sergeant Usher said.

Emery shook his head. "He was just a little creepy. A bit too intense and a bit too serious. But he never did or said anything wrong, and he was top of his class across the board."

Maggie looked to Usher. "You disagree?"

Usher looked down and said, "Not really. It was mostly just gut instinct. I started out at a men's facility for five years, medium to maximum security. Then I transferred and spent fifteen years in a female facility before I came here to teach. And I don't know if you've personally spent much time in prisons with your job, but the female facilities are much worse than the men's. I've seen a lot of bad people in my time. I think I'm a pretty damn good judge of character. And Clarence O'Neal always struck me as one of those people who deserved to be on the other side of the bars."

After refusing medical treatment for himself, Marcus helped the paramedics load Powell into the ambulance. Thankfully, Marcus could already tell that Powell was going to be okay. The warden had been coming around even before the paramedics arrived.

The ambulance hadn't made it a hundred yards before Marcus turned and moved back toward the intermodal shipping container. Members of the sheriff's tactical team had converged on the container when the parabolic microphones hadn't heard a noise in what the sheriff had deemed to be "too damn long." By Judas's design, the soundproofing had masked their screams. Luckily, Sheriff Hall hadn't been so easily fooled.

The sheriff stopped Marcus before he could reach the container and said, "My men are checking it for any other surprises. You were lucky to have survived that thing once. He could have had the whole place wired to blow, instead of just dropping some bees. It may still blow. We know he has access to explosives."

Hall laid a restraining hand on his shoulder.

Marcus shoved the hand away and pushed past the sheriff. He didn't have time to wait. He kept seeing the video of the woman drowning in the sand, a poor innocent young woman trying to claw her way to air, to the most basic strand of life, even after enduring unspeakable pain and torture. He imagined Renata and Ian Navarro dying in the same way.

"Hey, wait!" Hall said. "At least let me bring in the dog to check that it's not wired. He could still be watching. Waiting for us to go back in before he blows it."

Marcus said, "Just pull your men back to a safe distance." He didn't want them in the way as he searched the scene for the next clue anyway. He already knew what he would find. Another video. Another message. Another path to be dragged down kicking and screaming. Another game to play.

All these guys wanted to play games now. He missed his days as a Brooklyn homicide detective, when most murders were gang related or a marital dispute. He blamed reality television for all these crazies suddenly having delusions of grandeur.

Marcus slowed his speed and waited to enter until the five men in tactical gear surrounding the container had pulled back. Then he re-entered the long metal box that had very nearly become Scott Powell's tomb.

Some of the hornets still buzzed angrily around the compartment, but the majority of the colony had followed Powell and Marcus outside, where the swarm had been dispatched with the assistance of the tactical team.

One of the big yellow insects dive-bombed Marcus, and he cringed at the sound of its wings buzzing past his neck, but he did his best to ignore the distraction. He had already received an injection to counteract the effects of the stings and had bigger considerations than his own discomfort.

He moved to the back of the container first. He had

a suspicion of where he'd find the next clue. It wouldn't be hidden. This guy was through playing around in the shadows. He checked the small end tables and the chair Powell had been sitting on. Then he searched the broken hornet's nest. He kicked open each piece of the ruined nest. The hornets doubled their efforts at his further intrusion, and a squadron flew out from beneath one especially large chunk that he kicked over. He found the device inside the third piece. A pill-shaped cylinder just like the last one but missing the clear end, which had contained the poison. He twisted off the cap at one end to reveal the USB dongle of another flash drive.

Marcus wondered about the way the devices were concealed inside of something. The first inside Ray Navarro's stomach. This one inside the hornet's nest. Did that mean something? Something symbolic to the killer? Was it intentional or subconscious?

He double-checked the rest of the scene, and then he walked back toward the entrance, glad to be free of the buzzing and stinging. Sheriff Hall had formed a perimeter farther back. Hall didn't walk out to meet him. The sheriff waited for Marcus to walk back up the hill. Apparently, Hall hadn't abandoned the notion that the shipping container was a powder keg poised to explode.

Marcus held up the flash drive as he reached Hall and his men. "Do you have a computer here that we can watch this on?"

The sheriff nodded and shouted orders at one of his men. Then he said to Marcus, "Your partner called from Foxbury. He's wanting to speak with you." Hall held out Marcus's cell phone.

Marcus said, "Thanks," to Sheriff Hall and then called Andrew back. "Give me some good news," he said as the call connected.

Andrew replied, "We have a problem."

"When don't we have a problem?"

"Okay, then we have another problem to add to the list. Ackerman is in solitary confinement for putting six men in the infirmary. Reese even ordered outside specialists to be brought in to tend to the wounds that some of these guys sustained. Ackerman nearly killed one of them."

Marcus walked over and rested his hand on the nearest police cruiser. He fought back the urge to ram his fist straight through the cop car's hood. "How the hell did he manage all that? He hasn't been there one day, and he's already bypassed their whole system?"

"He says that he needs to speak with you immediately."

"I'm sure he does. Let him rot in there for a while. I should have never brought him into this."

Andrew said, "It was actually the Director's idea to send him in undercover."

"Yeah, but I agreed to it. And I've been pushing for something like this for months. Maybe he's just too far gone."

"Either way, whatever trick he used to bypass the system could help us. And he might have beaten some other useful information out of Lash's men."

"Lash?"

"Yeah, the guards pulled Ackerman off the ULF leader himself when they burst in."

Marcus cracked his neck. He felt like a greedy tick swelling up with blood and ready to pop. "I'll talk to him when I get back, but after that he's not even going to see a flicker of artificial light until this case is over. The most important thing now is that I've found another USB device."

"Same as the other one?"

"Close enough."

One of the sheriff's men returned with an armored laptop that looked like it had been unfastened from some kind of mounting system. The deputy, dressed in black tactical gear, rested the laptop on the hood of the cruiser in front of Marcus. He raised the lid and a virtual desktop flashed to life.

On the other end of the phone line, Andrew said, "Does it contain another video?"

"I'm about to find out," Marcus replied.

Marcus and Sheriff Hall were about to start the second Judas video when a silver Audi A4 sped to a stop in front of them, riding a tornado of dust. Bradley Reese, Powell's PR representative and future son-in-law, stepped from the car and scanned the faces of the remaining officers, disposal teams, and medical workers. When his gaze came to rest on Marcus, Reese raised his eyes and a finger as if he was going to ask his question while still fifty feet away. Then Reese moved with purpose in their direction.

Marcus growled deep in his throat.

"Great," Sheriff Hall said. "The cavalry's here."

Marcus said, "How long have you been on the job?"

"Heading toward twenty," Hall said.

Marcus laughed. "You started young. What's the exact number? You know you know what it is."

"Eighteen years and five months."

"You were full-time SWAT before coming here?"

"Yeah. How'd you know that? You been reading my file?"

"It's in the way you handle yourself. Point is, in all your years in law enforcement, including full-time SWAT, have you ever seen a bigger minefield of disaster than this case?"

"Not even close."

Reese arrived in front of Hall's cruiser. He wore a tightly fitting gray suit. One a bit beyond what Marcus assumed was Reese's pay grade. But that didn't necessarily mean anything. Reese had made a TV appearance that day. Powell's company may have bought Reese the suit as a job-related expense. Like providing a construction worker with a hard hat. Marcus could see the muscle beneath the suit clinging tightly to Reese's small frame. Reese was about five foot seven, and he looked like he was one of those blessed at birth with an unusually high metabolism. But Reese had done his best to make himself look bigger and more formidable than his genetics allowed. His hair was that deliberately messy look, which he had probably spent an hour preparing, organizing the chaos. And Reese's features were that of a chiseled B-movie star. Marcus detected a make-up smudge on Reese's collar—likely a byproduct of the earlier TV appearance and not a life choice—and the man had ink stains on his fingers. The ink stains seemed unusual, as if Reese had done a lot of writing by hand recently.

Reese announced, "I assume Mr. Powell is on his way to the hospital?"

Sheriff Hall said, "He's headed to Cornerstone Hospital. I can have one of my men drive you over there if you want."

"No, thank you," Reese said. Marcus couldn't place the man's accent. American, but too generic to tell where Reese had been born. Reese continued, "Our VP is in Italy right now, and we're not that big a company, so I'm about as close to being in charge as anyone now that Mr. Powell's been hurt. I figured that I should be here to represent the company's interests."

As Marcus considered his next words to Reese, he knew that they would have made Andrew cringe had his friend been present. But sometimes being rude to people could serve a very specific purpose. Putting a person's back to the wall or giving them a verbal shove could bring out much more of that person's true character than Andrew's honeyed, diplomatic tone ever could.

Marcus said, "You do like to slime your way into things, don't you, Reese?"

"Excuse me?"

"Might as well show the boss that you can be in charge, if given the opportunity. I bet this whole situation is killing you. After all, you've been working so hard with Powell's daughter to worm your way in, and now this mess could bring down the company you hoped to inherit."

Reese took a hostile step forward. "I have my job because I deserve it. Not because of my relationship with—"

"Which came first."

"What?"

"Did you start dating Powell's daughter before or after being given your current position at his company?"

"That's beside the point. What's your problem?"

"I just don't have time to hold the hand of a wormy little executive as he stumbles around deciding what to do. And in your case, trying to figure out what decisions make him look the best."

Reese jammed a finger into Marcus's chest. "I know how to do my job. You worry about doing yours!"

"Okay. If you know how to do your job, then shut down the prison and start moving out all those inmates immediately."

"That's ridiculous. We almost have this situation under control, and it doesn't affect the integrity of the prison itself. We've called in a few extra guards, but we're—"

"Did you hear what happened in there?" Marcus pointed toward the shipping container resting farther down the hill. "He used your software against us; which means that he has full access to it."

The correlation dawned on Reese's face, but he said, "We'll bring in some forensic computing experts and figure out how that could have happened. But our system is still functioning normally."

"People are going to die if you don't shut down the whole thing and get out now. Judas is using this prison and the controversy surrounding it as a stage. If you take away the stage, you stop the performance. I don't know what he has planned, but it's not going to be good for your company or your career."

"Even if I agreed with you, I don't actually have the power to make a decision like that."

"Then get in touch with the person who does. You mentioned a VP. Get him on the phone."

"I'll try to reach him, but he's probably in the air. He was in Europe with his family when it happened, so he might not be back until tomorrow. And the assistant warden at

Foxbury is really just a paper pusher. He has no decision-making power."

Marcus shook his head. "Just don't get in the way of me doing my job." Then he reached out and clicked a key on the armored laptop to play Judas's next message.

Reese said, "What's this?"

Marcus ignored him.

Judas's face, or at least the same tragedy theater mask with its downturned features of anguish, filled the screen. From behind the mask, the electronically disguised voice said, "If you're watching this, you passed the first test. But you have one more mountain to climb before reaching Renata and Ian."

The image changed to that of the woman in a glass box drowning in sand. The same woman from the previous video. In this video, the sand was up to the woman's waist. She was trying to push herself up onto the sand and somehow claw her way out through the ceiling of the enclosure. But a hood that had been tied in place covered the woman's face and her hands had been secured behind her back. Marcus could hear her sobbing as she fought for her life.

Judas said, "This is what Renata and Ian are experiencing at this very moment. They've already lost a husband and father. They've already endured so much. If they live, they will both likely have nightmares for years to come. But if you don't reach them soon, nightmares and PTSD will be the least of their concerns. Actually, they won't have any concerns at all."

To the recording, Sheriff Hall said, "Yeah, we get it asshole."

"It's a good thing that this is our final act. If you pass the test at the next location, you will have rescued them. But don't think for one second that you can get to them without following the rules of the game."

The image changed to a set of coordinates. Marcus used his phone to snap a picture of them. Judas said, "At these coordinates, you will find the entrance to an old mine. Only two people may enter the mine. The lead investigator—or whoever is in charge now, if he or she also happened to be allergic to stinging insects—and a representative from Powell's company, since Mr. Powell is now either headed to the morgue or a hospital bed. These two people enter alone. No one comes in behind them. You can bring your phones and radios with you this time, but they'll do you little good in the trials ahead. Ten feet inside the entrance, along one wall, you'll find an old table containing further instructions. Follow all of this exactly as I've described or Renata and Ian will die."

The video reached its end.

Sheriff Hall gestured toward Reese and said, "Well, I guess it's a good thing we just happen to have a representative of the company right here."

Marcus narrowed his eyes and said, "Yeah, what a happy coincidence. Mr. Reese, you're driving."

Reese took his place behind the wheel of his Audi A4, while Marcus sat in the passenger seat. Marcus asked Reese for his phone and then, from memory, typed the coordinates into the device's GPS app. He handed it back to Reese without a word, and neither of them spoke after that. Marcus knew how telling silence could be, and he wanted to let Reese sweat a bit.

But the maneuver was interrupted by the ringing of his phone. Marcus answered the call and said, "What did you find at the Academy?"

Maggie replied, "The candidates that Stan flagged weren't memorable, but they did give us the name of another possible suspect. Clarence O'Neal. He's a guard at the prison who could be a fit for our mastermind. I had Stan check on him, and Clarence has been making unusually high deposits."

"Okay, dig into him. See if he could be our guy."

"Way ahead of you. Stan also found that Mr. O'Neal owns a secluded property up in the foothills not too far from the prison."

Marcus watched the dirt road coming from the cargo container give way to asphalt as Reese headed toward their next sadistic game. He said, "You and Andrew should go check out O'Neal's place."

"I'm good. I'm already at O'Neal's trailer now."

"By yourself?"

"I have Major Ingram and Officer Dunn with me."

"Both of whom could still be suspects. Damn it, Maggie. I don't need to explain the reasons why going in there blind and naked is dumb. You know all the reasons. I have to deal with another of Judas's games, but Andrew could be there in a few minutes. Or I could have the sheriff see if any of his deputies are close by. Give me the address."

"We're fine. We're just going to check out the place and maybe ask some questions."

"Yeah, unless you find something or bullets start flying.

Is this about the argument earlier? Listen, I handled it poorly. I should have discussed my decision with you, but I made that decision from the standpoint of what was best for the investigation. It had nothing to do with you or wanting to sideline you. I wanted Andrew with me. And—"

"You're not helping. You think he's more capable than me?"

"That's not the point. I wanted Andrew with me because he's so good at smoothing things over when I piss someone off, and I thought that you and Dylan could use some time together. You're practically his stepmom. And—"

"But I'm not his stepmom. He's not my responsibility."

"Come on, Maggie."

"No, you don't get to treat me like I signed up for mommy duty."

"You don't want the job?"

"I didn't say that. But I'm not going to let anything get in the way of my real job. I have to be out there. Working the case."

Marcus gripped his phone so tightly that it made him wonder about the sturdiness of the device. "I don't have time for this right now. I'm sorry that you interpreted what I was saying as a suggestion. I'm ordering you to wait for backup you can trust. Our problems have nothing to do with that. I won't let you put yourself in danger in some attempt to punish me over an argument. If our relationship is going to cause this many problems in the field, then maybe we shouldn't have a relationship."

"Okay. Sounds good to me." Then Maggie hung up on him.

Marcus closed his eyes and growled. Breaking up with Maggie was not at all what he wanted. He loved her, despite any issues, arguments, or eccentricities. The problem was that he knew if they each had to choose between the other and the job. . . He would choose her, and she would choose the job.

Reese chuckled and said, "That was not the right thing to say there, my man."

"I am heavily armed and in a very emotional state right now, Mr. Reese. Choose your words carefully."

"It's just that I thought you were singling me out for some reason. Now, I realize that you're just not able to properly communicate your feelings."

"Say another word about what you just overheard, and I will calmly sit here until we arrive. But when we do, I will beat you within an inch of your life. Does that properly communicate my feelings on the matter to you, Dr. Reese?"

This was exactly the opposite of what he had intended when he chose to ride with Reese. He wanted to be on the offensive, not the defensive.

"What about you and Powell's daughter? I suppose you get along perfectly. That's the way it is in the beginning. It's a scientific fact. It's a chemical thing that wears off. But I guess in your case, it will last longer for her since you're just using her to get to Daddy anyway."

"You know what, I'm tired of you accusing me. I loved her with all my heart."

"Loved? Don't you mean, love? Why the past tense?"

"I said love. Don't try to trip me up and mess with my head. I love her. And she loves me. Her father gave me this job because he wanted to help me out since I'm going to be his son-in-law, but that's not why I'm marrying his daughter. It's just an added bonus, and I'm not a bad guy for accepting his help."

"I hear your fiancée is in India right now on some mission trip. What do you think about that?"

"I don't know what you mean."

"Just seems like a big commitment. A month long trip like that displays a level of dedication. Implies that this might not be her first or last journey. What do you think about her being away from you like that?"

"We're comfortable in our relationship."

But Marcus wanted to probe deeper. He said, "Did she check with you first? Before booking the trip?"

"Why does that matter?"

Marcus pulled out his phone and sent a text message to Andrew. As he typed, he said to Reese, "I was just curious which one of you wore the pants in the relationship."

Reese glared over at him. Marcus could see fire there. Maybe enough for Reese to be a killer. But then that look faded into something else. Something smug. With a smile, Reese said, "Now I see what you're doing."

"And what's that?"

"You're intentionally antagonizing me because I'm a potential suspect."

"Should I consider you a suspect?"

"I have nothing to hide. Ask me whatever you want."

"Powell said you were an orphan. What happened to your parents?"

"I don't know. They gave me up at birth. I was raised at an orphanage in Texas."

"Have you ever tried to look for your real parents?"

"No, and how the hell does this relate to your investigation?"

"You said I could ask you anything. What did you do before going to work for Powell's company?"

"I worked for an advertising agency in Dallas. My references are on file. Feel free to give them a call and verify."

The GPS announced a turn, and Reese followed the directions onto a gravel road. Then the computerized voice of the phone said, "Your destination is in two miles on the left."

Marcus cracked his neck and centered himself on the task at hand. Reese would have to wait. Maggie would have to wait. Right now, he had a game to play and a mother and son to save.

Clarence O'Neal's property sat in the shadow of a large, jagged rock face. Maggie examined the dilapidated buildings as Ingram allowed the vehicle to roll to a stop. The focal point at the center of the property was an old white and yellow double-wide trailer. Various buildings of sheet metal surrounded it. Some falling in on themselves. There was a fenced-in area housing a trio of old horses and one new metal building that matched the colors of the desert sitting behind the trailer and butting up against the rock face.

Maggie looked over at Ingram and said, "Remind me what you did before becoming a correctional officer?"

The big black man puffed up even larger and said proudly, "I was a Marine, ma'am."

"Good," she said and then pulled a compact Taurus .357

Magnum revolver from a holster on her ankle. "Then you know your way around one of these."

He took the weapon with a nod. "Yes, ma'am."

"What about me?" Jerry Dunn said from the back seat.

"You wait here like a good boy," Maggie said and then stepped from the rented minivan.

There were no lights on inside the trailer. The sun had just begun to set, and it cast strange shadows over the property. Her eyes flicked over each dark corner of the lot as she approached the front door. She banged three times and announced loudly, "Department of Justice. We need to ask you a few questions."

After a few seconds of waiting, she said, "Major, you told me Officer O'Neal has been off all weekend, right?"

"That's correct," Ingram said.

"Okay, let's check around back. I want to see what's in that new building back there."

"I noticed that. It looks to be the newest and most expensive structure out here. No windows though."

"I think we'll find it unlocked, if you know what I mean. You don't have a problem with that, do you?"

"Three of my men are dead. Not to mention the inmates who were under my care. My responsibility. One that I take seriously. Whatever needs to be done to stop this guy, I'm along for the ride."

Maggie patted him on the shoulder. "Good, I'm glad I have you here to watch my back."

He smiled, showing a mouth of perfect white teeth that stood out in stark contrast against his dark skin. "I'm glad to be of help."

Maggie rounded the side of the trailer, hand resting on

her holstered Glock pistol, ready to retrieve the weapon at the slightest sign of danger. The new metal building was fifty yards from the trailer across an expanse of scrub brush and cacti with a four-foot walking path cut through its middle. Maggie guessed the walls of the building to be fourteen feet high. The sheet metal was new and the color of sand, and the building emitted a low electrical hum. The closer they came to the building, the louder the humming. The whole place smelled like fertilizer, and the scent of animal feces was much too strong to be coming from the few boney excuses for livestock which were scattered about the property.

She announced herself as a federal agent and then checked the door. Locked. She reached into a back pocket and retrieved her lock-pick set. Marcus was the expert lock picker of the group—a skill that she suspected came more from a troubled youth than out of career necessity—but she was a quick study. In a matter of seconds, the door swung open, and she smiled back at Major Ingram. "Told you it would be unlocked. Now, let's—"

Maggie started to scream for Ingram to get down, but she quickly realized that the warning was too little and too late. The man who stood between them and the trailer was already squeezing the trigger.

She looked up into Ingram's eyes, met his gaze.

A half second later, a rifle shot rang out. Ingram's head jerked forward, and blood splattered Maggie's face.

She screamed as she dove through the now open door just as another shot meant for her head cracked against the metal building, piercing a hole through its skin, and clanging again as it passed through the building's far side.

Maggie kicked the door closed as she pulled her Glock.

She screamed as she wiped the blood from her face and scooted herself back farther into the building. She waited a breath to see if her attacker was coming through the door behind her, but then she rolled to the side and sprang to her feet. Another shot flew through the building's door at head height.

Maggie turned to check the rest of the building and instantly realized why they had received such a rude welcome. This new metal building was filled from floor to ceiling and side to side, from the ground up, with multiple rows of shelving units. And each of those shelving units was lined with marijuana plants and ultraviolet lighting.

She thought she saw movement farther into the rows, but her attention was drawn back to the more immediate concern of the man charging after her with the kind of rifle normally used to hunt elk.

She crouched low and held the Glock level at the door. She waited impatiently for a span of two breaths. But nothing happened. The man didn't kick open the door, nor did he cautiously push his way inside like a little boy checking his closet for a monster. He was waiting for her to make the move. She resisted the urge to grit her teeth or look over her shoulder.

Patience, she told herself.

Patience.

Another voice in her head screamed that someone could be sneaking up on her at that very second. A second shooter hiding among the rows of pot plants. A second shooter now creeping up behind her. Should she risk a glance?

Patience.

But the second shooter . . .

The man with the rifle kicked open the door and charged forward into the building.

For the first time, she got a good look at her attacker. He had pale white skin beneath a red flannel shirt and a shaved head with wild, random patches of longer hair. His eye sockets were dark and sunken. His frame was small and frail, but there was fire in his eyes.

Maggie had already estimated the level of his chest based on his height. She had aligned the barrel of her weapon with the spot she hoped would connect with his heart.

When the shooter kicked his way inside, all she had to do was squeeze. The hard part was not hesitating. And she didn't. She squeezed the blocky grip of the Glock twice in quick succession.

The weapon jerked with flashes of fire. Both shots connected with his midsection, and he fell forward from his own momentum, tumbling into one row of shelving units and toppling several of the plants.

Maggie spun back toward the inner part of the building, away from the first downed attacker. But there was no one there. Just more rows of plants and lights and irrigation systems. The thick aroma of thriving marijuana plants made her eyes water.

Maybe there was only one of them out here?

From the direction of the trailer, a man yelled, "We have your friend! Come out now, and we'll work this out. You have ten seconds, and then he dies."

Then she heard Jerry Dunn's voice. "Don't listen—" he said and then cried out in pain.

"Eight. Seven," the other voice screamed. "Six."

She approached the door and peered through the

opening without moving the door itself and alerting them to her location. She saw a short black man with a shaved head and a precise goatee holding pale-white Jerry Dunn by his shaggy hair. The newcomer was Clarence O'Neal. She recognized him from his file. Clarence crouched behind Dunn, using the young correctional officer as a human shield; which meant no clean shot for her. A wound on Dunn's head gushed blood; apparently, he had put up a fight.

"Four. Three."

She had no options. There was a confidence in the man's voice that told her that he'd carry through with his threat. She pulled the door back and stepped outside into the light from the setting sun.

She held the Glock up and at the ready and said, "Put the gun down. We can work something out."

A voice from the darkness behind her said, "I don't think so, bitch."

Maggie cursed inside but did her best to maintain a calm exterior as she raised her hands in surrender. There must have been another man hiding behind the corner of the building.

"Down! Now!"

Maggie dropped the Glock to the desert floor and said, "Listen, guys. I'm not here about all this. We're trying to stop a killer. It has nothing to do with your little operation. I'm sure we can—"

She felt the pain of a blow to the back of her head, and then she felt nothing at all.

★★★

There were several reasons why the Director had volunteered to drive the hour and forty-five minutes to Phoenix Sky Harbor International Airport and play taxi for his old co-worker Valdas Derus, who was now a special agent with the FBI's Behavioral Analysis Unit, but none of those reasons had to do with friendship.

Once they were inside the Director's rented Cadillac CTS Sedan and on the road, the Director said, "So are you comfortable with the role that we need you to play?"

"Not necessarily, but I'm here for Scott."

That was Val. Loyal to a fault.

The Director could still hear the slight tinge of a foreign accent betraying Valdas Derus's true Lithuanian roots, but Val had mostly lost the inflection. Although, the Director noticed that Val's accent had a tendency to get thicker and more exotic when a female was around. Val had been divorced for over five years now, and he still hadn't found a replacement. But not for lacking of trying.

Valdas was one of those guys who had somehow become more charming and attractive with age and had timeless features and flowing black hair with only a hint of salt with the pepper. Seeing Val made the Director feel even worse than he had after seeing Powell. Powell and Valdas both still looked young and vibrant despite their ages, while the Director knew he was fading. And the next person that asked if he was sick was going to get bitch-slapped. He knew they were whispering about whether or not he had cancer or something of the like. The truth was that he hadn't checked and didn't want to know. Until the pain got to the point that he couldn't work, he wasn't about to waste time with doctors.

The Director said, "Hopefully, we'll catch the guy before anything escalates, but if shit hits the fan, I need to know that you're on my side."

"I thought we were all on the same side."

"You know what I mean. I need you to create a buffer between the Shepherd Organization and the media, so that direct attention won't be paid to the SO. And don't forget, you'll get the credit if we actually do good with this case as well."

"I'm here, aren't I? I'm ready to do my part. Have you heard from the hospital?"

"I talked to one of the nurses while you were getting your luggage. They said Powell's going to be fine. In fact, against doctor's orders, he's already on his way back to the prison. Can't say as I blame him. I'm anxious to get back there myself. There's a tension in the air. Like something's coming. You can just feel it."

"You act like the place isn't going to be there when we get back."

The Director didn't want to admit to Val that he worried exactly that, and so he said, "My team's handling the case—and these kids are sharp, Val—but I want to help in every way that I can. I need to be there to do that."

"Surely they can survive another few hours without you."

"You would think. But I'd rather not find out. Especially with this group. They're every bit as reckless and stupid as we used to be."

Val laughed. "You make it sound like we're old men. I still am reckless and stupid. And you may not be stupid, Philip, but you've always been reckless."

The Director knew that there was a passive accusation

in those words, and his mind immediately jumped to the memory of Powell's last case with the Shepherd Organization. A case that involved a serial murderer dubbed the Cattleman, who liked to brand his victims with a big X on their left arm. He had murdered four members of a family outside of Amarillo and had kidnapped the family's youngest daughter. Luckily, she was able to escape and had provided the information that had ultimately led the SO to her abductor. It was a long and difficult hunt, but their team eventually caught up to the Cattleman and put an end to him.

The little girl, Debra Costello, had been scared and alone with no one in the world to help her. She had no family and would have gone into the system, but lucky for Debra, Scott Powell and his wife decided to adopt her and raise her as their own.

But now, he feared the worst for Debra.

"One of the main reasons that I wanted to meet you personally is to discuss something of a sensitive nature and get your take on it."

Val wore a tailored black suit and was picking lint off it in the passenger seat. He looked up from the inspection of his wardrobe and said, "I don't like the sound of that."

"It's about Debra."

Valdas said, "What do you mean? What happened to Deb?"

The Director explained about the woman in Judas's video, and that, even though her face was never shown, Marcus had recognized the scar on Debra's arm from a photograph he had seen on Powell's desk.

The Director said, "She was scheduled to be gone on

some mission trip to India. Supposed to have left a couple of weeks ago. But I contacted her friends from church. She never showed up for the trip, but they did get a call from her canceling on them."

"She must have been alive when she canceled."

"Maybe."

"What's maybe?"

"We checked the phone records and got the number she called and canceled from. That number is a burner cell, and it's also the same number that has been calling Powell and leaving him messages that make it seem that Debra's okay and is having fun on her trip."

Val leaned his head back against the seat and closed his eyes. "You're thinking that he forced Debra to record some messages for her father and is sending them out automatically to make it seem like she's alive? Why would he do that?"

"I have no idea."

"What about this new fiancé of hers?"

"He's our prime suspect, but that same burner phone has also been calling his number."

"So he could be getting calls that make it seem like she's okay as well?"

"Or he's smart enough to make it look like he's receiving the fake calls when really he's the one who set them up in the first place."

Val teared up and covered his mouth with a hand. After a deep breath, he said, "Do you think she's dead?"

"We don't have a body. So there's always hope. But yes, I think the odds are good that she's dead."

"Does Scott know?"

"No, and I'm not sure how to tell him. Or even if we should tell him."

"He needs to know."

The Director said nothing.

Val said, "You want me to tell him."

"It would be better coming from you."

"What is it with the two of you? You didn't even show up for his wife's funeral."

"I sent a card."

"He was your best friend."

The Director said, "He was my friend. But when he walked away from the SO, he turned his back on me as well. I didn't go to the funeral because I knew I wouldn't be welcome there, and I didn't want to add to his pain."

"I didn't know things were that bad."

"Old wounds. They may not be completely healed, but they don't hurt anymore. Powell had a different path. A different view of the world. But he's followed through with some of those dreams, and I respect what he's built here. I'd like to see him keep it. I'd like to stop some maniac from burning it to the ground. Maybe if I can do that for him, then he'll forgive me for whatever reason he left in the first place."

Traffic came to a complete stop on the interstate, some kind of road construction ahead. The Director looked over at Valdas, whose face was a mask of shock and disbelief.

"What?"

Valdas said, "Are you saying that, after all these years, you still don't know why Powell left the SO?"

"Well, I have some ideas."

"You could have asked him."

"He turned in his resignation, and I accepted it. He walked out of my office and never looked back."

"You could have gone after him. Confronted him about it. Or even just called him at some point over the past ten years."

"This isn't a love story. We're two grown men. If he wanted to talk, he knew the damn number. Do you know why he left?"

"Yes, I do."

"Will you tell me?"

"No, I will not."

"Why not?"

"Because you're two grown men, and if you want to know, you can damn well ask him yourself. You know the number. Now, how can I help you find the man who took my goddaughter?"

A large, blue and white sign read Foxbury Mine Company– No Trespassing.

Marcus could see the entrance to the mine around a few dirt mounds farther down the road. There was old gravel covering the path that he guessed was once a rocked roadway. He directed Reese to park the Audi about a hundred and fifty yards from the entrance. Their four police escorts, including one black tactical van, pulled alongside them, and the officers filed out, securing the perimeter as best they could in an orderly and professional manner.

Marcus wasted no time. He scanned the officers for Sheriff Hall and said, "Get Reese suited up with some body armor, just in case."

Reese held up a hand. "That didn't do Mr. Powell much good. Besides, I'm pretty quick, and I'd rather have full range of movement."

Marcus cocked an eyebrow and said, "Listen, Bradley, we're not going to be doing Greco-Roman wrestling in there. You're wearing the vest."

Sheriff Hall handed Reese the body armor and then held out a black shotgun with a pistol grip to Marcus. Hall said, "As requested, Special Agent Williams, one Remington 870P loaded with special breaching rounds."

Marcus took the shotgun, checked the weapon over, and gave a nod of approval. Reese glared at Marcus but accepted the black tactical vest that one of the sheriff's deputies held out to him. He slipped the straps over his shoulders with deliberate slowness, and Marcus decided to let Reese catch up. He turned toward the mine's entrance and moved off, checking his Sig Sauer pistol one last time before going into battle.

He heard Reese start pulling faster on the vest's straps and cursing under his breath. "Wait up," Reese yelled.

But Marcus didn't slow his pace. He wanted Reese to fall in line behind him like a shuffling puppy following at the heels of its master.

Because Bradley Reese was one of two things. Their killer. Or someone whose ego could get in the way of the investigation. Either way, Marcus knew that he didn't like the man. He just hadn't figured out why, yet.

Reese caught up and said, "Did I run over your cat or something in a past life? What is your problem with me?"

"Just do exactly as I tell you in there."

"Okay, I get it."

Marcus added, "And keep your mouth shut."

"Okay, you the man. I bet you're a joy to be around really early in the morning."

Marcus ignored the comment. The entrance to the mine was large enough to drive in a truck, but he could see that the tunnel narrowed after thirty feet. The old wooden support beams had been reinforced with concrete. He guessed that this was an old mine which had undergone a retrofit somewhere in the past ten to fifteen years. Maybe some old man struck gold down there. He didn't know what they even mined in Arizona and, at the moment, he really didn't care.

He refused to lose sight of his goal. His mind kept flashing to the Navarro woman and her son. The glass cage. The crushing weight of the sand.

As Judas had promised, they found further instructions and supplies sitting on an old wooden table to the right of the entrance. There were two flashlights, a map, and a cheap tablet computer. Marcus knew they could try to trace back the tablet to where it was purchased, but he doubted it would lead anywhere. Judas might have bought it off the street or a pawnshop or any one of a million Walmarts. All places where he could have paid anonymously with cash.

Reese picked up a flashlight and shined it on the map. It looked like the blueprints of an ant colony. Marcus scanned the map for a few seconds, committing the entire drawing to memory, and then he picked up the tablet computer.

He touched a button on the side of the device, and the tablet came to life and immediately started playing another video from Judas. The eerie white theater mask filled the screen, and Judas said, "Take the tablet to the spot marked on the map."

Marcus tapped on the screen again, but the same video just repeated itself. He tried pushing different buttons. Maybe he could bypass Judas's program? Maybe he could access another video before Judas wanted them to? But with each press and hold or combination of the two, the video repeated itself. He doubted there would be any Internet signal down in the mine, so whatever Judas wanted to show them must have been contained on the device. He rotated the tablet and flipped it over. Judas must have wiped it and loaded his own custom-built operating system. He considered the implications. It meant custom programming work. Maybe something that Stan could trace back through the code? Maybe there was some kind of log showing what networks the device had accessed?

With everything Marcus tried, Judas said, "Take the tablet to the spot marked on the map."

After ten or so repetitions, Bradley Reese said, "I think he wants us to go to the spot marked on the map."

"I told you to keep your mouth shut."

Marcus picked up a flashlight, left the map, and headed for the mine's inner entrance. He pictured the map in his head and imagined the next series of turns visually in his mind.

Reese said, "Hey, you forgot the map!"

"No, I didn't. In fact, I memorized it."

Reese snatched up the old map from the table. "If it's all the same to you, Memory Man, I'll take it along just to be sure."

Marcus didn't reply. He kept heading farther into the mine, toward whatever twisted game awaited them. But his focus wasn't on the danger to himself. He could only think of the falling sand and a boy the same age as his own son crying out for help.

The Director parked the Cadillac in the Luhrs City Center parking garage, and then they had to walk what seemed like five miles to reach the damn building. The Director was sucking air and seeing his life flash before his eyes before they had made it half way. Valdas looked like he could have carried the Director from the car and still not been half as out of breath as Philip felt at that moment.

As they walked up, Val said, "You didn't tell me that their office was in Luhrs Tower. I've always wanted to get a closer look at this place."

The Director had forgotten that Val was an architecture enthusiast. He looked up at the building between gasps. To him, it looked like a fourteen-story office building and not much else.

Val continued, "I love how the designer combined the Art Deco styling with regional Southwest and Spanish colonial influences."

They reached the front door, but the Director was feeling light-headed and didn't think he could muster enough strength to pull the massive thing open. Struggling to breathe, he said, "Yeah, it's great. Grab the door."

Valdas pulled open the door, but the Director could see the questions in his old partner's eyes. He stumbled through the opening and fell onto a bench in the building's lobby, trying to catch his breath and get the world to stop rocking back and forth like a sailboat in rough seas.

Val took a seat beside him and said, "We're not that old yet, Philip."

"What's that? I couldn't hear you because my brain is slowly dying from lack of oxygen."

"You haven't even been to the doctor, have you?"

The Director said nothing. He just leaned back and closed his eyes and wrestled for control of his own body.

"You're a smoker. It could be emphysema or something like that."

"I quit."

"The damage was long done by then, my friend. There may be some kind of medicine that could help."

"I'm fine. Just fighting a bit of a chest cold. Probably from lack of sleep."

With that, he patted Valdas on the knee and said, "Good talk. Let's get back to work."

They took the elevators up to the seventh floor and stepped out into the Phoenix offices of Prison Systems International. The Director had been shocked that the CEO of PSI, Robert Gordon, was actually able to meet with them in Phoenix. PSI was a global titan in the world of prisons and prison-related industries, and the Phoenix office was a mere outpost for them. He had actually been expecting and hoping to meet with an underling, some junior vice president. Those guys didn't have their line of bullshit perfected yet. The lies were easier to spot.

The office's styling spoke volumes as to the company's position in the marketplace. Even though they had exited on the seventh floor, the ceilings reached up high enough that the Director knew this was both the seventh and eight floors combined. The outside walls were exposed brick. The inside walls were mostly metal and glass with a textured stucco filling the gaps. The reception area was two stories tall, but some of the rest of the second story appeared to be loft offices and a huge conference room. The designs were elegant and modern and looked like they cost a fortune, and the whole space smelled like a freshly cut cucumber.

After a few moments in the reception area, they were greeted by a young brunette wearing a conservative skirt that was a size too small and a revealing black and white top that reminded the Director of a Rorschach test. He noticed Valdas admiring the young lady and putting a little extra swagger in his step. She led them up to the executive boardroom which occupied a portion of the loft. She then directed them toward a pair of chairs facing a large black wall.

She said, "Have a seat. Mr. Gordon will be with you in a moment."

Valdas said, "I love your shoes. Gianvito Rossi, right?"

Her eyes lit up, and she gave him a big smile. "Yeah, how did you know that?"

He shrugged. "I just appreciate beautiful things when I see them."

The young lady blushed and eyed Valdas seductively as she closed the doors. Once she was out of earshot, the Director said, "I just threw up a little in my mouth."

Val grinned and asked, "Jealous?"

"Hardly. All that flirting, dating, and dealing with another person's baggage. Whole thing sounds exhausting.

My wife died a long time ago, and I have no desire to hunt down another."

"Aren't you lonely?"

"You saying that you're not?"

Val smiled. "Touché."

Abruptly, the black wall in front of them came alive and faded up from black to a picture of a man in a dark purple suit sitting in an office somewhere.

"Gentleman, I'm Robert Gordon, CEO of PSI. How can I help you?"

The Director said, "What the hell is this? When I contacted your office, they scheduled you to meet with me here at this time to answer some questions. Did something change?"

Gordon said, "No, that's why I'm here. Ask away."

"I thought you would actually be here."

Gordon laughed. "In Phoenix? I'm afraid not. I'm actually in Cologne right now. But I have another five minutes where I can answer any questions you have."

The Director looked to Valdas, who shrugged. The Director sighed and said, "I know you're some big-shot executive and all, but if you didn't have the courtesy to travel your ass down here, then you shouldn't have made me hike my wrinkly old ass all the way here, especially when people's lives are in danger."

Gordon turned serious. "I'm sorry. I didn't mean to offend you. I'll make a note for my secretary to do a better job in the future explaining when I will be attending a meeting via videoconference."

"What do you know about Foxbury?"

"I'm familiar with the concept, and Mr. Powell's vision of

the prison of the future. He approached one of my people about a partnership and investing at one time. I wasn't terribly interested then, and nothing's changed since."

"Are you familiar with the shooting incident that occurred there?"

"Yes, my secretary prepares me a news brief every morning. A real tragedy."

"We think that it's a professional job. That maybe someone is trying to sabotage Mr. Powell's company."

"Are you suggesting that PSI had something to do with this shooting incident? That's absurd. To be perfectly blunt, if I wanted Mr. Powell's company to go under because I thought his ideas were a threat, I would simply buy him out and liquidate everything. Or if we thought Foxbury was actually a good idea, which we don't, we could have purchased the concept from him. And, no offense to Mr. Powell or his company, but we would probably have done a hundred times better job in our execution."

"But let's just say, what if you did see Powell as a possible threat, but your ego was too big to actually buy anything out and admit that you should have listened to him in the first place. And then let's say someone approaches one of your executives and tells them that their organization is going to be taking down Foxbury, and they can do it in a way that makes sure Powell's company goes out of business. Or they can do it in such a way that makes him look like a victim. And all you have to do is pay a modest fee to swing things in one direction or the other? I would say that getting involved at that point may seem tempting to someone like you."

"An interesting fiction."

"What if I also told you that we had one of your execs willing to testify that you did pay to ensure Powell Prison Technologies went out of business?"

Gordon's shiny exterior faltered for a brief second, and the predator beneath shined through. The CEO said, "I would want to know that man or woman's name and see a detailed account of their accusations. So that we could disprove any such allegations."

The Director stood up and walked toward the screen. He said, "I'm going to give you one chance, Mr. Gordon. I just want to stop this madness. I know that even if we come after your company on this, you'll probably get off on it or pin it on some underling. I'm not naive. I know how the system works. But I also know that lawyers are expensive and scandals like this hurt stock prices. So, if you know anything about this incident or anything else happening at Foxbury and you tell me right now, we'll make it look like you were never involved. I just want to stop anyone else from getting hurt."

Gordon leaned back in his chair and eyed the Director for a few long seconds, but then he said, "I'm sorry. I would gladly help if I could, and my heart goes out to the victims of such tragedies. But I don't have any information that could help you. That's the truth. And anyone who says differently is lying to you."

A few minutes later, as they were leaving Luhrs Tower and walking back to the parking garage, Valdas said, "You didn't tell me that you had one of PSI's executives willing to testify."

Between wheezes, the Director said, "That's because I

made that up on the spot. I was fishing for something, but sometimes the fish just don't want to bite."

A second after Maggie regained consciousness, she rolled to her feet. Or, at least, she tried to roll to her feet. The dog chain wrapped around her wrists jerked her back down in the same way it would have done with a dog sprinting after a mail carrier. Her face struck the filthy linoleum of the trailer's kitchen when she fell. She quickly pulled herself up again, more cautiously this time. The air was heavy with what smelled like a mixture of cat urine and paint thinner. She hardly noticed the throbbing pain in her head over her mind screaming about the germs on her cheek from it striking the floor. Maggie could feel each individual virus strand, the millions of teaming creatures squirming and burrowing on her skin, trying to find an entry point, trying to dig their way into her flesh.

She rubbed her cheek violently against her shoulder in revulsion.

Jerry Dunn said, "Are you okay?"

She looked up to see Dunn chained in a similar manner across the room from her. Their captors had fastened her chains to some kind of center post in the trailer's kitchen. She guessed the countertop section above her served as the dining room table. Dunn was secured to some exposed pipes on the opposite side of the trailer's living room. Their wrists were behind them, and the chains bit into her skin like tiny, hungry serpents. No position provided comfort.

She tested her restraints. The chains on her wrists couldn't be slipped and attempting to do so caused her great pain.

She fought down the part of her mind which screamed at her that she had no idea where this chain had been and that right now this rusty old dog chain was playing the role of an express train carrying a billion tiny invaders into her body.

Dunn said, "Agent Carlisle? What are you doing?"

Giving up on the chains, Maggie backed up to the built-in countertop and pressed her weight against it, checking for any give. The trailer was in disrepair and old, and so she wasn't surprised when she felt the whole cabinet system move slightly. She could probably break the center post and the counter system apart with relative ease. But if she did, it would create a hell of a lot of noise, and she had no idea who was still within earshot.

"Agent Carlisle, please be careful."

"I'm just trying to see if I can slip these chains. You should be doing the same on your end."

Jerry started stuttering something, the words sticking in his throat like peanut butter. Maggie felt a rush of sympathy for the man. Jerry hadn't been trained for anything like this. He could have been a damn good correctional officer, but that didn't prepare him for their current predicament. And if he wasn't their killer, then he was another victim who deserved her protection. She stopped pushing against the trailer's cabinetry and said, "Calm down, Jerry, everything's going to be fine. What are you trying to tell me?"

Jerry centered himself and said, "You're about to spill a bunch of chemicals, and if this place is what I think it is, that wouldn't be a good idea."

Maggie released her hold on the cabinet system and peeked her head up over the counter's edge. The counter and two tables beyond it were covered with glass jars and chemicals and what looked like the home chemistry set of a very disturbed child. She turned back to Jerry and found that more of the same filled the trailer's living room. Clarence O'Neal and his friends were entrepreneurs. They not only had the marijuana plants in the shed, but they also had a meth lab in the trailer. Why not? Might as well double down on your criminal endeavors. Silly to put all of your drug-dealing eggs into one basket.

Jerry said, "From what I've always heard, these chemicals and labs like this are highly unstable. You see them blowing up on the news all the time."

"I'm aware, Officer Dunn. Thank you."

He said, "How's your head?"

"I'm fine."

"That's good. I'm really sorry that I let myself get captured like that. I wasn't watching for someone sneaking up behind us, and the two of them had me dead to rights. There was nothing I could do. Nothing I could have done even if I had been armed."

"It's okay, Jerry."

"Maybe if I wasn't like this. Then I would have been able to fight back or I could have made some move on them while they were forcing you to come out."

"Jerry, it wasn't your fault. And you're right. None of us was expecting this. There's nothing you could have done. Your limp wasn't a factor."

"It's more than a limp."

"I know. A car accident?" Maggie had already read in Jerry's file that his parents had been killed in a car accident, which also caused damage to the part of Jerry's brain in charge of motor function. His file said that none of Jerry's impairments caused him to test any slower than a normal cadet did. In fact, his scores were above average. If she could keep him calm and following her orders, she knew that Jerry could be a real help in getting out of this situation.

"It happened when I was a kid," Jerry said.

"It doesn't seem to slow you down. And that's good because I'm going to need you to step up."

"Of course."

"Where are the two guys?"

"They chained us up and then left us here."

"Did you hear any vehicles pull up or leave?"

"No."

"Then they're still here somewhere, which isn't good. I was hoping that they would have run. Cut their losses and bugged out. But if they're still here, it means that they're covering things up. They plan to clean up the scene out back. They're betting my office doesn't know exactly where we are."

Jerry said, "Does your team know exactly where we are?"

"How long was I out?"

"Maybe fifteen minutes."

"That's not long enough that they could be sure we don't still have backup on the way. Did you see the guy who shot Ingram?"

"I saw them checking his body. He was dead."

"I mean, did you see the way he looked. He was so skinny and pale. I bet he was the one left here to do the cooking and was dipping into their stash. That's probably why he resorted to violence so quickly. He was paranoid and out of his mind on meth."

Jerry said, "Okay, but what does that mean for these other guys? They didn't seem out of their minds, at least, not on meth."

"It means that these two are probably pissed at their friend for screwing everything up for them. They wouldn't have pulled the trigger like their friend did. They haven't killed us yet, and that alone proves that they're a bit more levelheaded. But they will still come back to the same conclusion as their buddy. They have no other options. If they can possibly cover this up, they will. They're going to kill us. If somehow a bunch of officers show up here to rescue us within the next twenty minutes, then we'll become hostages. If we don't have backup here in the next hour at the most, those men out there will murder us and pretend like we were never here."

"But someone will track it back to them."

"Probably. But they'll take that chance. They'll cover it up as best they can. And that means that we don't just get killed. We vanish without a trace."

"I don't want to vanish without a trace."

"Neither do I, Jerry. Which is why we're going with door number three. You're going to do everything I tell you, and we're going to place those men under arrest."

"I don't think they're going to come quietly."

"Then we'll kill them, Jerry. But you don't need to worry about that. You just need to do exactly as I say, and I'll handle the rest. Can you do that? Can I count on you?"

"Yes. I'll do whatever you need."

"Good. First, I need you to . . ."

Maggie stopped speaking as she heard the footsteps coming toward the trailer's front door. She knew then that there wouldn't be any time for plans. The entrepreneurs behind this little drug-production factory had come to an executive decision. They had decided to tie up the loose ends sooner rather than later.

Marcus raised and aimed the shotgun as light flooded the tunnel they had been walking through. He squinted around the rock room as his eyes fought to adjust. The small tunnel had given way to a slightly taller room serving as the nexus of three different tunnels. He pictured this part of the map in his head. It had shown some of the other shafts as being flooded. It had also displayed one area where an abandoned entrance had been closed off, but a mine shaft holding the original elevator was still in place. He estimated that was about where they were now. Right beside the old mine shaft. He didn't see any motion detectors, but he guessed that was how the lights had activated. That or the presence of the tablet. And either solution spoke volumes about Judas and his level of skill and planning.

He took a step farther into the lighted space, and the tablet computer dangling from his left hand sprang to life. Another video message. Judas said, "The tunnel ahead of you splits off into three directions. The agent in charge will enter the far right tunnel. The company representative will enter the middle tunnel. Inside, you will both find clear walls built into the tunnels. Each of you will enter and shut the door behind you. Have a seat in the chair, and you will receive further instructions. You're very close now. Your goal is just around the next bend."

Reese looked genuinely worried. Marcus made a note

that Judas had referred to them by their positions in the game and not by their names.

"Should we do as he says?" Reese asked.

"We don't have much choice. But don't worry. We're going to be fine. If he just wanted to kill us, there are a lot of easier ways."

With a nod, Reese headed toward the middle tunnel. Marcus gripped the breaching shotgun firmly as he approached his own tunnel. The dimensions of the square opening were maybe six by six. And, ten feet inside the shaft, Marcus found the entrance to his "glass" box. A portion of the polycarbonate had been fashioned into a small door. He checked the hinges. They were identical to those used earlier inside the intermodal shipping container. The box had two sides of bullet-resistant, high-pressure polycarbonate that looked to be four inches thick. He had no idea what that stuff cost, but it couldn't have been cheap. The other sides of the box had been fashioned from the tunnel itself. Marcus could see the chair in the center of his tiny room. Another small metal table sat beside the chair. A two-way handheld radio sat on the small table. Marcus would have rather seen a syringe or a gun. The presence of the radio meant that he and Reese were supposed to speak and work together, or were going to be pitted against one another. And Marcus still hadn't decided whether Reese was another victim in this or the mastermind behind it.

He took a moment to examine the enclosure, searching for flaws or weaknesses, before sitting in the metal chair. It was bolted to the stone floor, but he didn't see any other wires or potential traps.

As he sat, the tablet came to life again. Marcus didn't even twitch at this. He had been expecting it.

What he wasn't expecting was the creaking open of a chute in the ceiling behind him. His right hand went to his Sig as his gaze traveled over his shoulder.

On the tablet's screen, Judas said, "I'm now speaking only to either the lead investigator or the company representative, since only one of you could have carried the tablet computer into the tunnel with him. The other can't hear this message. However, if you wish, you could pick up the two-way radio beside you and let him or her listen in. Just push the big black button on its side, and you can communicate with your partner. I'll give you a moment to call out to him and tell him to listen, if that's what you've chosen."

Marcus didn't move. He didn't pick up the radio and call out to Reese. He just waited for a few seconds to go by.

Judas said, "Sitting beneath each of your two-way radios, you'll find a coin. A Tyrian shekel to be exact. The same coin that many historians believe was paid to Judas Iscariot for his thirty pieces of silver from biblical lore."

The radio squeaked to life beside him. "Agent Williams? Can you hear me?" Reese said.

From the tablet, Judas continued, "This coin is your lifeline. Through it, you can find redemption, be the hero and the savior. The game is simple."

Holding the tablet computer, which kept playing the video message, in his left hand, Marcus scooped up the radio and said, "Maintain your position for a moment, Mr. Reese."

Judas said, "You each have a coin and a small tray in

front of you mounted into the rock wall. That's where you will cast your vote. To live or to die. A very simple choice that we each make every day in every small decision; to live a life of meaning and legacy or to slowly die and fade away. I've just boiled that lengthy death down into one choice with a binary outcome. You may have noticed that there were three tunnels."

"Agent Williams, what's going on over there? A trapdoor opened in my ceiling," the scared voice of Bradley Reese announced over the radio.

Judas said, "You may have wondered what was down that far left tunnel. That's where you will find Renata Navarro and her boy. I have placed a similar coin in their tray. But you see all that sand needs to go somewhere, so I need the two of you to decide who will live and who will die. The person whose coin is in the tray will be spared. The others will die."

"Agent Williams!" Reese said.

Marcus clicked the radio's button and said, "Don't say another word." He hoped that response was vague and menacing enough to shut Reese up for at least a few more seconds.

Judas continued, "So I'll let the two of you choose who should be sacrificed. But, you may be wondering what would happen if you both placed your coins. The game is set up so that two matching decisions means the two of you will be sacrificed. So if you both place your coins, you both die. If you both don't place your coins, you both die. But then you may wonder what happens if all three of you place your coins. Then you all three live or you all three die, depending on whether or not all three tunnels have their coins in place or not. But now the question is did I place the coin in Renata and Ian's tunnel or was I lying? You have sixty seconds to discuss your options and place your coins."

Maggie cursed under her breath as she saw that both of their attackers were climbing into the trailer. She had hoped that one of them would disagree with killing them or just not want to participate in murder. That would have made what she was about to do much easier. But she also supposed that the killer whose trick she was about to employ wouldn't have worried about minor deviations. Ackerman would have just adapted and overcome, and that's what she was going to do as well.

She heard his voice in her head. That's the spirit, little sister. Hearing his voice made her angry. But the anger fueled her adrenaline. And she needed the adrenaline for what was about to happen.

Clarence O'Neal—an impeccably dressed black man, not a button or hem out of symmetry, the habitual actions of a former soldier—spoke first, clearly taking charge over his partner. Clarence held a black semi-automatic pistol in his left hand. He said, "We tried to think of another way. We really did."

Maggie said, "Well, you tried. That's what's important. But you know, Mr. O'Neal. I thought you would be smarter than this."

"It's Officer O'Neal, and I don't think you want some sad attempt at tricking us or buying time to be your last words, do you?"

Maggie felt the reassuring little button just beneath the

big toe of her right foot. During her last adventure with Ackerman, he had taken a switchblade knife and cut it into the toe of his boot so that he could eject the blade out past his toes. She had taken things a step farther, adding a level of comfort and safety, making the adjustments necessary to conform to a sensible woman's shoe. But the idea behind the little toy that she now hoped would save their lives was definitely Ackerman's. Although she never planned on him finding out that she had ever learned a single thing from him. She hoped never to see him again altogether if possible, but she knew the chances of that were slim.

She said, "I just figured that a criminal mastermind like yourself would realize that you don't want to be inside this room at the time of our murders."

Clarence's partner chuckled at the words: criminal mastermind. Clarence scowled at the other man and said, "Why is that?"

"Because you can't inflict fatal gunshot wounds on two people in a space like this without getting all kinds of evidence all over you. I told them you weren't smart enough to have planned the prison shooting."

"I planned the prison shooting? Why would they think that?"

Maggie shook her head. "Maybe because of all the oddities in your financials due to your drug business here and the fact that you're the only psychopath that the academy instructors could remember."

"They called me a psychopath?"

"They called you much worse than that, Mr. O'Neal."

The other man said, "Let's just get it over with, Clarence. She's trying to mess with your head. Just shoot her."

Maggie fake cried and said, "Please, don't kill us. I'll tell you what the task force knows about you and your operation." She lowered her voice and dropped her head low. "I'll tell you where it is!"

Clarence said, "Where what is? What did she say?"

He leaned in closer.

Maggie fake-cried some more and mumbled, "I'll tell you where it is."

Clarence leaned closer.

Maggie pushed the button with her big toe to eject the knife blade from her shoe and then kicked Clarence O'Neal in the abdomen. When Ackerman had done this, he had stabbed his target right in the neck, but from the look on Clarence's face, her kick had made its point just as well.

Still, Maggie had hoped that one of their attackers would have had cold feet. Then their greatest threat would have been disabled by her actions. But now, although Clarence O'Neal was likely incapacitated, his partner was still a threat.

Clarence grabbed her boot, the toe still lodged in his side, and held it there with all his strength. The look in his eyes didn't speak of planning or anger, just shock and pain. He was acting purely out of surprise and natural instinct. But O'Neal's instinctive reaction was also successfully holding her in place—one foot stuck to Clarence's side, and the other dangling awkwardly.

Her hands were still secured behind her back, and she balanced her weight on her shoulder and struggled to pull herself free before Clarence's partner could come to his senses and walk over and shoot her.

She tried to pull the boot free from O'Neal's iron grasp,

but he was too strong. With her right foot wedging a blade into Clarence's side, her left foot was in the perfect position to kick the muscular little man in the crotch. Which she did. Twice.

He doubled over and cracked his head on the countertop. This caused him to release his grip long enough for Maggie to pull her foot free and kick away from him.

She could only think of one move. One solution that could save her life. Clarence's gun.

She kicked and clawed against his feeble attempts to restrain her. She scooted back under the counter and tried to pull her hands up and under her feet. She glanced out and saw Clarence's partner waving his gun back and forth in a shaky up-and-down motion. He caught sight of her watching him and squeezed the trigger. But apparently his deceased partner wasn't the only one dipping into their drug reserves because Shaky's aim was way off. Clarence screamed again and grabbed his arm, the stray round having clipped him.

She heard glass breaking above her as the poorly aimed bullet ricocheted around the kitchen. The chemical smell grew stronger and then black smoke started rolling off the countertop and filling the trailer.

But she couldn't worry about that now.

Maggie tried to imagine where Clarence's gun would have fallen.

He had been holding it with his right hand. He had then grabbed her boot with his left hand and, considering the iron grip, he had probably held onto the gun in his right hand.

Clarence was now on his knees, one hand to his side and

one to his shoulder, screaming at his friend. She didn't see the gun.

She finished pulling her hands out from beneath her feet as she spotted the black pistol. It had fallen, at some point, and had slid beneath the trailer's old refrigerator. The fridge was a grimy yellow, and it had no bottom plate.

Maggie did her best to ignore her own internal warnings of how many viruses and bacteria and insects and small mammals had built their overlapping little colonies of disease and infestation beneath that old refrigerator. She pushed every other concern away and convinced herself on a deep animal level that not getting to that gun posed a far greater risk to her health than any number of infections.

She dove for the fridge, sliding across the linoleum and snatching up the gun from its hiding place beneath the appliance. O'Neal's partner had barely recognized that she had moved when she raised the gun and shot him six times in the chest and stomach.

She then turned her attention to O'Neal, but he was no longer helpless on his knees, clutching at his wounds.

Apparently, some ancient instinct of self-preservation had activated within him because he was now ignoring his injuries completely. He rocked back on his haunches and launched himself toward her like a lion going for a gazelle's throat.

She raised the gun to fire, but he was on top of her before she could shift her aim. Her shot sailed over Clarence's shoulder and through the roof of the trailer.

She tried to maneuver his weight off of her, but Clarence's eyes had the crazed look of a wounded animal approaching death. Her father had taken her hunting with him once in Wyoming. She had seen that look in the eyes of a dying predator before. She knew the danger.

Clarence slammed her arms against the front of the fridge and knocked the gun away. Then his hands found her throat and wrapped around it. His fingers were like the coils of a snake, choking the life from her.

She kicked and clawed and fought against his grip, but her hands were still restrained by the dog chain, which limited her options.

He was winning. Despite all her training. All her extra work. All the hours of sweat and pulling triggers and living and breathing for moments like this and, despite all that, he was winning. That's how pointless it all was. She thought of the results of her medical tests. Of her fight with Marcus.

The room was growing dim.

She tried to scrape the old dog chain against Clarence's wrists.

Despite all her training, she was going to die at the hands of some small-time drug dealer in a revolting old trailer outside Middle of Nowhere, Arizona. Forget that noise. She had more to do with her life. She had more dragons to slay. She had yet to find the man who took her brother. She refused to let this Breaking-Bad wannabe take her down and keep her from all the work still left to be done.

Then she remembered the knife sticking out of her right shoe. Clarence O'Neal had his hands wrapped around her throat, choking the life from her and, although she couldn't reach his face or neck with her arms, she could reach him with her feet.

She kicked up her right leg and drove the toe of her

foot into the side of Clarence O'Neal's neck. He released a bloody gargle, and his grip faded to nothing.

She pushed him off and called out, "Jerry, are you okay?"

Unfortunately, the voice that answered was a different one than she expected.

None of it made any sense. Judas's instructions were conflicting and overly complicated, but Marcus supposed that was how they were meant to be. That was the whole point. Judas wanted to prove his superiority not just because he was better at some pointless little mind game. He wanted to prove his superiority by transcending the games altogether. By being the gamemaster, moving people around like they were nothing more than chess pieces.

Marcus stood up from the chair and jacked a round into the breaching shotgun that he had requested from the county's tactical unit. He dropped the tablet onto the chair and took aim at his door's hinges. Marcus had always known that the only way to deal with a killer playing games was simple. Don't play. Rise above. Beat them at their own game only as long as you have to and then turn the game on its head.

Judas had just spouted a lot of nonsense to confuse them, but he had revealed one detail that Marcus was betting to be true. Renata and Ian were being held down that third tunnel. And that meant that he didn't need to play this game any longer.

"Agent Williams!" Bradley Reese's voice said over the radio. "I heard that whole transmission. He played it in here too. I heard you choose not to share all the info with me.

Then I heard that you can sacrifice me to save yourself and the woman and the kid. Is that your plan? You going to—"

Marcus squeezed the trigger and the specially made breaching round exploded into the hinges of the polycarbonate door. Metal sprayed over the tunnel floor and sparked off the glass. He repeated the shot against a second set of hinges at the top of the door. Then he kicked the door and found the spot holding it on the opposite side, the locking mechanism. He fired again into that area of the glass. The door came down with another kick, and Marcus raced into the room connecting the three tunnels.

He figured that he had at least thirty seconds left before time caught up with Judas's deadline. He supposed that right now, Judas would have wanted him and Reese to be arguing over how they should place their coins. Arguing over the nonsense of Judas's instructions and doubting one another. It was a good game. One that Marcus was glad not to be playing. And he suspected that even if they had played and won somehow by random chance, Judas would have still rigged it for them to lose. Because the game wasn't the point. Marcus knew that it was the betrayal that was important to Judas. Not just the betrayal between the two people, but the betrayal of every system of belief that person held. Judas wanted to flip people's worlds on their heads and have them do everything perfectly but still lose in the end.

Which was why, before they had even stepped into the mine, Marcus had decided to go with door number three and bypass the game altogether. Now, free from his own enclosure, he decided to release Renata and Ian first. Not just because of the whole "women and children first" thing, but also because he figured that he would have a few extra seconds with Reese. Even if Judas had the right and center chambers rigged to fill with sand quickly, Renata and Ian were nearly submerged before this part of the game had even begun. They would only have a moment after the countdown ended. Reese, on the other hand, would have a few more seconds at least. His section of the tunnel would have to start from scratch and fill to the point that the sand engulfed him. Then enough time with him submerged and deprived of oxygen would have to pass to cause brain damage. Marcus believed that he could beat that time and save everyone if he acted decisively now.

He ran past Reese's tunnel to where Renata and Ian were being held. After only a few strides into the tunnel, he saw the mother and son beyond a slight bend. He watched their faces light up at the presence of a potential savior.

"Stay away from the door and cover your eyes," he yelled to them.

He gauged when they were a relatively safe distance from the door, and then he raised the shotgun. He fired twice in quick succession, destroying both of the hinges. The pressure of the sand pushing against the barrier snapped the locking mechanism, and the sand inside came flooding out like a tidal wave. Marcus backstepped away from the onrushing sand, but it still nearly toppled him over.

He regained his balance and was about to rush over and help Renata and Ian, but then Marcus saw a red light flashing overhead and heard an alarm bell ringing.

He didn't think enough time had passed since Judas had given his instructions. But, then again, maybe he was wrong. Perhaps Judas had lied about the amount of time they had.

Or opening this door had triggered some kind of fail-safe.

In any case, the alarm bells started ringing and, a second later, he heard Bradley Reese let loose a strange, fading scream in the neighboring tunnel. He looked back to Renata and Ian and watched helplessly as another, larger wave of sand fell from the ceiling above them.

Shaky, Clarence O'Neal's partner stood up and rasped, "You bitch!" as he tore off his shirt and the bullet-resistant vest beneath.

Maggie cursed her luck. Not only did she stumble across drug dealers, but they also had to be the ultra-paranoid kind who wore body armor and were pumped up on stimulants.

She scanned the linoleum for the gun O'Neal had knocked from her hands. Shaky was looking for his own gun as well. They both saw O'Neal's gun at the same time. They both went for it. Two people injured and out of breath. But Maggie knew she was faster. She wanted it more. She would reach the gun first. Then the dog chain caught her again and jerked her back. The gun had apparently landed just beyond the reach of her restraints.

Shaky laughed as he picked up the pistol and aimed it at her head. Through scum-filled teeth, he said, "Any last words?"

"Yeah," she said. "I feel sorry for those little dogs."

He tilted his head just like one of those little dogs, and she continued, "You know, always running out and getting yanked back on the chain and then they keep forgetting that they're attached and they—"

The ear-piercing pop of a gunshot reverberated through the trailer.

Maggie blinked a couple of times and said, "Took you long enough. He wouldn't have let me stall much longer."

Jerry said, "I've never . . . I think he's dead."

Maggie looked across the kitchen at where Shaky had landed. He had a nice, clean hole in his forehead. "Yes, Jerry, he's definitely dead." She pulled herself back onto her knees and added, "You had to do it. It was him or you. He was going to kill both of us."

"I know." But Jerry didn't seem convinced.

"Can you get out of your chains? I think I could probably knock over this—"

And then the front door burst open, and two armed men stormed inside.

```
FILE #750265-6726-693
Zolotov, Dmitry - AKA The Judas Killer
State Exhibit F
Description: Diary Entry
```

Now that I look back on it, I realize that killing that dog was the pinnacle of my career as a murderer.

Everything before and after was just the rise and fall. Every kill after that, at least those from when I was boy, was just some part of me chasing that initial feeling.

And chase it I did.

I killed maybe six people that summer.

I varied the genders and ages. Tried out different things to see what I liked. It was easy to manipulate people. Especially when you were just a little boy and didn't pose a threat.

But I never found that serenity again, and I quickly learned that, for me anyway, it was about much more than the killing. The feeling I was chasing didn't come from murder, but from proving something to myself.

Unfortunately, my search for meaning drew unwanted attention from law enforcement. I had been careful. Had left no evidence. But some cop traced back some of the missing-persons cases to the fair circuit and came around asking questions. That cop took notice of me and my father because of some reports that victims had been participants in our games. Up to that point, we hadn't drawn the attention of law enforcement with our human mouse race.

Many states had provisions exempting carnival games from gambling laws. The other states that hadn't enacted such laws didn't enforce gambling rules on the midway. And if any gaming official ever did come around, it was merely to fish for a bribe. That was until I drew the attention of a cop who was probably owed a favor, which led to the eyes of the gambling commission falling upon Father and "The Judas Game."

We were in the country illegally, and I think Father was wanted for questioning by the police in Kansas regarding an incident with an underage girl. The last thing that my father or I, or anyone else on the midway for that matter, wanted was attention from the cops.

Fate or manifest destiny or pure luck and coincidence or whatever irresponsible force was to blame then dropped another variable on us. Father had an old friend back in Russia who had inherited a dilapidated theater in a decent part of the city. Apparently, sometime in the unknowable past before my birth, Father had actually pursued an acting career. And he had actually made friends with someone. This past colleague wanted Father to write a play for his newly acquired performance venue. He couldn't pay us up front, but the main thing would be that Father's ego would be fed and fat and happy.

So Father and I fled the land of milk and honey and bribe-resistant law enforcement and headed back to Moscow. And that's when I met Stasi.

The wave of sand threatened to drive Marcus farther away from the frightened mother and her child. So he fought forward against the current. The particles rushed over him and tore at his skin like sandpaper. His eyes burned. Through the haze, he saw Renata and Ian gasping for air as the wave threatened to carry them farther down the tunnel.

He reached out and grabbed them both under his left arm as he shielded his eyes with the breaching shotgun and his right arm. He held up the mother, and she held up the child. And a stubborn will to never surrender held up Marcus. Together, they steadied each other until they were out of danger.

Once they were free of the wave and the sand was slowing down, Marcus said, "Stay here," to Renata and then ran toward the center tunnel.

He hoped that he wasn't too late to help Reese.

There still should have been plenty of time to save him,

despite Judas's extra surprise. Still, the closer he came to Reese's enclosure, the deeper the sinking feeling grew in his gut. As he turned the corner and saw that there was no sand in Reese's tunnel, the sinking feeling jolted him like he'd been on an elevator that had slipped a cord.

When he didn't see Reese in the tunnel at all, the elevator dropped completely.

And when he saw that the floor of Reese's enclosure had actually been a false bottom and had dropped away like a trapdoor, the sinking feeling became more like striking pavement.

He hit bottom just like Reese probably had a few seconds earlier. And that's when he realized what had been so disturbing about Reese's scream. Reese had been falling into a dark hole, getting farther and farther away. The fall had created an eerie echo effect. He hadn't thought much of it at the time, but a part of him had registered it as strange. Now, that same part of him, that same tiny detective, checked off a box and declared that mystery was solved.

Marcus reloaded the breaching shotgun and fired three more blasts into Reese's door—instead of kicking it, he pulled it toward him and away from the hole. He made sure that it fell back into the tunnel instead of down into the shaft. He didn't want shattered bullet-resistant materials raining down on Reese, on the off chance that he was still alive.

Leaning over the hole, Marcus yelled, "Reese!"

There was no reply.

"Bradley Reese! Can you hear me?"

No reply.

Marcus felt a sudden wave of guilt.

He hadn't known Reese very well or for very long, and he hadn't liked him much in the time that he had known him. But that didn't mean that the guy was all bad. And it definitely didn't mean that he deserved something like this. Marcus considered what Reese's last thoughts would have been. Probably something about Marcus betraying him and choosing to let him die. Reese probably blamed him at the end. He wondered if he should have clicked on the radio and let Reese listen to Judas's video. Maybe he should have been nicer to him. Maybe he should have told Reese to put his coin in the tray, just in case.

He second-guessed himself for a moment more and then went back to Renata and Ian. As he helped them toward the mine's entrance, recalling the map from memory, he stopped and said, "Wait here for just a minute. I need to check something."

Then he moved back toward the three tunnels and entered the first—his tunnel from the game. The floor in his enclosure was also gone. Just like Reese's, it had been built to function like a large trap door.

Marcus stared at the depths of the pit into which he would have fallen, but he wasn't seeing his own mortality. He was seeing lost opportunity. He could have had that tablet computer analyzed, but now it was in a million pieces at the bottom of a mineshaft.

As he gazed into the darkness, trying to see the bottom, he realized that just because he had refused to play Judas's game didn't mean that he had won.

Episode 3

After freeing Maggie and Jerry Dunn from the dog chains, Andrew had the correctional officers he had deputized help the pair out of the filthy little trailer and over to their vehicles, which were parked a safe distance away in case the whole place exploded. By the time they were all clear, the kitchen was in flames. The fire trucks were on their way, but he didn't think there would be much left by the time they arrived.

Maggie was the first to speak. "Did Marcus tell you to come help me?"

"It's called backup, Mags. It's kind of a thing we cops do."

"We're not cops. And does Marcus always call in for backup and accept help from people? If he had taken our help last year, he would have never been taken prisoner in the first place."

"Is that what's going on? You're mad at him for not putting up more of a fight when he was taken?"

"No, of course not. Listen, we had no reason to think that Clarence O'Neal was cooking meth and growing herb back here. I had two other people with me."

"One of whom is now dead."

She shook her head and gritted her teeth. Andrew's ex-wife used to make the same face when she'd get angry with him. "We had no reason to think that we would be walking into a situation like this."

"No, you had reason to believe that you were walking up on a serial murderer who likes to work with sophisticated technology and explosives. Hell, Maggie, you barely survived these guys. It's a damn good thing that you didn't find our killer."

"That's enough."

"No, it's time you heard this. I know what Marcus did for you in Pittsburgh."

"He told you?"

"He didn't have to. We covered up the whole thing so it doesn't really matter, but remember, I was a medical examiner. I know a thing or two about the meaning behind the angle of stab wounds. What the hell is going on with you?"

"You know, I had a brother once. And he died. I don't need a surrogate. I don't need you in my business."

Andrew said, "You should talk to Emily about it."

"I'll do that."

"I'm serious. If you don't talk to her about this, I'm going to tell the Director."

"You do what you feel you need to do."

Andrew closed his eyes and took a breath. "You know, we all used to be like a family."

Maggie pushed him aside and moved toward her vehicle. "Things change," she said.

"What are you doing?"

She said, "I'm going back to the prison. Clean up this mess for me, will you. That's what you're good at. You're like our janitor."

Andrew wasn't sure what to say to that. His mother had always said that if you don't have anything nice to say, then you shouldn't say anything at all. So he said nothing at all.

He watched Jerry Dunn walk up and ask her for a ride.

"Sure," Maggie said, and then she climbed into the minivan and sped off.

Andrew looked around at the burning trailer and the metal building full of pot plants. He thought about the dead bodies contained in both of them.

With a shake of his head, he said, "So now I'm the damn janitor. My professors from medical school would be so proud."

Debra Costello lived in a luxury apartment not far from Catalina State Park and Mt. Lemmon. It was a beautiful two bedroom inside a new, gated community. A nice, safe environment for a young lady designed to keep danger at bay. Unfortunately, the Director knew that the people who hurt you most often were the ones you welcomed inside.

They had torn the place apart searching for any clues. Unfortunately, the only thing they had found so far were some small traces of blood. The Director was working on dismantling Debra's couch for any evidence when Val called out from the bedroom, "Come take a look at this."

The Director made his way down the hall to Debra's bedroom. It was beautifully decorated and well kept. He hadn't seen Debra in years, but from everything he had learned in the past few days, Powell had done an excellent job in raising her. She seemed to be a kind and responsible young woman.

Valdas sat at Debra's computer. He looked over his shoulder and said, "Look at this, Philip. I discovered a program running on her computer." He brought up the program and clicked an icon that displayed a horn with sound waves coming out of it.

Out of the computer speakers came a young woman's voice. "Shoot . . . Missed you again, Dad. I'll try later tonight. Everything's going great though . . . I love you."

The young lady sounded stressed about something, but if he hadn't known any better and he were the message's recipient, the Director would have assumed that she was just exhausted from her trip.

Valdas wiped tears from his eyes and said, "That was Debra's voice. You were right. I traced back a cable plugged into her MacBook and found the burner cell phone connected to it. He had a program on here that would somehow leave messages from her making everyone think that she was safe. If you consider that and the blood . . . Debra has to be dead."

The Director didn't know what to say. He had no words of comfort to offer that wouldn't sound hollow.

Valdas collected himself and said, "I've been thinking about this, Philip, and I've decided that it's time we tell Scott about his little girl."

"It will destroy him. He's already dealing with a lot."

"I would want to know. And him not knowing isn't going to bring her back."

Valdas pulled out his cell phone and navigated his way to

a video conferencing app. The Director said, "I figured we'd wait until we got back to the prison. Tell him in person."

"We still have more work to do here. We tell him now."

Both of them sat down on Debra's bed and Val held up the phone so that their picture was displayed in the top corner of the device's screen. The phone was one of the new oversized models, and although the Director thought it was a step backward to have to lug around an even bigger device, he had to admit that the extra screen size was appealing.

When Scott Powell's face appeared on the phone's display, Valdas immediately said, "We have some bad news . . . "

Then Valdas started crying again. This time uncontrollably. He gestured at the Director to continue on.

With a look at Valdas meant to say thanks for throwing me under the bus there buddy, the Director said, "It's about Debra, Scott. We think this guy took her."

"She's in India. I've been receiving calls from—"

"He faked them. We just found out how." The Director went on to explain how Marcus had seen the scar in the video and all that they had discovered since.

When he was done, he could see Powell weeping and the jumpy video looked like the device was enduring an earthquake. The Director felt helpless. He felt like all of this was somehow his fault.

After a moment, Powell's tear-soaked face reappeared on the screen.

The Director said, "We're going to find this guy and put him in the ground. I promise you that."

Powell was silent for a moment, but then he said, "You still don't get it, do you? If my daughter is dead, taking another life isn't going to bring her back. I told you when we went up against the Cattleman that I wanted him alive. That I wouldn't be part of your shoot-first-ask-questions-never mentality any longer. I wanted then and I still want these men to stand trial. I want them to see justice. I wanted the Cattleman to see justice, for Debra's sake, but you murdered him."

"That was a clean shooting. Obvious self-defense."

"You put his back against the wall on purpose and manipulated him into doing what you wanted. You wanted that man dead, and he died."

"And what the hell is wrong with that? The world's a better place without him in it!"

"That's not for you to decide. I actually believe in second chances and redemption, Philip. You look at criminals and see weeds that need to be pulled so that healthy crops can grow. But I don't see them as weeds that need to be pulled out and tossed away. I see potential. I see men and women who with a little help and a lot of love can still be a light in this world."

"You are so naive. Most of those men would rather cut your throat as look at you. And the justice system is a joke."

"I one hundred percent disagree. You are right that some people can't be helped. Some people deserve to be in a hole somewhere, whether that's a cell or a grave. But that's not for you to decide, Philip. Only dispassionate, objective people can decide something like that. There can be no justice where there is passion."

"But there can be vengeance."

Powell said, "Kill all of them you want, and it will never bring back your wife."

"I'm not a fool."

"No, Philip, you're a zealot. You're chasing a white whale that doesn't exist. You want to know what kind of man you really are? We were best friends, and when I left the SO, I was so afraid for my life that I kept copies of all of our case files as insurance against you. Because I was worried that a man who used to be my best friend may slip into my home and murder me and my family in our sleep . . . just because he thought it was for the greater good. You think that life is transactional. That for every sin that's committed equal retribution should be extracted, but that's black-hole logic that only leaves the world a cold and dead place. Killing won't bring back the ones we've lost. It will only tarnish all they've left behind, and all they lived for."

"Well, while you're teaching psychos how to read, I'm still out there in the trenches and the mud, bleeding, and watching good people die at the hands of your charity cases. You can spare me your self-righteous bullcrap. You can tell Judas, the man who more than likely murdered Debra, all about your wonderful new programs when I catch the son of a bitch!"

The Director grabbed the phone from Val's hand and threw it against the wall. It ricocheted across the room with a crunch. He stood there panting and feeling light-headed again.

Val was quiet for a moment but then said, "That went about how I expected. And you owe me a new phone."

As the Director stormed out of the room, he said, "Send the bill to Powell Prison Technologies."

Maggie parked the minivan and then suffered through a

probing pat down from a young male guard at the next security checkpoint before being allowed entry into Foxbury. The guard gave Jerry a wink when he thought Maggie couldn't see him, but Jerry didn't come to her rescue. He just diverted his eyes and then followed behind her like an orphaned puppy which had finally found its mother.

As they crossed through the manufacturing facility and down the tunnel to Foxbury's main building, Maggie observed her newfound partner. He was cute in a younger brother sort of way with his shaggy black hair and Eastern European skin tone. But she definitely wasn't buying what he was selling, and it was probably best if he knew that sooner rather than later. As they walked, Jerry started to say something twice, but both times he seemed to think better of it. She hoped he wasn't planning on asking her out. She didn't ask him what was on his mind, and she didn't really want to know.

Every time she looked at Jerry, she thought of her real younger brother. He would have been about the same age as Jerry was now. She supposed that if Ackerman was correct in his assessments of her brother's case, then her brother could still be out there. She wondered what he would have been like now, or was like now.

They passed through the corridors of the prison's main building. The halls were teeming with sweaty inmates, and she could feel their hungry eyes following her. She did her best to ignore them, but their crawling gazes felt like centipedes creeping over her skin.

The guard behind the glass allowed them through a checkpoint leading up to the CCE and Powell's office. She finally permitted herself a second to relax. She took a deep breath, but when she did, she caught a big whiff of the cat-urine chemical smell from the trailer. Some of those putrid scent molecules must have still been stuck in her nostrils and, with them, billions of microscopic invaders climbing up her nasal cavity. She rubbed at her nose, as if that would help somehow.

The elevator doors closed, and Jerry said, "So do you have a—"

Maggie cut him off. "I'm a nun, Jerry."

"I thought you were a—"

"I'm on loan from the Vatican to help the DOJ with special cases."

He seemed to process this for a moment and then said, "Are you teasing me?"

"Yeah, but in a good-spirited way. You saved my ass back there. I won't forget that. But yes, I do have a boyfriend."

He seemed to take a second to process that information and then said, "Okay. But I was going to ask if you have a badge that actually says Department of Justice."

"Oh. Well. I . . . "

"I thought it sounded pretty cool, if you did. Like you were a member of the Justice League like Batman and Superman."

She felt three inches tall. "Yes, I do have credentials that say Department of Justice." She wondered if this was the slowest elevator ever made. They stared at each other for a couple of seconds, and then she pulled her creds from a pocket and handed them to Jerry. The elevator dinged. He opened the leather flap and looked at the badge and ID.

"You can just keep that," she said and stepped out through the elevator's opening doors. She couldn't take another second inside that box. It felt like four years of her high school gym class had just flashed before her eyes.

She heard Powell shouting nearby and was happy for the distraction. She rounded a corner and saw Scott Powell—who was speaking with his hands as much as his mouth—say to Spinelli, "How in the hell is that even possible?" Spinelli was at her terminal in front of the main display and looked as if she was about two seconds away from curling up into a ball and pretending to be dead.

Maggie came up behind Powell but didn't say anything. She wanted to see if he gave away anything more. He didn't. He noticed her between tirades and said, "What happened to you?"

Maggie had been fighting to ignore the drying blood and the filth from the trailer still staining her jacket. "I fell. What are you doing out of the hospital?"

Powell looked unsteady, as if he could fall over at any moment. If she had to guess, she would say he was strongly disobeying doctor's orders by even being out of bed. He said, "I wasn't about to stare at some hospital room ceiling while my dreams burned."

"Fair enough. But don't take that out on her." Maggie gestured toward the cowering cyber queen.

Powell glanced at Spinelli and closed his eyes. "I apologize, Lisa. I know it's not your fault."

Spinelli said, "I understand. It's totally fine." But the young blonde thanked Maggie with her eyes.

"Tell me what's happened," Maggie said.

"It's about your friend, the agent you have undercover."

"He's not my friend. What's he done now?"

Powell said, "It's not so much what he's done as what

his intervention has exposed. Earlier, while we were at the shipping container, Ms. Spinelli called me about the incident involving your non-friend and our resident celebrity, Mr. Lash. I instructed her to hold back certain information from your team."

"You have to be kidding me. People are dying."

"I just wanted to make sure that no one went off half-cocked before we had all the information."

"You just wanted to make sure that no one shut down your pet project and burned your dreams."

Powell nodded and said, "Yes, that to. But it's in the past now. We have considerations that are far more important. We need to go speak to your non-friend. If he confirms my fears, I'm going to follow Agent Williams's advice and evacuate Foxbury."

Maggie, Powell, and Jerry Dunn took the elevator down two floors and then walked through the old lobby. It was a large, open space with a staircase leading up to a reception area. Ackerman was just down the hall from there in the Administrative Segregation Unit, the place where troublemakers went after being subdued.

Ad Seg at Foxbury was actually four separate holding cells with one shared hallway. The cells were all padded and each one had a large window for looking inside. She had seen something similar at a prison in New Jersey where they were using holding areas like this as segregation and suicide watch. She wondered if the residents here could even commit suicide. Would the system allow them to harm themselves or shock them into submission for trying?

A small metal shade that could be slid off to the left covered the monitoring window of the first cell. She guessed they were keeping Ackerman in darkness. Probably treating him as they would any other prisoner, in order to maintain his cover. That was fine with her. She knew Ackerman wouldn't mind the dark and, even if he did, she could have cared less about his well-being.

Jerry pulled the metal shutter to the side and flipped a switch to turn on the lights inside the cell. She was glad to have Jerry there. She had yet to let her mind wrap itself around the events that had taken place at Clarence O'Neal's trailer. She felt nauseous and shaky every time the thought of how close she had come to dying caught up with her. An experience like that formed bonds quickly. And Jerry Dunn had been there when she had needed him. She was glad he had stayed and wanted to help.

As Jerry stepped aside, Maggie looked through the viewing window at Ackerman.

He had his right arm in the air, blocking some of the light to help his eyes adjust to the sudden illumination. Then she noticed that a makeshift patch, fashioned from a torn strip of his prison jumpsuit, covered one of his eyes. She wondered if he'd hurt it in the fight with Lash. He was shirtless in a crouch with his back pressed against a corner of the room. He looked feral and powerful. He stood and approached the viewing window. His muscles were coiled and bulging, and he had no trace of fat on him, but his body was also covered with layers of scar tissue. She knew each of those scars had a story. Some of them had come from his father, Ackerman Sr, who was at that very moment withering away in a Supermax prison. But she also knew that many of those other scars had come from his victims and law enforcement fighting back.

She said, "Where's your shirt?"

"In the corner. It's hot in here."

"Put it on."

"Do my scars make you uncomfortable, little sister?"

"Your existence makes me uncomfortable."

Ackerman said, "You took your time getting down here. Where's my brother?"

"We're trying to do our jobs, not babysit. The world doesn't revolve around you."

"You can't prove that."

"What's with the eye patch?"

"I'm maintaining my night vision. I read somewhere recently that the reason pirates wore eye patches was actually for strategic purposes. So they could maintain perfect night vision, which it takes a half hour in darkness or low light to achieve. Say a pirate boards another ship. The people down in the hold would have an advantage over the conqueror because it was often very dark down in the belly of those ships. When the pirate entered, he would essentially be stepping out of the sunlight into darkness and fighting people who could see where he was essentially blind. So, along the way, some above-average swashbuckler realized that he could wear an eye patch and maintain his night vision in one eye. Then he could just switch the patch to the opposite eye or flip it up and continue on with the looting and pillaging."

"Okay, but why are you wearing one?"

Ackerman said, "It's a surprise."

"I don't like surprises."

"It's not for you. And I think you have more important questions to ask."

She said, "How did you bypass the security system?"

"I didn't bypass anything. I provoked Mr. Lash into prematurely revealing his hand. He had a device in his possession which disabled the security system in that room."

She looked to Powell with a question. But the warden was staring off into space, and there were tears in his eyes.

"Mr. Powell? Are you okay?"

Powell nodded and said, "Yes, we found the device he mentioned. Your undercover agent here managed to kick a breaker and trigger a secondary alert system. Otherwise, I'm not sure what would have happened."

Ackerman said, "They would have killed me and disposed of the body. I'm sure they had at least some plan for that. But you see, that's the problem."

Powell said, "Attempted murder is usually a problem."

"Work with me, Maggie. Why is an attack like this a problem?"

She said, "There are a lot of problems here. Just tell me."

"Think about it, little sister."

She resisted the urge to tear the door open and smash Ackerman's face in. She said, "It's obviously pretty disturbing that Leonard Lash is in possession of a device that can bypass the prison's security."

"Yes, and why would he ever give that secret away? Why would he ever give away that tactical advantage?"

"We would never have known about the device if you hadn't kicked that breaker."

"Wrong," Ackerman said. "They would have been able to dispose of my body and slip away, but they couldn't just make the system and everyone here at the prison forget that I ever existed. I'm betting that as soon as they turned off their cloaking device, the prison's monitoring system would have flagged that my restraints were no longer reading a pulse."

Powell coughed and leaned against the glass. He looked like he was going to pass out. "Are you going to make it?" she said.

"I'm fine," Powell said with a bit of a sharp edge to his voice. "I was just going to say that he's right. I have no idea how they planned to get away with killing or even injuring him."

Maggie finally saw it.

She said, "They were going to leave the device in there with you and stuff you into one of the machines."

"Probably something like that."

Powell shook his head. "No, that would have prolonged it a bit. But the laundry staff starts at 5:00 a.m. They would have found the body almost immediately. Then we could have just watched the tape of who entered and left the room. We would have had the murder tracked back to Lash before breakfast."

Maggie checked her Apple watch. It was nearly two in the morning. She said, "It's because they knew things would already be in motion by that time."

Ackerman added, "I'm surprised it hasn't happened yet. I've been expecting it to come at any moment."

"Expecting what to come?" Powell asked.

"The conclusion of your experiment, Mr. Powell."

"I know we have some issues here, and we're going to—"

Ackerman said, "You still haven't put these pieces

together yet, have you? The shooting incident was to remove opposition and ensure that there wouldn't be any power struggles once the lights went out."

Maggie said, "But the games?"

"A distraction. He has Marcus racing all over the countryside like a horse with its eyeballs scooped out."

Maggie grimaced. "Thanks for that image."

"Is that not a saying?" Ackerman shrugged. "Anyway, the point is that the theatrics are to keep everyone's focus away from the prison, where the real game is about to begin. And he's successfully sent the lead investigator and all the tactical units far away from Foxbury."

Powell said, "Who is he? Who is Judas?"

Ackerman shrugged again. "I can't do everything for you."

Maggie said, "We need to evacuate."

Powell rubbed at both his temples. Tears were forming in his eyes. "I've already ordered all non-essential personnel moved out. Which wasn't too difficult at this hour. Most of the doctors and barbers and such are already at home in bed."

Maggie said, "We'll need to coordinate with the sheriff's department to transport the prisoners somewhere. Or maybe it would be easier to just use the sheriff's department as extra guards. Completely bypass the software."

Ackerman knocked his fist four times against the reinforced window. He said, "If I may interject, you only have one chance at stopping this."

Maggie was about to beat the answer out of him when the lights dimmed and then extinguished completely. A flashing red glow replaced the warm white light of the fluorescents.

Maggie said, "What is this, Powell?"

"It looks like a lockdown. Like a threat level red was triggered." He snatched the handheld radio from his side and called out for Spinelli. But there was no answer other than the static hum of dead air.

Ackerman started laughing. He walked over to the corner and picked up his shirt. He slipped it over his shoulders, popped his neck, and stretched his arms. Then he walked over to the security door to his high-security padded cell. He pushed through the door like the cell was just his bedroom and he was coming out to join the family.

Ackerman said, "As I was saying before Foxbury returned to the stone age, you can't let them take the control room. It might be your one shot at stopping them from taking over completely."

Powell said, "The restraint system should still be active."

Ackerman rolled his eyes. Then he punched Jerry Dunn in the face. It was a quick jab that caught everyone by surprise and left the young correctional officer on the ground.

Maggie rushed forward to help Jerry and screamed at Ackerman to get away from him. She pulled her gun and pointed it at Ackerman. "Get back in that cell!"

Ackerman took a step toward her. "Or what?"

"I'll do it. I will kill you. Just give me a reason."

"I'm sorry, little sister. I didn't mean to imply that I didn't think you had the balls to pull the trigger. I just wanted to hear you say the words. I'm glad to inspire such passion in you."

"Get in the cell."

"It doesn't lock anymore."

"We'll figure something out."

"I don't think so. You need my help."

"I don't need anything from you."

Ackerman sighed. "We don't have time for this. Mr. Powell, where was Leonard Lash taken after our scuffle?"

"He and all of his men were taken to the infirmary."

"And they would still be there now?"

"That's right."

"And where is that located?"

"Just down the hall from here."

Ackerman nodded. "So we're sitting directly between the infirmary, where Lash was being held, and the control room, where he'll be headed now."

Powell said, "I suppose so."

Maggie asked, "Why is the control room so important?"

Ackerman said, "Let's talk about that in a moment. Right now, you should probably concern yourself most with the group of large, angry African-American gentlemen who will be storming into this room at any moment with the intention of ending our lives."

Marcus told Ian Navarro, "My son, Dylan, he's about your age. He's actually here in Tucson. Maybe we could get the two of you together before we fly back to DC."

The scared little boy didn't acknowledge him. He hadn't spoken a word since Marcus had carried him from the mine. Ian and his mother, Renata, sat in the back of an ambulance parked just outside the mine's entrance. Renata had latched onto Marcus in much the same way he had seen kidnapped children do when reuniting with their parents.

He didn't blame her after all they'd been through. She was just looking for any stable ground to stand on.

Renata said, "I'm sure he would love to meet your son."

Marcus said, "He's big into Legos and action figures. He takes an old suitcase full of them with him everywhere he goes. You into Legos, Ian? Dylan loves using them to create his own little worlds."

A paramedic said, "We're good to transport them, sir."

"Great." Then to Renata he said, "If you need anything, you have my card. Don't hesitate to call, even if you just need someone to talk to. I don't give very good advice, but I'm cheap."

She smiled and said, "Thank you, Agent Williams. I don't know how to thank you. You . . ."

She started to tear up, and Marcus said, "I tell you what. You send me a Christmas card and a family photo every year, and we'll call it even."

As the paramedics loaded them up and closed the doors, Renata gave him one last nod of thanks and, for the briefest of moments, Marcus felt like a good man who did good things.

From behind him, Sheriff Hall said, "Nice call with the breaching shotgun."

"I have my moments."

"We're working on recovering Reese's body and the tablet, but it's going to take some time. The insurance company says we have to call in cave rescue and mining experts."

"You're a by-the-book kind of guy, aren't you, Sheriff?"

Hall got that far-off look again, same as he had during the briefing. Marcus said, "What's bothering you?"

"It's nothing. Just thought this kind of thing was behind me."

"Where were you on the job before this?"

"Detroit."

"Detroit SWAT? That had to be rough."

"It had its days. What about you?"

"Brooklyn Homicide."

"Wow. One of the best departments in the country. And I hear it's becoming a hip place to live now."

"Yeah, a lot's changed there since I was a kid."

Sheriff Hall gave a nod. "The world never ends up being the way we thought it would be."

One of Hall's men, of the full-tactical-gear variety, ran up and announced, "Sir, I think something's wrong at the prison. We just lost all communication."

Demon stared at the block wall and waited for the first part of the plan to begin—a plan that he had helped devise. Of course, no matter how much hand he had in the design, he would never have set foot inside Foxbury. He was only here now because the law demanded it. His law. A cardinal sin had been committed, and retribution would be swift and come directly from him. That was the law. It was what the Legion demanded.

And it gave him a chance to get out and stretch his legs a bit. Spread his claws and keep them sharp.

As he watched the block wall, it started bleeding. The grout between the blocks became veins. The aged concrete became as flesh. Then the veins burst, and maggots spewed out of them. Thousands of tiny bodies. They were all screaming. They each had their own small voice. They were screaming his name. His real name.

And then the falling maggots struck the concrete floor of his cell. They burst into black tar and morphed into millions of tiny flying creatures, all of them different. Different faces, characteristics, and numbers of limbs.

He could feel the tiny creatures more than he could see them. And he could hear their songs. Their siren calls. Telling him to bite into his own wrists.

He ignored it all, as best he could. But there was always something there, something strange right outside the corner of his eye. Something shrieking, growling, calling his name, or hurling insults.

The Legion was currently criticizing him for letting things go this far. Maybe he should have stepped in earlier and put an end to Judas and his machinations. But he had been curious. And he enjoyed a good piece of theater as much as anyone; as long as it was a tragedy, and everyone died in the end.

The lights in the hall flashed to red, and he heard the lock to his cell click as it disengaged.

The dark man had been crouching like a spider in the corner of the room, but now he stood and moved toward the door.

Demon stood and followed.

Ackerman felt like a curtain of blood had fallen over the sun. The red glow permeated everything. He supposed the system had been built with a fail-safe evacuation setting. Something the new program hadn't overwritten. Some switch built into the foundation programming, which told the emergency lighting to kick on in the case of all hell breaking loose. And, as Ackerman watched the red glow, he felt as if hell truly had come to Foxbury.

Hell had come to Foxbury.

That made him smile.

Not because it sounded like the tagline for a movie. Or because he had any desire to see Hell.

It made him smile because this Hell had come to Foxbury shortly after he had arrived. And that reminded him of John the Revelator and his story of the rider on the pale horse. And I looked, and behold a pale horse: and his name that sat upon him was Death, and Hell followed with him.

Ackerman liked thinking of himself as the pale rider of death. He had just started to imagine what that might have been like when he heard the rapid rat-tat-tat of automatic weapons fire.

It was too early for the sounds to be from the guns of law enforcement tactical units. Only the tower guards would have ready access to such armaments. It could have been some capable guard who had sprinted to their central armory and had then sprinted back with such a weapon. But it was the final and most likely scenario that disturbed Ackerman the most.

He thought of the bomb left for Ray Navarro. The mastermind would have done something similar here. Only this time it was likely assault rifles left for Leonard Lash and his men.

He should have thought of that.

Now, he would be facing a group of men more heavily armed than he had anticipated.

That didn't disturb him because of the added danger. He couldn't have cared less. He would adapt and overcome on the fly. It was what he was best at. What disturbed him was the fact that he had made such a tactical error.

He considered the implications and decided to stay the course.

A moment later, Leonard Lash and two of the members of his goon squad, a pair who were still able to walk, burst into his holding cell. They covered the corners and tried to act the part, but Ackerman could tell that these men had been given no formal instruction. Their movements were sloppy and undisciplined, and they had never lost the bad habits repeated confrontations literally beat out of you.

The ULF enforcers found no one around the viewing area of the Ad Seg hallway. Ackerman had gotten Maggie and the others out of his way, so that he could handle the situation with Lash.

He honestly didn't know what his brother and his team did without him.

He sat in the corner of his padded cell just as he had been when Maggie had arrived a few moments earlier. The ULF enforcers swarmed in and covered him with their M4A1 assault rifles. Ackerman didn't move. He didn't make eye contact. He didn't even look up. He didn't acknowledge them in any way.

Lash stepped in after them with a black Glock pistol dangling from his left hand. Lash said, "Not such a big man now, huh? That's the thing I love about guns. They level the playing field between more evolved and more feral beings."

"Whoever said that being less feral equates to being more evolved?"

Lash said, "You don't act like a cop. And you obviously have skills. So who do you work for?"

"I take orders from no man."

"Everyone answers to someone."

"I answer only to God. I fear no man. 'You will not fear the terror of night, nor the arrow that flies by day.' Psalm 91 verse 5."

Lash said, "I don't have time for this. Tell me who you are and maybe I let you live."

Ackerman laughed. "You know, Leonard, your biggest sin will also be your downfall."

"Who do you work for?"

"It's the same sin that led to the angel Lucifer's downfall as well."

"Are you with Demon's group?"

Demon's group?

Ackerman still wasn't sure how his new friend, Demon, fit into all of this, but Lash had just confirmed his suspicions about Demon leading some type of group.

"Do you know how Lucifer sinned?"

"I don't care."

"He thought that he could be the biggest fish in the pond. But the truth is that there's always a bigger fish, at least from our limited perspectives on dimensional space. And the sooner one accepts that, the quicker they can find where their piece fits into the grand puzzle of creation."

Lash just smiled and said, "Kill him."

★★★

Maggie looked through a crack in the frame as she nudged the door open with her foot. They had moved into a room that looked like the nurses' old break room, which was just down the hall from the Ad Seg cells, located down the hall from the infirmary. It was a whole medical wing which had once housed the doctors and nurses of an insane asylum, and now the space had been revived and housed the prison's medical unit. Different but still the same. Things had a way of coming back around.

Jerry Dunn hovered over her shoulder. He whispered, "You and your undercover agent seem to have a bit of a strange relationship."

She said, "He's a strange sort of guy. And he's not an agent."

"Then what is he?"

She thought about that, but anything she wanted to say wouldn't have been appropriate.

"He's a special consultant."

"So he's like an expert on prisons or something?"

"I'm watching for Lash. Do you know if these are the only Ad Seg rooms?"

From behind her, Powell said, "There are two identical Ad Seg units in this wing. Each with four cells. The one your consultant is in and another closer to the infirmary."

"Good. Then they'll check that one first and give us all an extra second to prepare."

Jerry said, "You seem to really trust your consultant."

She glanced back at the shy correctional officer and said, "Why would you think that?"

"You gave him your gun."

"I didn't exactly give it to him."

"You could have tried harder to stop him from taking it or questioned that he had a plan or would handle the men who were coming to kill us. But you just went along."

"He's a good guy to have on your side in a fight. The problem is that he's never actually on your side. He's only ever on his own side. If your goals align with his, then you're fine. But let's just say that I don't always align with his goals."

Jerry said, "Oh, that's good."

"How is that good?"

"I thought that maybe the two of you had a thing."

She scowled at the young man. "He's not my type."

"What is your type?"

"The kind of guy who doesn't ramble in my ear during a crisis situation."

Jerry backed up a step, and she felt guilty. It was a strange feeling. Like she had just kicked a puppy.

"I'm sorry, Jerry. I didn't mean to snap at you. You're a sweet kid, but I am seeing someone."

"Someone on your team? Agent Williams?"

She said, "Do you work for *National Enquirer* all of a sudden?"

He hung his head. "I'm sorry."

And there was that look again. One puppy through the uprights. She said, "No, Jerry, again, I'm sorry. And yes, I'm dating Special Agent Williams."

"So the boy you mentioned earlier, Agent Williams's son—"

"Dylan."

"Yes. Dylan. He's kind of like your stepson then?"

"I suppose he's something like that, but nothing legal yet. I need to be listening for—"

"I'm sorry. I just really respect that. After my parents passed away, my uncle took me in and raised me like his own. He and his wife couldn't have kids and. well, I guess it's just special for someone to take on that kind of responsibility."

Maggie did her best to focus and keep the tears at bay, but Jerry's comment about his uncle not being able to have children had struck too close to home. Her eyes couldn't contain them. The tears flowed freely. She wiped them away.

Jerry said, "Did I say something wrong?"

"No, your comment just made me think of something that I've been trying to forget. I just found out that I'm infertile. I can't have kids. Just like your uncle and his wife."

"Oh no, I'm so sorry. But you know, I think sometimes God opens up holes like that in our lives to make sure that we have room for something or someone else. Like with my uncle taking me in. And, in your case, so you would have room in your life to let in new people."

"Shut up. Someone's coming."

She looked down the hall and watched as Lash and two of his men entered the room where Ackerman was waiting. She reached down and retrieved her backup weapon from an ankle holster. She had inherited the compact Taurus .357 Magnum revolver from Marcus, as a gift.

She stepped into the hallway and said to Jerry, "Who said I gave up all my guns?"

Ackerman had initially intended to use Maggie's gun only to threaten Lash and his men. He had promised his brother not to kill anyone, and bullets could be very unpredictable. Up close with a knife, he could have stabbed these men twenty times without doing any serious, permanent damage. But even a perfectly aimed bullet could ricochet off a bone and slice an artery, ending the target's life.

He supposed it was a chance he would have to take. And how could his brother fault him for taking down three armed men? It would be a "clean shoot" as the cops would say.

Still, he had given his word, and so it would break the spirit of that oath if he didn't at least try to wound them. Just a slight maiming. Maybe they would no longer have the use of a hand or would require kidney dialysis. But that definitely still counted as being alive.

As he crouched in the corner of the padded cell, he could feel the weight of Maggie's Glock against his leg. He had tucked the gun between his calf muscle and his thigh, into the crook of his knee, so that he could access it with ease. Tucking the gun into something like a waistband could cost a few milliseconds if it snagged on clothing. And in situations like this, milliseconds mattered.

His adversaries thought that they possessed the advantage, but Ackerman had set up the cell to be in his favor. He had pulled the metal shade closed and had removed the lights in the hallway. Which meant that the cell's only light source was a naked bulb in the corner of the room encased in clear plastic beneath a metal cage.

He knew that he had the element of surprise because they had no idea that he was armed.

And he knew that he could take all three of them before they realized what was happening. The no-killing part was what made matters more complicated. But he wasn't concerned. He had always come out on top in such situations.

And Ackerman had a theory as to why.

Gunfights like this, point blank range, were about reaction times measured in the tenths of seconds. He had come to believe that his lack of fear gave him an advantage of at least a few milliseconds over nearly every other living creature on the planet. He gained valuable reaction time while the brains of other organisms struggled against the pointless forces of implication and consequence and fear.

But there was none of that for him. He just saw what needed to be done and did it. There were, of course, logical variables that his brain still calculated like the organic supercomputer that it was, but if reaction time meant the difference in such a duel, then Ackerman had an inherent advantage.

He waited until the last possible second before springing into action.

The two untrained ULF revolutionaries squeezed their assault rifles tighter to their shoulders, preparing to fire.

And he lunged forward and to the right and swung the gun up and across in a very controlled and calculated arc.

But he wasn't shooting at Lash and his comrades.

He was aiming for the light in the corner of his cell.

He squeezed the trigger in a quick double pull, sending two projectiles through the metal grate and shattering the red emergency bulb.

Darkness fell over them.

He rolled away again and one of the ULF enforcers fired their assault rifle. But the man's aim was wild. He was literally firing blind into the spot where Ackerman had once been.

The room wasn't completely dark. There was some ambient light still coming from down the hall. And Lash held a small flashlight in his left hand. But it was dark enough that night vision became a matter of tactical significance.

And Ackerman was ready. Like the pirates of old, he pulled the makeshift eye patch from his right eye. He raised Maggie's Glock. And then, squeezing his left eye shut, he aimed and used his perfect night vision to fire three bullets into three strategic, pre-calculated points on each man's body.

When it was done, there was a lot of screaming and cursing. None of it coming from him, since he didn't find either particularly helpful.

He stepped forward and finished disarming the trio of men while regarding his handiwork.

At some point in his life, he had flipped on the TV at some seedy motel and watched an action star shoot the guns out of the hands of two attackers. But Ackerman knew that was not the way to disarm an opponent. First, modern firearms could sustain multiple rounds from even high-powered rifles and remain functional—still firing, still able to take a life. Second, it created shrapnel that could kill the person you were trying to disarm.

The correct move, in his opinion, was to go for the dominant shoulder, which forced the attacker to lose their aim for sure, and then either drop their weapon or, in most cases, completely lose control of their arm and their senses.

As he looked at the three writhing men and covered them with the Glock, he thought of the past. He thought of the man he had once been. Once upon a time, these three would have been ready to play a game. He laughed to himself. He had truly been the angel of death in those days.

And his name that sat upon him was Death . . .

Maggie rushed into the cell waving around a snub-nosed revolver. She looked at the three writhing and cursing men and said, "I thought you had a plan?"

Ackerman said, "This was it."

"So your plan was to face down three dangerous criminals armed with assault rifles. And to do it alone, outnumbered, and outgunned. And end up shooting the three of them. With my gun."

"You say all that as if it was a bad plan."

She shook her head. "You had three other people who could have helped you. And I had a second gun. We could have caught them by surprise, snuck up behind them, distracted them. But instead, you have to face them down alone."

Ackerman considered this and said, "I see your point. I suppose I'm still adjusting to working in a team-based environment."

She said, "It figures that you'd be a ball hog."

Ackerman took a step forward and placed the barrel of the Glock against Lash's forehead at a spot between the ULF leader's eyes. Lash just glared back and clutched his wounded shoulder.

Ackerman said, "You know, we could end all this fuss right now. We could put two more into my friend Leonard and remove the financial backing of this little revolution. No one would doubt that it was self-defense. That would sure throw a wrench in their plans. All it would take is one squeeze of my finger. With all the people I've killed, what's one more?"

Maggie said nothing.

He waited a couple of seconds and then looked over at her. Ackerman had merely been playing around with Lash, making him feel that his life was in danger. Ackerman expected Maggie to quickly tell him to stand down, but that order never came. He could see in her eyes that she was considering it. She was trying to think of a reason not to just put a bullet through Leonard Lash's brain.

He waited, and finally she said to Lash, "Get on your feet." Then to him, she added, "Now, what's so important about the control room if the system is already down?"

He stared at her a moment and let the tension settle in the air. He wanted her to know that he knew what she had been thinking.

Ackerman said, "I'll explain on the way. Let's hope that no more tests arise between here and there. Because Mr. Lash and his men won't be the only convicts headed for the control room, and time is not on our side."

Demon had studied the blueprints and knew the layout of Foxbury well. In order to reach the control room, he would have to pass directly through all of the residential wings. His own apartment was, of course, at the farthest end of the facility opposite his destination.

The corridors he discovered on the way there represented many different levels of chaos and, to his eyes, varying pictures of hell.

In one, there was screaming, and burning toilet paper and the aroma of blood and sweat.

Another corridor was empty. It looked serene and mundane, like everyone had just stepped out for lunch.

Down a third hallway, he found a single dead man resting in a spreading pool of blood. The dead man was lying roughly in the center of the corridor, roughly halfway between one end and the next. Someone had stabbed the man repeatedly in the abdomen. And Demon knew enough about forensics and wound patterns to see that most of the stabs had occurred post mortem, or after the man's death.

This killing hadn't been some kind of riot-related, wrong-place-wrong-time kind of thing. This killing had been fantasized about. This had been an old debt come due.

When Demon first spotted the body and the blood, he hadn't been sure if it was real. But upon viewing the murder scene, he knew this was a true corpse. It wasn't a trick of his mind or his condition. That had been a living person and was now a rotting pile of meat.

He knew for sure because demons didn't kill this way. Only men killed liked this.

Demon removed his prison-issue shirt and threw it to the side. He kicked off his shoes and rolled up his pant legs a cuff, for better range of movement.

Judging by the color and abundance of the blood, the dead man's killer must have nicked a primary artery. Demon stepped out into the pool of blood and lay down on his stomach. He rolled in the blood. He took handfuls of it and smeared it all over himself. He painted his entire torso with it. The blood was still warm, and it made him feel powerful, unstoppable, immortal.

He made sure that every inch of his flesh was coated in fresh blood. Then he stood, stretched out his fingers on both hands, and tensed all his muscles.

He heard a noise at his back and spun around to see two men standing at the end of the hallway. They stared at him with their eyes wide and their mouths agape.

Demon looked down at his own naked torso, which was now covered in another man's blood. Then he looked to the pool and back to the pair of awestruck convicts.

He said, "Come on in, boys. The water's fine."

Maggie had taken charge and organized their group as best she could. She had given her Glock pistol to Powell and her .357 Magnum to Jerry Dunn and instructed them to lead the way to the Control Center East. Then she hauled the three UFL prisoners into the middle of the caravan, with her and Ackerman taking up the rear with the M4A1 assault rifles.

She hated giving Ackerman a gun at all, but he had proven himself before. And Maggie chose to swallow her pride a bit, rather than put herself in greater danger. The bottom line was that, in a crisis like this, Ackerman was the kind of guy you wanted on your team. Although, she hated to admit that in even the smallest way.

She could see the questions in Ackerman's eyes. He knew that something was up with her. She said, "So what's so important about the control room if the software is down?"

Ackerman said, "We haven't had a chance to just chat recently. How are things?"

Maggie clamped down her jaw so tightly that she felt

something pop in her eye socket. She said, "Things are just great. I'm filthy, bloody, and covered with billions of disease-spreading microorganisms which are currently injecting me with Lord knows what kind of exotic diseases. Not to mention the fact that I signed up to be an investigator, not an action hero!"

"You seem tense."

She said, "Ack—"

She stopped herself as she realized not to use his real name. But what was his false name? Then it hit her. She had given him a name to represent an old friend of hers. She had wanted to remind him that she hadn't forgotten or forgiven. Now that had backfired on her as she was forced to remember her old friend and the fact that she wasn't entirely innocent in his death.

"Alexei, I don't have time for your crap. Now what about the damn control room?"

"You still don't see the potential of this? Think about it a second. This place is wrapped in concentric circles of security and covered by cameras at every angle. If they get that system back online and turn it against their keepers and the outside world. . ."

Maggie said, "They would be able to see any attack coming. So they would be able to force a prolonged stalemate."

"Foxbury is the perfect storm to become the FBI's next infamous and bloody standoff. If Lash or whoever is involved takes that control room, then there will be no resistance. There will be no rescue. They will own Foxbury."

The ramifications of such a sophisticated security system being used to keep people out rather than in had just started to sink into Maggie's head when Powell called back, "We hear voices ahead. Several of them."

Lisa Spinelli tried to throw up as quietly as possible, which was not an easy thing to do. When the security system went down, she had decided to go straight to the source and access a terminal connected directly to the servers. Whenever possible, always go to the source. Her brother, Peter, had taught her that.

Once, back in their young and stupid days, Peter had tricked a professor's grading system. He did it not by hacking the encrypted database but by loading a Trojan onto the teacher's computer, which then changed the printer font to one of Peter's design whenever the Spinelli name was detected. Which basically gave him the power to turn c's into a's and d's into b's. And the funniest part was that the school's secure server had everything correct, and when the teachers checked their programs, everything would seem in order. Until the grade cards were printed.

They had eventually been caught, but it was still a lot of fun while it lasted. And the lesson that she and Peter had taken away was that eyes couldn't be trusted. Only source code could be trusted.

So she had opened up the maintenance hatch in the back corner of Control Center East and had climbed down into the server room, which was located directly below the CCE.

She had just started the long and arduous process of backtracing the intrusion and the corrupted code when the screaming started.

And by the way her coworkers in the CCE had screamed,

they must have seen Satan himself up there. And then Satan must have tossed them into a wood chipper.

If she lived through this, she would never forget the sound of those screams. It had been like she had overheard a wizard transform men and women into squealing pigs and then into whimpering canines and then into silence. Into the silence they fell.

She began to weep and then threw up again.

But once her fit of near-silent heaving was over, she returned to work at the terminal. Maybe she could still save Foxbury, and her own life along with it, by doing what she did best.

The voice that called to her from the top of the access hatch dashed those hopes. The voice was deep and raspy with a thick Scottish accent. "Come on out of there now, love," the voice said. "You won't like it if I have to come down after you. You have thirty seconds."

She burst into tears and spent the first ten seconds freaking out and trying to wake up from this nightmare. The next ten seconds were wasted on trying to find a weapon. As if she would have had the slightest clue of what to do with any kind of weapon. Then she used the last ten seconds to ascend the maintenance ladder back to the control room.

In the CCE, the overhead fluorescents were all out, but the light from the display screens, which now showed only an army of loading and error messages, filled the space with a blue glow. Chairs and equipment had been toppled. Terminals and keyboards had been smashed to pieces. The whole room smelled strongly of rust, like the old 1978 Mercury Bobcat she had driven in high school. The car had been born ten years before she was and, by the time it had come into her possession, it was more rust than car. The smell of the CCE reminded her of driving to high school on a hot day.

When Spinelli saw the first of her coworkers' bodies, she let out an involuntary shriek and quickly clamped a hand over her mouth.

The man's name had been Bill. She had seen pictures of him at his son's soccer games. She had given him advice on an anniversary present for his wife. And now he had been torn apart. She tried not to let her eyes linger for too long on the body and the mutilation, but she had seen more than enough. Bill's insides were now his outsides.

And Lisa Spinelli had a terrible feeling that she was about to endure a similar fate.

A voice from across the room—a voice with that same Scottish accent and same frightening rasp—said, "Come sit with me."

She willed her legs to move. She ascended to the next level of workstations, moving toward the voice.

The man who had summoned her was turned away so that she could only see him in profile. He sat in one of the many office chairs lining the row of terminals. The same kind of uncomfortable chair that Mr. Powell had purchased in bulk at a heavy discount to stock the retrofitted prison. From where she was standing, the light from the wall of monitors lit his profile and obscured his features. He was just a vague black outline of a man.

He kicked out the chair beside him and said, "Sit."

She complied immediately, and then she looked across at him. It was the first time she had gotten a good look at the man who had murdered her coworkers. The face she saw across from her truly was that of the devil. His features were distorted. His skin was caked in dried crimson. The whites of his eyes glowed in contrast to his other features, which were covered in blood, both dried and freshly spilled.

They sat in silence long enough to give her cause to jump when he said, "I'm in a grumpy mood, Ms. Spinelli. That's not your fault, but I'm going to take it out on you just the same."

"How do you know my name?"

"I know lots about you, Lisa. And I know lots about your brother, Peter."

"What do you know about Peter? Did you kill him?"

"Simmer down now, lass. I didn't kill your brother, but I think you know why he died."

She said, "He would never."

"Oh, please. Darling, he sold out even cheaper than we had budgeted for. And you know it's not even the first time he's done something like this."

"My brother was a good man."

He laughed. His teeth glowed like the whites of his eyes. "There are no good men. Just those who have done evil and those with the capacity for it. Those who have already screwed you over, and those who are about to."

"Why are you doing this?"

"Because the Legion demands it."

"That's cool. I'm a big fan of the Legion. What exactly do you want from me?"

He leaned forward in his chair very slowly. She could see a strange glimmer in his eyes. A lust. A hunger. He said, "Do you really want to know?"

She couldn't find words.

He continued, "I would like to wear your flesh. And I mean that in every possible way. I want to tear you open and slip inside of you."

She laughed nervously and said, "That's very flattering, but I am engaged. And we're in love. Umm. So I'll have to pass, but let's still be friends."

He chuckled slowly. "I like you, Ms. Spinelli."

"Is that a good thing?"

He leaned forward and sniffed her hair. "Let's just see where it leads us."

Marcus sat atop the passenger seat of the sheriff's SUV. He had ridden to the scene with Bradley Reese, and it hadn't felt right to use the man's car, especially after the way he had treated the dead man. That was, if Reese was truly dead, a fact he wouldn't fully believe until they found a body at the bottom of that pit.

He said to Sheriff Hall, "How long until you can retrieve the body from the mine?"

Hall said, "I have someone at my office working on figuring out the proper legal way of doing it."

"Can't you just find one of your guys who has been rock-climbing before? Send him down that hole?"

"Oh no. Insurance would never allow that."

"Come on, I know you're an elected official, but—"

Hall said, "About that. I consider myself a straight shooter."

"I can see that."

"And so I need to come clean about something."

Marcus said, "Tell me it's not as bad as you're making this sound. I really don't need any more complications."

"Yesterday, a man came into my office. He had made an appointment under the guise of representing a civic action committee wanting to sponsor my next campaign."

Hall paused a second as he guided the SUV onto the highway, lights flashing and sirens blaring. Raindrops pelted the windshield. Andrew had told Marcus earlier that they were here for Arizona's monsoon season, which ran from June to September and often promised some short but heavy downpours.

Once on the highway, Sheriff Hall dug into his pocket and pulled out a business card. He handed it across to Marcus. One side of the card was a painting that Marcus recognized as a hellish scene painted by Hieronymus Bosch. The other side was even more disturbing. It detailed a hellish torture session in a flowing, precise, handwritten script.

Hall said, "The man who came into my office said that's what would happen to my two daughters if I didn't comply."

Marcus said, "Have you had the card analyzed? Dusted for prints, DNA, traced back the card stock?"

"Yeah, but everything so far came back negative."

"What did this man want you to do?"

"He wanted to be on the next transport going into Foxbury. And he wanted me to put together some fake transfer documents."

"And you complied?"

"You have to understand, at the time I thought Foxbury was the most secure place on the planet. He showed me a live video feed of a man in a black mask with a sniper rifle.

Then the video panned over to what he was looking at. It was my daughters' school."

"How do you know it was a live feed?"

"The man with the scars spoke to the other two men."

"But it could have been a recording, and he just set it up to appear live."

"I suppose, but the time of day corresponded with it being a live feed. The girls were at recess."

"How do you know it was two men? Did you see both of them?"

Hall said, "No, but from the way the video was shot, it looked like at least two men. Or one man and one woman."

"So if you had tried to arrest him, then he kills them right then. And if you don't get him into Foxbury, he kills them in the way he explained in detail on this card."

"Right. He gave me instructions from there on what to do. And I did it. I figured having him locked up in Foxbury would at least buy me some time. Now, with all this going on, I can't help but feel responsible. I'm thinking of stepping down as sheriff."

Marcus rubbed the bridge of his nose. "No, Sheriff Hall. You're a good man who was protecting his family. I don't want you to step down. I just wish you had said something sooner."

"I didn't know what to do."

Marcus said nothing.

When they reached the outermost security checkpoint, Sheriff Hall stopped the vehicle and met briefly with his men. They were already establishing a perimeter, but Hall was more concerned with taking back the prison. He picked a handful of men from the tactical unit to enter Foxbury through the manufacturing facility and regain control. Marcus geared up alongside Hall's tactical team and jumped into the back of their SWAT van.

Sheriff Hall was at the front of the van, sliding into his tactical gear with as much ease and habit as most men have when slipping into a pair of mesh shorts. Marcus dropped down beside him and said, "Just like riding a bike."

Hall said, "Listen. I really appreciate your understanding."

"You probably shouldn't thank me yet. You see, one of the reasons I don't want you to step down is because now I have something to hold over your head. We may have to do some things that the insurance company is not going to like. For instance, going down into the mine to verify that Bradley Reese is actually dead at the bottom of that hole. And I don't care if you have to tie a rope around your secretary and lower her down there in order to get it done. Just make it happen."

Ackerman and Maggie traded places with Dunn and Powell. An old metal door with a small, reinforced security window inset in its center separated them from the next corridor. Ackerman moved up to the window first.

He popped his head up for about a second and then pulled himself back out of sight. In that quick glance, he had analyzed and quantified the entire scene.

He returned to where Maggie was covering the door like a pro, the M4A1 assault rifle at her shoulder and fire in her eyes. He was so proud of how she was coming along.

She said. "What are you grinning about?"

"Nothing important."

"So, about the corridor full of bad guys . . . You saw . . . "

"I was just thinking about that time when we were in Chicago and—"

"First of all, don't make it sound like we were working together in Chicago. I was there working. You were creepy stalkerizing us."

"That's not fair."

"How many bullets were exchanged between our group and you while we were in Chicago?"

"Several, I suppose. But it's not really a party without a little exchange of gun fire."

"It doesn't matter. Just shut up. You always do this. You think it's funny that other people are afraid and you're not. It amuses you that I'm scared to death right now."

"No, little sister, it most certainly does not."

She said, "What did you see?"

"There are five enemies in the corridor. It appears that they have instructed some of the other convicts to remain in their cells. They are also armed with Tasers that they acquired from the guards they are holding hostage. Beyond this point is a larger corridor, likely a nexus point for a couple of Foxbury's different wings. There are a few stairs leading up right after you go through the door, and they have the high ground. My assessment is that they are using this as a holding area for hostages before moving them on to one central location."

"You think they're that well organized?"

"I think a very powerful man is facing a death sentence, and even after appeals and all the circus, he can't hope for anything better than his sentence being reduced to life in prison. Or twenty years, which is close to the same thing. He doesn't like any of those options."

"We can't go in there guns blazing. Not with hostages."

"Well . . . We could."

"I won't risk it. Using your rifle is a last resort. This is not time for shoot first and ask questions never."

He said, "The longer we wait, the more complicated things get. They could be reinforced or the dynamics could change. And we don't have time to go back and find another way around. I'll give you another five seconds to decide before I take action."

"Stand down. You will take no action without my go ahead."

"I'm trying very hard to work in a team-based environment right now."

She said, "How about you start working in a do-every-damn-thing-I-say environment. And by the way, your promise to Marcus not to kill anyone should still apply."

"I won't kill anyone. Unless, of course, one of them has some kind of medical condition. I can't always account for every variable. I mean, shit happens."

"I don't want shit to happen! We're going to double-back and find another way around."

Ackerman nodded, and then he ejected the magazine from his rifle. He held it out to her. She looked confused, but she took it from him.

He leaned forward and said, "I know you're scared, little sister, and you think that my lack of fear clouds my judgment. But believe me when I tell you that I don't want you to be afraid, and although I lack fear, that doesn't mean that I compensate with stupidity. Let me demonstrate."

Then he kicked through the door into the next corridor.

★★★

Little sister thought that he just rambled about and rushed headlong into every situation but, if anything, he overanalyzed. And he never took on a fight he couldn't win. After all, losing was just an excuse for not cheating hard enough. Everything he did was calculated, weighed, and then often put instantly into action. There was no second-guessing or morality or fear of pain or death. There was just analysis and action.

He decided that he would walk back through this encounter with Maggie afterward and explain his every calculated move. That way she could perhaps understand that although his ways were often a mystery to her, they were very sensible from an objective standpoint.

He would use this as a teaching moment.

He had that in mind as he stepped up the stairs toward the group of men on the landing which joined several hallways. The far side of the nexus held seven hostages. Five inmates-turned-revolutionaries stood between the hostages and Ackerman. If each enemy had retrieved a Taser from a guard that meant that two of those were still available for use. He scanned the area, and his eyes found the electricity-based weapons sitting on the ground near the line of hostages.

These guys were making it too easy.

He debated about even using the Tasers, just to make it a bit more challenging.

He said, "Hello, gentlemen."

Ackerman had come to realize that his lack of fear also gave him a tactical advantage in that he was never afraid to fail. He considered all the possibilities and their potential outcomes, but he didn't fret over how things would turn out. This gave him a tactical advantage because he always entered every situation assuming that he would win. He may have to adapt and improvise his game plan. That was inevitable. But why even consider defeat? Ackerman felt that it was amazing what one could achieve when that person knew from the start that they were going to win. No doubt. No fear. Just analysis and action.

The first opponent stepped forward, aimed the Taser at Ackerman's chest, and said, "Don't move!"

Ackerman kept moving forward.

He held the empty assault rifle up like a white flag of surrender.

The man who seemed to be in charge of the gathered group was a behemoth of a man with a military bearing. But the rest of the group seemed to be a mix of colors and gang affiliations. Ackerman supposed this was the reason for the shootings—ensuring alliances, just as he had predicted.

The big man who seemed to be in charge kept the Taser trained on his target and said, "Don't you move, you crazy bastard."

Ackerman considered the man's voice and tone and then gave his face a second look. He laughed out loud when he realized who it was. His old friend from the prison yard. What was his name? Bozo?

Ackerman said, "My dear Bozo, so good to see you again."

The man's voice was little more than a rumble as he said, "Bozo? You call me that one more time, and I'm gonna—"

Ackerman laughed and replied, "My apologies. I forgot that's not actually your name. I was just calling you that in my head earlier."

Bozo leaned down into his face. He could smell the big black man's sweat. The odor reminded him of a dive bar he had demolished once in Chicago. Bozo said, "I find that name offensive and racist."

That genuinely surprised Ackerman. "I apologize. That was never my intention. Offensive? For sure. But racist? Never. I actually think you may be confused at what I'm referencing with that name. At any rate, the name was simply intended to convey my view of you as some sort of clown or dancing buffoon. Any other undertones were purely accidental, and I'm truly sorry for that."

"My name is Winston."

"Then that's what I'll call you."

The smart play for this group would have been to surround him and work together to restrain him. But these were mere foot soldiers following Lash's orders, and he supposed their presence as convicts at Foxbury to begin with spoke to their poor decision-making skills.

Winston repeated himself. "Don't move."

Ackerman kept walking forward. He said, "Are you familiar with the infamous Nazi scientist Hans Eppinger?"

Winston said nothing. The big man just kept his feet moving and his eyes on the assault rifle. He said, "Where did you get that gun?"

"From your boss. But Mr. Lash is fine. Don't worry. Anyway, Hans Eppinger tried to see if people's bodies would somehow adapt to drinking seawater. Or at least I suppose that's what he was after when he forced ninety gypsies to drink nothing but seawater."

"Where is Mr. Lash?"

Ackerman supposed that Maggie was currently listening in and thinking that he was merely talking to hear the sound of his own voice. But, in reality, he was using the conversation as a distraction while he analyzed the coming fight. He already knew how things would play out; down to what order the opponents would be dispatched and what available weapons he would use to achieve that. He had sized up each adversary, their strengths and weaknesses, and he had chosen a fighting style to implement. Indonesian Silat, which was a fighting art that he employed on a regular basis and had been studying extensively as of late. Unlike many of the other disciplines, it assumed that the opponents you were facing were trying to end your life. With that in mind, Silat was brutal, and it aimed for all out destruction of one's opponent.

He would have to explain all of this to Maggie during his post-fight analysis.

He said, "It's reported that the suffering gypsies would lick the freshly mopped floors to find drops of fresh water. All the subjects died horribly, of course. Perhaps Eppinger was merely in the data-gathering phase at that stage of the game. Doesn't matter. The point is that it's amazing what normal, intelligent human beings will do, what ignorant schemes they can be talked into, when under the influence of an egomaniacal narcissist."

Ackerman knew it wouldn't be long now before Winston took action. He could see the big man's wheels turning.

Winston would eventually figure out that he was holding a nonlethal weapon, and the safest course of action would be to stun and subdue Ackerman before asking any other questions.

Ackerman said, "What did Lash offer you to go along with all this madness? Money? Freedom?"

Winston pulled the trigger.

Ackerman saw the move coming long before the big man pulled the trigger. It was predicted by Winston's eyes, posture, and breathing. But Ackerman wasn't worried about the Taser. He wasn't concerned about the electric shock he would receive. He had practiced this move to perfection with everyone from security guards to federal agents.

Electricity-based weapons required a connection from the intended target's body to a power source of some kind. In the case of the typical pistol-grip Tasers, the weapon fired barbs into the flesh of the target, which connected by wire to the power source in the Taser's grip.

When Ackerman saw the big ULF enforcer tense to fire, he released his grip on the assault rifle, letting it fall to the floor. After that, all he had to do was send his arms into motion before the kiss of the Taser reached his skin. He jerked his arms up to about head height, each aimed with an arcing path toward the point of impact of each electrode. He wasn't fast enough to catch the prongs before they struck, but once his arms were up, the rest was like surfing. All he had to do was ride the wave.

Truth be told, this was his favorite part.

Something so soothing about the muscle-tensing touch of electricity.

He felt the prongs penetrate his flesh, and the shockwave began. Eventually he knew his body would betray him, and he would succumb to the current if he didn't ride the wave of electricity with his falling hands. He guided his soon-to-be-useless arms like a pair of paratroopers gliding toward an objective. Then he used his remaining muscle control to tangle his fingers around the wires and, just before the wave crashed, he let his arms fall to his sides, yanking the barbs free of his flesh.

With the electrodes in hand, Ackerman thrust them back at their master. Winston wore a long-sleeve T-shirt and prison-issue pants. The best point of impact would be his torso, but Ackerman opted for exposed skin and jammed the prongs he had just ripped from his own flesh back into Winston's neck.

The big man's eyes had already been wide and fearful, but they went wider. He was out of the fight for at least a few seconds, which meant that he was out of the fight altogether.

Ackerman held Winston up for a second and then shoved him back toward his friends.

At this point in the dance, Ackerman faced a choice. Go for the improvised knife sticking out above Winston's waistband, probably something fashioned from broken glass. Or use the assault rifle as a bludgeoning tool. Considering that he had promised not to kill these men, the knife would be the obvious choice. He could be very precise with a blade.

But he decided to go with the assault rifle.

Less mess.

He snatched up the weapon and swung the empty gun by the barrel toward his next closest threat. It struck the man across the face and drove him downward toward a brick wall. The man collided with the brick in such a way that Ackerman had to wonder if the blow was fatal.

How was he supposed to keep from killing anyone when all these people were so damn fragile?

As he suspected, both the second and third attackers had prematurely pulled their triggers and missed. So that left only one real threat, since victory was insured by limiting the number of Tasers to one. He could easily handle the stings of one Taser, but in numbers they could immobilize him.

The first and second of the hostage takers were now down or at least stunned and momentarily out of the fight. The third was still on his feet. He was a big, dumb-looking white guy with Aryan ink. He hadn't changed position by two feet during the entire confrontation.

He threw a punch at Ackerman. A big, dumb, slow haymaker.

Ackerman grabbed the wrist with his left hand and snapped the man's forearm using his own forearm as leverage. The big Aryan howled in pain, and Ackerman shoved him aside.

The fourth man stupidly tried his Taser, but he was also blocking his final ally from attacking.

The fourth man fired, and Ackerman once again turned the electric serpents back on the snake charmer. Just as he had done with Winston, he jammed the hooked prongs into the man's neck and shoved him aside.

The final man had the stance and technique of a boxer.

He feigned two fake punches, Ackerman blocked a third, and a fourth connected with Ackerman's jaw.

He stumbled back and gave a nod of respect. He said, "Nice moves. I had you pegged as a boxer, but you were a bit more than just mildly competitive, weren't you?"

The final enemy narrowed his eyes and said, "Two-time Golden Gloves winner."

Ackerman said, "Good for you. But I don't really care for boxing. Too violent."

Then he sprang forward.

Golden Gloves was ready. He feigned a big punch with his right and then faked an uppercut with his left. But then Golden Gloves wisely chose to throw no punch at all, and he instead focused on defense.

His strategy didn't matter.

Golden Gloves wasn't ready for Ackerman to lunge not at him, but instead at the wall to the boxer's left.

Ackerman expertly pushed off the wall with the side of his foot and, launching himself into the air, he used his downward momentum to drive his elbow into the side of the boxer's head.

Ackerman connected with the blow, but Golden Gloves wisely wrapped him up. It was second nature for a trained fighter to wrap up his opponent if necessary.

But Ackerman had counted on that training. He had exploited that ingrained tendency.

Golden Gloves wrapped up Ackerman's arms, just as he had planned. And then Ackerman did the thing that all modern boxers feared. He bit the man's ear off.

★★★

FILE #750265-6726-694
Zolotov, Dmitry - AKA The Judas Killer
State Exhibit F
Description: Diary Entry

The stage production of The Judas Game was a moderate financial success. Although, I wasn't impressed with it. It was a drama about a youngest brother trying to cheat his way to riches by stealing a portion of his father's wealth. The critics weren't impressed either. It just didn't resonate. Like Father was trying too hard to be something he was not.

Although, if I were Father, I would have wanted to be someone else as well.

The production made just enough money to buy Father a bit of goodwill when his next two plays flopped completely. At that time, he started working at the theater as a stage manager while he toiled away on what he called "his masterpiece."

While Father had been failing as a playwright, I worked behind the scenes as a stagehand. I was a teenager by that time and so, like most boys at that age, thinking about girls occupied most of my time.

But there was one girl in particular who caught my eye the first moment I saw her, and it wasn't long before she and I were deeply in love. Her father was one of the actors, and she filled in with some bit parts from time to time. Her name was Stasi, and she was the most beautiful thing that I had ever seen. Her hair was the color of maple syrup, and she smelled like strawberries. But she tasted better than either of those.

Stasi was the one thing that I've had in my life that truly felt real. With her, for a time, the hole that was in my soul was filled by her light and our love. We would sneak away into the shadows of the catwalks, high above the stage, and we would lie there on the metal, side by side, staring down through the grates, and talking about where we would live and how many children we would have. I could have died in her arms. I used to lay my head on her chest and listen to her breathe in and out, our hearts beating in unison. It was innocent and beautiful.

Her father, much like mine, was an abusive drunk, and I always suspected that he visited Stasi in the night. Sometimes she would come to me in the morning, crying and wanting me to hold her. She never told me, and I was too scared to ask. Too afraid of what I would do when I learned the truth. What I would do to him. And I knew that, no matter how perfectly I orchestrated his murder, there were elements beyond my control that would threaten the perfect sanctuary that Stasi and I had found in each other.

I felt like Stasi and I were living in a bubble that would inevitably pop, and I was too afraid to move or change anything for fear of that perfect world bursting around us.

Until I met Debra, I didn't think that I could ever love like that again. But Deb reminded me so much of Stasi. So much pain in her past, but so much joy in her future. You could just see it in both of their eyes. They each held a light inside that had refused to be extinguished, no matter what the circumstances that the darkness threw at them.

I envied them both. I always wondered what was inside of them that wasn't in me. I was born into darkness, and I embraced it out of survival and necessity. But they had refused to let it stain their souls, and their courage and strength astounded me.

I would have died to protect Stasi, just like I would have died for Debra after her, and so when Stasi asked me to run away and start a new life, I had no hesitation. I would have followed her anywhere.

So we made our plans. And then we made our escape.

The SWAT van was wheels up when Marcus received a text from Andrew. It said, *Thirty seconds out. Don't leave without me.*

Marcus yelled up to the driver and told him to wait. Then he started counting seconds. It was two and a half minutes before the van's rear doors parted and Andrew climbed inside.

Marcus had hated to wait, but he was damn glad to see his friend. He said, "Took you long enough."

Andrew, out of breath, said, "I peeled out of there as soon as I got your message. The cops on the scene think it could be a state record, by the way."

"Go team."

"We obviously can't be involved in the arrests."

Marcus said, "Sheriff Hall and I understand one another."

"She barely made it out of there alive."

"That's what I heard."

"I told her that I knew."

"Knew what?"

"That you covered for her in Pittsburgh. I saw the pictures of the body. Up-close pictures of the wounds. I can tell things from wounds like that. Things about the person who did the stabbing."

"I believe you. Do you have a point?"

Andrew said, "Let's start with what I know."

The van started to roll out, and Marcus said, "Have to take a rain check on that."

Andrew said, "I'll be quick."

"This really isn't the place or time."

"Another girl went missing, but you knew she was already dead."

"I had a hunch."

"We were all following different leads. I went to the warehouse district. You were following up on the ATM thing. And Maggie was checking out a lead on the van. You told me that Maggie called in for backup and waited at the scene and the two of you went inside together. Then you were attacked and defended yourself, killing the suspect."

Marcus said, "What is this, an IA investigation?"

The van bounced over the scorched earth of no man's land and moved through the final gate leading to the manufacturing facility. The plan was first to secure that building and the tunnel leading into the prison. It was imperative that they maintain a foothold here.

Andrew said, "This is your friend asking for the truth. I don't understand why you're covering for her. It was self-defense. She wouldn't have gotten into any real trouble. Probably just a psych eval and some mandatory vacation time."

The van rolled to a stop. "You don't stab someone eleven

times in self-defense. You do that out of anger," Marcus said, and then he stood up and jumped down from the back of the van.

Sheriff Hall held back with Marcus and Andrew while his SWAT team prepared to blow the front doors.

To Andrew, Marcus said, "You wearing your vest?"

"Never leave home without it," Andrew said. "It's saved my life too many times. But we're not done yet. Why did you cover for her?"

"This reminds me of that time in Chicago when the Prophet blasted you with that hand cannon."

"Yeah, I remember."

Marcus said, "What does it say about us that memories like that qualify as our good times?"

One of the tactical team announced that they were ready to breach. Sheriff Hall looked to Marcus for confirmation, which Marcus gave with a nod. The group stacked up with the sheriff and the two federal investigators on each end.

As he mentally readied himself to breach, Marcus felt oddly relieved to be out of that conversation and into a situation he could better understand.

Maggie and the others rushed up to help secure their new prisoners, who were bleeding and screaming on the ground. She looked at Ackerman, whose face was covered in blood; not his own but from the man who's ear he had bitten off.

She could think of nothing to say to Ackerman, who just stood there oblivious to the world of humans like a dog who had just pissed on the floor for reasons that had probably seemed perfectly sensible within the mind of the dog.

Warden Powell looked at the carnage and said, "Where precisely did you recruit this gentleman, Agent Carlisle?" Powell's Louisianan drawl had gotten stronger. He looked pale and exhausted. The exuberance she had seen when he had initially showed her his work was gone. It had been drained away as if someone had pulled the stopper on a bubble bath and all that was left were some surviving bubbles clinging pathetically to life at the bottom of the tub. Powell added, "Was he spec ops or something?"

Ackerman, face still covered in blood, said, "You realize that you're talking about me, and I'm standing right here. And no, Mr. Powell, I was not a soldier of any kind. I like to think of myself as more of a Jedi Knight."

Maggie laughed aloud. She said, "First of all, you are far from a Jedi. You're not even Boba Fett. And second, you've never even seen *Star Wars*."

Ackerman said, "I read the novelizations."

She rolled her eyes and directed her attention to the former hostages. They had just rescued seven of the approximately twenty-five guards inside the complex. That was a major win. Perhaps with a united front and Lash in custody they could still end this uprising before it could get its feet under it.

She helped the men up, and they retrieved their weapons from the fallen inmates. She said to the guards, "Have you seen where they're keeping any other hostages? Or does anyone know where they were taking you?"

The most senior of the correctional officers stepped forward. He was a bearded forty-something man with a beer gut and Bob Newhart eyes. He said, "They're rounding up everyone still here, guards and staff, and herding them into the chow hall. And I don't know why, but I heard them say that we all would get new accessories for our wrists and ankles."

She turned to Ackerman, who was wiping the blood from his mouth onto his sleeve. She said, "You were right. Their plan is to turn the security system against us."

He said, "That's a silly thing to say. Of course I was right. But now I foresee an even bigger problem. Mr. Powell, I need to know how your electric restraints remain charged up."

Powell, with just a twinkle of renewed vigor, said, "That's actually one of the coolest things about our system. The restraints never have to be hooked up and recharged. They're powered through a type of inductive charging which uses a magnetic field to wirelessly refuel any kind of device. It's a technology designed by a company called WiTricity, which was founded by a team of physicists from MIT with the goal of bringing wireless electricity into the mainstream. It's pretty amazing stuff that will soon be a big part of our everyday lives."

"I assume that requires some kind of base station to set up the magnetic field. Where are those base stations located?"

"There are four of them throughout the prison in spots that every resident will visit on a daily basis. When they enter those areas, their bracelets and anklets automatically receive juice from the base station. The four current base stations are in the chow hall, the education unit, the yard, and the manufacturing facility. And, of course, we receive an alert if any resident's restraints are low on power."

Maggie said, "Why does it matter how they're charged?"

"Because if I had full control and my fingers on the switches," Ackerman said, "and I essentially possessed the power of Zeus within these walls, I know exactly what I would do."

The tactical team swept the rooms of the manufacturing facility like the professionals they were, clean and tight and efficient. But they also encountered no resistance. They encountered no one at all. The gate guards had said that Warden Powell had ordered an evacuation of all non-essential personal right before communications went dark.

The western control center was empty. Two of the sheriff's men stayed behind there to see if they could get security back online, while the rest of the group moved as one through the manufacturing facility toward the residential buildings.

As they worked their way down to the tunnel, Marcus couldn't believe this case had fallen into his lap only a couple of days ago. It felt like he had been chasing Judas for years.

They arrived at the tunnel's entrance, and the team leader sent two of his men to scout ahead.

To the tactical team leader, Marcus said, "Do you have enough explosives to blow the door?"

The armor-clad officer said, "We should be able to—"

The noise of automatic gunfire and the screams of combat echoed up the tunnel in a maelstrom of sound and fury.

A small security station sitting beside the elevator regulated access to Control Center East and Powell's office. Every time

Maggie had entered Foxbury's nerve center, the same officer had been running the station from behind the security glass. He had reminded her of Matt Damon, but with red hair and if Damon had gained seventy pounds for a role. Each time that man had given her access, he had been excessively polite and friendly to her.

Maggie didn't think she had even responded with more than a nod. She had been too wrapped up in her own problems to have paid any attention to him.

When the doors all unlocked and all hell broke loose, the elevator guard would have been an easy target. She noticed blood on the floor. The rolling desk chair was on its side. It didn't look good, but she hoped that Ginger Matt Damon had simply been taken hostage.

She found the control for the elevator. A big green button marked UP. She pressed it and then joined the others in front of the elevator. The doors buzzed and pinged and parted. She was the first inside. Powell told two of the guards to stay there and hold the station.

The elevator doors closed, and Maggie felt the elevator rise. But it was a painfully slow two floors. The elevator was old and creaky, but it was also sturdy, a big industrial-designed people-mover. Not fancy but dependable. She felt a bit of a kinship with it. Just like the old elevator, she also felt like she was struggling to keep up.

They had plenty of time to prepare for what they would find above. She and Ackerman stacked up in front of the opening with their rifles at the ready. She could feel someone behind her, just a bit too close. It was Jerry Dunn, still holding her snub-nosed .357 Magnum and looking anxious.

The eastern control room was dark except for the glow of the computer terminals and the display wall, which all showed blue Powell Prison Technologies logos and error messages. Maggie and Ackerman fanned out and gave a cursory sweep of the space, while she directed Dunn to check the conference room, which occupied one of the control room's uppermost corners.

She was about to finish with her side of the room when Dunn screamed and cursed. He stumbled out of the conference room, gagging and hunched over as if he was going to be sick. He slammed the door shut behind him.

Maggie ran up the stairs, reopened the door, and discovered what had upset Jerry. The conference room table was piled with bodies. She didn't look long, but she guessed it was a collection of four technicians and two correctional officers. The smell was already overwhelming. She eased the door shut.

Jerry Dunn punched the wall and said, "I'm tired of seeing friends die!"

Maggie rubbed his shoulder and said, "I know, but hold it together for me. I'm going to need your help and your head in the game."

Dunn wiped his eyes and smiled. "Sure thing, coach."

She gave his arm another squeeze, and then she joined Ackerman on the next level of the tiered room. Ackerman sat at a chair in front of one of the terminals with his feet up on the desk. His hands were behind his head, and his eyes were closed.

She said, "What are you doing?"

Ackerman didn't open his eyes. "Guarding the control room."

"Doesn't look like it."

"I'd like to see you try to steal it from me. Also, there is a young woman hiding inside a desk in the next row of workstations."

Maggie shined the flashlight of her phone in that direction, but she saw nothing. She listened. She heard nothing. Maggie said, "How do you know that? Do you smell her or something?"

Ackerman opened his eyes and growled deep in his throat, like a dog deciding whether to bark or bite or any combination of the two. Maggie found the mannerism disturbing from Ackerman because it was something she had seen Marcus do on occasion. She didn't like seeing similarities between the two, biological brothers or not.

Ackerman said, "No, little sister, I don't smell her. Well, actually, I do smell her a little, but the big giveaway are the Hail Marys she keeps repeating. Of course, she stops now. It's like when your commissary card stops working, and then when you take it to the guard it starts up ag—"

"Frank, I get the idea. You can go back to being deeply disturbed now."

"Sure thing," he said and placed his feet back onto the desk and closed his eyes.

Maggie listened again, but this time she heard some soft crying. She traced the sound back to a small inset in the computers covered by some panels that matched the desk's surface. Lisa Spinelli was tucked into the space amongst a jungle of cords.

Maggie said, "Ms. Spinelli? Lisa, listen to my voice. You're safe now. Relatively speaking, of course."

Spinelli said, "Give me another thirty seconds."

"We need you, Lisa."

"Thirty seconds."

"Okay."

She looked for the lighting controls. They were in the far corner of the room in a poorly planned location, which should have been fixed during the retrofit. But then she remembered hearing that this control room had initially been four floors of offices and treatment rooms. During the retrofit, they had combined four floors. So she supposed the controls were actually just poor planning or lazy electricians. Once she reached the controls, she was able to light the room a bit better. With the space now lit, Maggie noticed the blood for the first time. It coated several spots and was splattered everywhere in a pattern indicating arterial spray. Something horrible had happened here. And this wasn't the work of revolting inmates. This was someone who took pleasure in death and blood and suffering. Someone like Ackerman.

When the thirty seconds were up, Lisa Spinelli's head popped out, and she rejoined the world. She had only been standing there on trembling knees for a couple of seconds when Powell caught sight of her. He had been stabbing at one of the computers in the next row. Powell ran down to Spinelli and took her up in a big hug. He said, "I thought you were dead. But I was too scared to look through that pile of bodies and find out for sure if you were there. I'm so glad you're okay."

"Yeah, me too. I need coffee."

He patted her back and said, "We'll get you some coffee, darling. No problem."

Maggie said, "Ms. Spinelli, can you tell me what happened here?"

Spinelli swallowed hard and said, "I didn't see anyone get killed. I just heard it. But it sounded awful. There must have been a whole crew of them."

Ackerman said, "This was all the work of one man."

Maggie hadn't noticed him move from his relaxed position in the desk chair, but he was now on his feet and looking down on them from the next tier.

Maggie looked back at Spinelli and said, "You didn't see anyone?"

"No."

"Or where they went? It's strange that anyone would take this place and then abandon it."

"No, I'm sorry."

Ackerman said, "Where were you when this happened?"

"I was in the server room, below us."

"But the elevator—"

"You can only access it through a maintenance hatch in the back of this room."

Ackerman laughed. "Ms. Spinelli, you're a lifesaver. I was about to start shooting my way through the floor."

Maggie said, "What are you talking about?"

"Earlier, while you thought I was slacking off, I was actually listening to see if the person who did all this is still here. I didn't want a Trojan horse hiding among us."

"And you found a Trojan horse?"

"Yes, I believe so. I heard something directly below us, but I didn't know about the server room. Our friend is probably waiting down there for an opportune moment."

"You know who's down there?"

"His name is Demon."

* * *

Maggie stared at the two access hatches for the server room. One was five foot by five foot wide and designed to drop in equipment. The other was a two by two tube and ladder like you'd find leading to lower decks on a ship. Spinelli had already explained the layout of the room. Although, Maggie wasn't excited at the prospect of dropping down into a sealed room with nothing but server clusters and the man who had just murdered a bunch of people and stacked them on a table like he had hunted them for supper and was just waiting to skin and cook them.

She covered the hatch with her rifle and then gave Dunn the nod to open it. When he did, she said, "We know you're down there. Leave any weapons behind and come up slowly. You have nowhere to go. We have Tasers and will subdue you by force if necessary."

She waited for a moment and then heard movement below. A voice replied in a thick Scottish accent, "No need for that. I'm coming up."

Watching the man called Demon ascend from that hatch was one of the most surreal experiences of Maggie Carlisle's life. Everything had a reddish tint because of the emergency lighting. The hatch cover swung away from them, toward the wall. The ladder rungs had been positioned so that Maggie would immediately see Demon's face when he emerged. And when that happened, the killer certainly looked the part. He was shirtless and coated in blood. His dark hair was slicked back with it. It was under his fingernails and in his nose. His feet were exposed, but he wore the blood as shoes. Even with the gore, she could see the scars beneath, and those were more disturbing than the blood. The scars spoke of a long and checkered past. Lots of wins and losses. Lots of battles. Lots of times he killed and survived to kill again.

Maggie looked across the room to where the guards had herded Lash and his lieutenants. She was fine with holding the ULF leader like that, but this Demon was a different story. They would have to come up with something more secure.

Demon ascended slowly and then stood with his hands raised, his arms bent into non-threatening ninety-degree angles. She felt his gaze slithering over her. Then this creature—which a few seconds prior had emerged from a hole in the ground covered in blood like some kind of under-dwelling monster—smiled and said, "I can see why you like her, Jerry."

Everyone kept their weapons trained on Demon. Maggie said, "Friend of yours, Officer Dunn?"

Jerry replied, "No, and I think I would remember him. I haven't even seen him here at the prison. He must be a new transfer."

Demon again looked at Maggie. He said, "She does have a certain something, Jerry. I'll at least give you that. You may have found a keeper this time. That last girl you screwed up a mission for was nothing special."

With more than a little apprehension, Warden Powell stepped forward with a set of restraints they intended to place around Demon's wrists. Maggie didn't let her aim waver from Demon's heart. If he sneezed, she would end his day.

Without allowing her aim to falter, she said, "Jerry, what's he talking about?"

She allowed a glance in his direction. Jerry's gun was pointed at Demon, but his eyes were on the floor.

Demon said, "Well, what are you waiting for?"

Then, with only a slight hesitation, Officer Jerry Dunn grabbed Spinelli by the neck and, yanking her over as a human shield, placed the barrel of Maggie's .357 against Spinelli's temple.

Jerry said, "Weapons down. All of you."

Maggie stared at the floor as they were lined up and restrained in the same spot where they had been holding Lash earlier. Now, with their roles reversed, Lash and his men had secured all of them and forced them to their knees.

To Demon, Jerry said, "I was just waiting for the right moment. I don't even know why you're here. Are you checking up on me?"

Demon said, "It's not you who's brought me. Just keep your mouth shut. We'll talk privately later." Demon continued, turning his attention to Maggie, "The kid genuinely had you fooled, didn't he?"

She glared at Jerry, who wouldn't meet her gaze. She had noticed that his speech impediment had faded away completely. Although the limp seemed to be real. She said, "He was very convincing."

Demon smiled and said, "I know, he's so cute. You just want to put him in your pocket and take him home and let him sleep at the foot of your bed. Notice that I did not say in your bed. He uses that innocent routine on the girls, though don't let him fool you. He's not as dopey and helpless as he wants you to think. He had raped and murdered eleven women when I found him, and I helped him hone his craft on a few others. He's incredibly capable. But he's a killer and a sexual predator who fixates on women to the point of obsession. You're not the first. Not even close."

Jerry Dunn stepped forward and said, "I get the point, boss."

Maggie made a mental note of that word. Boss. His use of that word held all kinds of implications. Not only that Demon was in charge, but that it was also in the capacity of employer to employee.

Demon said, "I'm not sure that you do. Given that this is a pattern of behavior, and not just an isolated incident. You need to get on with your mission. Pretend that I'm not here. Can you do that? Or do I need to slit her throat to take away the distraction?"

Ackerman said, "I won't allow that to happen."

Demon said, "You've been quiet . . . and surprising. I understand Jerry fooling her. But he fooled you as well?"

Ackerman laughed and said, "No, I've been aware of Officer Dunn being a traitor for some time now."

Maggie turned her glare from Jerry to Ackerman. She said, "Bullshit. If you knew he was playing us then why didn't you stop him?"

Ackerman said, "Because you just ordered all of us to surrender. If you were trying to signal me to attack somehow, then I missed it. We definitely need to work on our communication skills, regardless."

"I meant before that. Before that thing came out of the hole."

Ackerman looked at her with confusion in his eyes. He said, "Was that meant to be some kind of double entendre or innuendo, because, if so, then I totally didn't get it. This is what I'm saying with the communication skills."

"Why didn't you do your thing on Jerry at any point if you knew that he was a traitor?"

"Because I thought you were working an angle on him."

"I don't buy it. You may have been suspicious, but you had no real way of knowing."

Ackerman said, "As soon as I saw the control room and the way security is lined out, I knew that it was him. Once you reach this room, you can lock down the elevators and isolate yourself. It looks like an old system. Something built into the original elevator designs. It wouldn't be connected to the security system. Not dependent on their technology. If that is engaged, then only someone already in here could give someone outside access; hence the necessity of a traitor in our midst to give access to the prisoners. Specifically, access for Lash and his men."

Demon added, "But Jerry abandoned his post."

Jerry said, "Let's talk about this in private, please. And I obviously still left it unlocked. Our friends here need to get bracelets and anklets, we need to get the security system back up, and we need to make sure that Lash's men have secured the manufacturing facility."

Demon looked at Ackerman for a few long seconds and then said, "Don't make me kill all of you. The plan requires hostages, so it's actually not something that would help my end goals."

As they walked off, Maggie whispered, "You didn't know for sure that Jerry was the traitor."

Ackerman said, "I asked one of our correctional friends, and he informed me that there are always two men on guard up here. There's a log and a calendar by the door. I checked them. Jerry was scheduled to work security here in the control center during this shift."

"Well, aren't you the detective."

"No, little sister, that's your job, but I do like to play. And I like to win. Remember this for me, please. When the time comes, you need to stall your admirer using his devotion and his insecurity. I'll come for you. Don't worry."

Maggie said, "What? You criticize my communication skills and now you're talking in riddles?"

Lash kicked Ackerman in the stomach. It was a solid effort from the ULF leader. Lash had lowered his toe and buried his shoe in Ackerman's gut. A firm, painful blow that left Ackerman doubled over.

"Leave him alone," she screamed.

Lash kicked her too and said, "You two are lucky that you're federal agents and we need some VIP hostages. Mr. Demon convinced me to spare you. But you're convicts now. You're in my world. I make the rules, and I say that convicts don't speak. If I hear either of your voices again, I will kill you both, hostages or not."

Maggie kept her mouth shut. She waited for Ackerman to make some smartass comment, but he said nothing. That surprised her a bit, but then she thought of what Ackerman had told her earlier: fearless didn't mean stupid.

With staggering speed and efficiency, the inmates had locked down Foxbury and isolated it from the world.

Marcus considered the time and money spent planning and coordinating something like this. The first of the sheriff's men through the tunnel had been ambushed by armed men and pushed back. Then they had tried to approach over land, but they encountered fire from a high-powered rifle in that direction. A part of him knew that they were already too late to stop the uprising, but his family was in there, and Marcus needed to do something.

To Andrew and Sheriff Hall, he said, "Maybe we can toss smoke grenades down the tunnel and take it by force."

Hall said, "I have no doubt we could take the tunnel and reach the door, but what if it's locked or we find a trap or heavy resistance on the other side. We don't know enough about what we're walking into."

Andrew said, "He's right. We're blind here, and who knows what they're planning. They're obviously more organized than we thought."

Marcus said, "We're like an hour into this revolt, and they have armed men guarding the perimeter. I'd say they're about as organized as it gets. And we're still just playing their game. We have to get in front of this."

The sound of footsteps echoed from around the corner, followed by the leader of the tactical team. The man was blond with blue eyes, short, and stocky. He carried himself in a way that spoke of experience and confidence. He said, "We think they're using some kind of jamming devices for cell phones and radios. I have one of my guys trying to figure out a way to break through the jamming or at least figure out a way for our team to stay in communication."

Andrew said, "What about the computer system? Were your men able to get anything done with that?"

"So far, they're completely locked out."

Marcus pulled a device out of his pocket that appeared to be a thumb drive. But it was actually much more than that. He handed the small device to Sheriff Hall and said, "Have your men plug that into the USB port of any workstation. It connects to the Internet through its own cellular signal and will allow our IT expert to access the system here remotely."

Andrew shook his head and said, "He can plug it in, Marcus, but it won't do any good. At least not until we figure out the jamming. If the cellular signals are being blocked, then Stan won't be able to connect. And I'm betting its military-grade jamming equipment."

Sheriff Hall added, "Of course it is. Nothing but the best for these assholes."

Marcus considered their options. They could take some men and try to approach the prison from its far side. But that way was nothing but scorched earth and wide-open spaces. A sniper would spot them easily and could finish them at his leisure. Then again, if they acted quickly, they would still have the cover of darkness.

Marcus said, "Sheriff, you're pretty intimately acquainted with Foxbury's security, correct?"

"Yes, sir. That was part of the agreement for allowing this place into my county."

"I imagine your county got a pretty sweet deal out of it."

Hall said, "It seemed so at the time."

Marcus asked, "Do you know if they have access to night vision or thermal—"

One of the SWAT officers interrupted Marcus, yelling, "We have someone coming down the tunnel!"

★★★

Marcus pulled his Sig Sauer pistol, dropped into a crouch beside a machine that reminded him of a giant version of a toy he had watched Dylan use to squish Playdough, and shined his flashlight in the direction of the tunnel. The big machine smelled strongly of rubber and grease. It wasn't new, which didn't surprise Marcus. Powell had probably purchased all of this industrial equipment in bulk for ten cents on the dollar.

The others performed similar maneuvers and took up positions beside various pieces of equipment around the mouth of the tunnel's access point. The exit reminded Marcus of the tunnel to the bullpen at Yankee Stadium. If that had been the case and he was nine years old again watching Andy Hawkins pitch to Wade Boggs, then the tactical team would have had the reliever—who would have been Dave Righetti in that memory—covered from every angle.

The man who stepped from the tunnel wasn't Dave Righetti. But Marcus did recognize him, and he was a minor celebrity.

The man's name was Oren Kimble, and Marcus had seen his case on the news. Kimble had slaughtered twenty-seven people and injured thirty-two others at a shopping mall outside of Akron, Ohio. Kimble had walked in with an assault rifle and a bag full of pipe bombs and extra mags. He was probably the second most famous prisoner at Foxbury.

Kimble had his hands up and said, "Don't shoot. He told me to deliver a message."

Marcus said, "Everyone hold position."

Andrew instantly moved behind Kimble and checked him visually for any weapons, explosives, or traps. He and Andrew had practiced and performed this dance several times. There was almost always more than meets the eye, and they had to remain ever vigilant considering the type of criminal they hunted.

Andrew gave Marcus a nod and then took up a position behind the inmate. Marcus kept his Sig to his eye but stepped out to meet Kimble.

He said, "Who sent the message?"

"Officer Jerry Dunn."

Up close, Oren Kimble didn't seem scary at all. Nothing like the way the media portrayed him. Kimble seemed like a scared kid, one who had once upon a time found himself at a mall with an assault rifle while off his medication.

"What's the message?"

"He told me to give you this and come back." Kimble reached for his wrist.

Marcus saw Andrew tense, and he said, "Slowly, Mr. Kimble."

Kimble stopped altogether and glanced over his shoulder, apparently just now noticing Andrew's presence behind him. Not great instincts from the kid. Marcus supposed that was why Kimble was in Foxbury, considering that he had been taken down from behind by a security guard and a soccer mom, instead of getting to have his big moment of suicide-by-cop glory.

In Marcus's experience back in Brooklyn, the offenders who committed suicide by cop were just stupid kids who felt unloved and unwanted and felt the need to go out in a blaze of glory. Those offenders never truly considered how their actions affected others, including the cops who finally ended them. Clean shooting or not, justified or not, killing always screwed with a cop's head.

Kimble pulled up his left sleeve to reveal the bracelet that all the inmates at Foxbury wore. The difference here was that Kimble had two shock bracelets, one latched to his wrist, and one hanging there unconnected. Kimble removed the extra bracelet and held it out to Marcus.

Marcus hesitated for a second as he weighed the dangers, but then he accepted the device.

The instant that his skin made contact and Kimble's grip released, the speaker on its side came to life. There was at first a vibration in the bracelet. His first instinct was to drop it, but then he realized it was just signaling an incoming announcement.

"Agent Williams. Good to see you again," said the voice coming from the shock bracelet's speaker. Marcus recognized the voice as belonging to the shy young man he had met earlier in the day.

Jerry Dunn said, "'The device works like a speaker phone. You can respond."

"Are you watching us on the camera system of the prison, or does the bracelet have a built-in camera too?"

"If you're asking whether or not I am in complete control of Foxbury Correctional Treatment Facility, including the building you're standing in, then the answer is yes. I am in complete control."

To emphasize the point, all of the lights in the building returned to normal. The red emergency glow transitioned to white, and the sprinkler system activated.

★ ★ ★

It rained on them for maybe ten seconds. Just long enough to make sure they were good and wet. To Marcus, the cool water felt kind of refreshing.

He said, "Cute."

He heard Jerry laughing on the other end. Marcus listened a moment, not to Jerry's laughter but to the background noise of the control room. Then he said, "Your speech impediment seems to have cleared up."

"Do you have a problem with people with speech impediments?"

"No, I have a problem with people who don't have the balls to be themselves."

"Sticks and stones, Agent Williams. That little demonstration I just gave you was merely a taste of the mythological level of power I now wield. I'm like the god of lightning here. And Thor has a message for you. Actually, it's less of a message and more of a declaration. Foxbury is mine now. I will politely ask you to vacate the premises. Pull your men back to the outer perimeter and wait for my demands."

"Demands imply hostages. How do we know that you're really in control over there?"

"In control?"

"We have to know that we're talking to the right guy."

"Get out now. It's the last time I'll ask nicely."

Marcus said, "And if we refuse to abandon the manufacturing facility?"

The small speaker sat silent for only a few seconds, and then Jerry said, "You ever play that game 'Imagine If.' Great for road trips. Let me just demonstrate. Imagine if I had captured all of the guards and staff and had attached these bracelets and anklets to their hands and feet. And then imagine if, at any point, I had the power to do this to any or all of them."

Marcus said, "Sheriff? How powerful are the shocks these restraints can administer?"

"Umm, something's happening with my . . ."

Oren Kimble started by dancing around and trying to remove his wireless restraints. And then he started screaming. Then convulsing. And then Kimble's eyes rolled back into his head.

They tried to help. They stepped on his hands and feet and then his chest to keep Kimble from harming himself during a convulsion. They tried to pry the bracelets off him.

But then he started smoking.

Marcus said, "How much electricity can those things possibly hold?"

The sheriff was trying to keep down Kimble's left foot. He said, "They get their juice wirelessly somehow."

"How do we turn that off? Can we cut power going to them?"

"I don't know how it works. Seemed like magic to me."

"Maybe we could—"

The electrical output and Kimble's seizure stopped more abruptly than it had begun. His convulsing ceased altogether. All at once. One second, Kimble was spasming, and the next, he was still.

Everyone stepped back and looked at Kimble's smoldering, lifeless body. Andrew moved forward and cautiously checked him for a pulse. He shook his head. Kimble was gone. Probably died at the same instant the shaking stopped. Or, rather, the electrical output ceased when the system no longer registered a heartbeat. Saint Nick was always watching. He knew if you were alive or dead.

Over the speaker of the bracelet, which Marcus had discarded to help Kimble, Jerry Dunn said, "You have thirty seconds to leave my domain, or I will send someone else down the tunnel for you to watch fry. And this time, it won't be a mass murderer. It will be a guard or technician. Maybe Warden Powell. Maybe Ms. Spinelli. Maybe your undercover consultant, Mr. Alexei. Or perhaps Agent Carlisle. I could send any of them down the tunnel. They are all in my custody. They are all my prisoners. My subjects. Do I need to send one of them on the long walk in order for you to understand?"

Marcus gritted his teeth. They had failed. He had failed.

He said, "Wheels up, everyone. We're pulling back."

The guard shack at Foxbury's outer perimeter had a small break room, maybe fifteen feet wide and twenty feet deep. It was equipped with everything from vending machines and microwaves to a kitchen table and refrigerator. A large whiteboard dominated one end and was filled with announcements from the shift commander. Marcus supposed it was as good a place as any to be their siege headquarters.

Once they pulled back, the sheriff had taken charge of his men and went to work establishing an airtight perimeter. They had reinforcements coming in from every surrounding branch of law enforcement. But it took time to mobilize people and resources, especially in the middle of the night. Still, the perimeter had its own security system independent of the main prison, so it was highly unlikely that anyone could escape the outer perimeter undetected, even without extra boots on the ground.

The correctional officer's break room smelled like burnt coffee, and it made Marcus crave a cup. He found the pot in the corner, a big old commercial unit, the kind found in restaurants the world over. As Marcus reached the machine, he saw that someone had left just enough coffee in the bottom of the carafe to create a mess. The remnants were still heating and bubbling, staining the glass carafe with a burnt black tar that would have to be scraped out.

Marcus took one look at it, snatched it from its cradle, and threw it like a fastball. It exploded against the white block wall a few feet away.

He heard everyone else inside the guard shack go quiet, but no one said a word. He didn't turn around. He just stood there feeling like an idiot, like a child throwing a tantrum. After a moment, the volume slowly faded back up as everyone went back to what they were doing.

From behind him, Andrew said, "I understand how you're feeling, but did you have to take it out on the coffee pot?"

"It had it coming."

"The Director asked if you would have a problem with Valdas taking over from here in regard to negotiations and rescue operations."

Marcus said, "That's why he's here. And there's nothing that I can do to help Maggie and my brother at this point. Unless we can get ahead of our friend Judas."

"What do you mean?"

Marcus walked over to the large whiteboard. A small tray hung from the board's right corner and held an eraser and some markers. First, Marcus used the rectangular eraser pad to clean the officers' assignments and announcements. Then he picked up a red marker from the tray and wrote, "Jerry Dunn."

Andrew, knowing the drill, sat on the end of the break room table and said, "He's obviously calling the shots."

"Or is at least a willing participant."

"You think he's some kind of patsy?"

"I don't know. Let's talk facts. Jerry Dunn was here at the time that Peter Spinelli was killed."

Andrew snapped his fingers and said, "By the way, Stan told me earlier that he found Peter Spinelli's offshore account. He was the one who gave up the software. Or that's the working theory at least."

Marcus made a dash beneath the "Jerry Dunn" heading and wrote, "Did Not Kill Spinelli."

Then he said, "Peter was stabbed with professional precision and pushed into traffic. That, to me, always felt like a job Judas did himself. That steered me away from Dunn in the beginning. He couldn't have been in both places at once."

"Maybe one of Lash's followers took out Peter."

"Maybe. Or maybe Dunn isn't Judas."

"Then who's our mastermind? This Demon guy who Sheriff Hall encountered?"

Marcus wrote "Demon" on the board as a new heading and said, "I don't think so. I still think there is something there with Reese. I hate to think that, because I was a jerk to the guy and, if he isn't Judas, I probably got him killed. But I still can't shake this feeling about him. And until someone finds his body at the bottom of that pit—"

Andrew raised his hands and said, "I'll stop you there. Sheriff just asked me to tell you that one of his men had cave diving experience. He found a body in the location you gave them. I was coming in here to let you know."

Marcus balled up his fists and counted to five. "A positive ID for Reese?"

"Who knows how long before they get the body up for official confirmation, but the sheriff said the description matches."

Marcus rubbed at his cross tattoo and said, "I don't know what to think here, brother. I feel like my instincts have been off. I should have caught this sooner. It never should have reached this point."

Andrew looked around, picked up a napkin from the break room table, and held it out for Marcus. He said, "In case you wanted to cry about it."

Marcus slapped his hand away and said, "Screw you."

Andrew dropped the napkin and said, "You've done a great job on this case. There's not exactly any field manual for something like this."

"Yeah, but that's the job."

"Maybe. Then again, maybe your instincts aren't that far off. Maybe Reese isn't our Judas, but that doesn't necessarily mean he wasn't still involved somehow. We know his fiancée is missing and probably dead. Maybe he was being coerced. Or he's an accomplice or partner. Something."

Marcus said, "We still have Reese's car. Sheriff's guys

took it back to their station. We should have them tear it apart. See if they can find anything."

"If there are any of them still at the station."

"It's a big department, but we definitely are all hands on deck."

Andrew paced in front of the whiteboard and tapped his teeth. "So what's the end game here?"

"It has to be about Lash."

"All this just for an escape?"

"There's definitely more to it than that. This isn't just business. There's a strong personal element."

Andrew picked up a blue marker and wrote "Lash" on the board as a new heading. "Maybe Lash wants to not only escape from prison but have no one looking for him long enough to get out of the country."

Marcus nodded. "Okay, so Lash hires someone to orchestrate a standoff. This thing could go on for days. All the while we're out here thinking that Lash and everyone else is still inside the building."

"And by the time anyone knows Lash is gone, he's sitting on a beach in a non-extradition country," Andrew added.

"Which means we need to figure out how Lash—or Judas or whoever—plans to slip past our perimeter."

"But what about Demon? Where does he fit in?"

"A guess?"

"Humor me. What's your theory?"

Marcus said, "My guess is that he's the commander or supervisor or whatever they call it in their business for a group of mercenaries hired to stage a big spectacle and extract Leonard Lash. But I think Lash hired some very bad men to break him out."

"If Jerry works for Demon, then why did Demon involve the sheriff? His guys obviously had the access to get him inside."

Marcus turned back to the board and said, "I don't know. But I do know that Jerry Dunn is right in the middle of it."

"What did you have in mind?"

"I was thinking breaking and entering."

Jerry Dunn's apartment was on Twenty-Ninth Street in South Tucson. He rented out half the second story of a squat, brown building that also housed a dry-cleaning business and a nail salon. The forty-something woman who ran the dry cleaner also owned the building. She had nothing negative to report about Jerry, not that Marcus had expected she would. She brought down the key in the middle of the night and gave her consent for them to search the premises. Not that it mattered at that point. They were going in one way or another.

Andrew was the first one up the stairs. Key in hand, he unlocked the second apartment door they came to. He twisted the knob and pushed, but the door wouldn't budge. He said, "Jerry must have installed his own deadbolt or something."

Marcus said, "Step back. I'll kick it in."

"Hold up a second."

"What?"

"Maybe he rigged the door?"

Marcus said, "If Dunn had it rigged to blow, then why would he have it locked? But more importantly, there's no keyhole for a deadbolt on this side of the door, so what's blocking us. And how did Dunn secure the door from the other side?"

"He could have locked it up and then climbed out the fire escape."

"Or there could be someone else in there. Someone who has himself barricaded."

"So what's the play?"

Marcus cocked his head to both sides, cracking his neck. "I'll go in through the fire escape. You cover this exit, just in case."

"Don't forget to let me in."

"You can go up the fire escape, and I'll wait here, if you'd prefer."

"No, my leg, remember."

"Right. Milk that for all you can."

"I intend to."

Marcus took the stairs in a fast jog and didn't let up his pace until he was in the alley pushing a dumpster up to the wall in order to allow him to access the retractable ladder. Climbing up the fire escape reminded him of Claire Cassidy, his one-time fiancée and Dylan's mother. He had performed a similar maneuver many times back in Brooklyn when she still lived with her parents.

The thought of Claire reminded him of Dylan. And thinking of Dylan only added to the anxious dread that had been eating away at him since they had been driven from Foxbury. Was he failing his son, just as he had failed his friends still trapped inside the prison? He had never been there for Dylan as a father. He wanted to raise him right, to be a good dad. But what did he know about being a father? His adopted dad had been killed when he was Dylan's age, and his biological father was currently locked away in the kind of place they would have incarcerated Osama bin Laden, if he had been captured and convicted. And his grandfather, Louis Ackerman, wasn't exactly a model parent. The fact was that he came from a long line of people who royally screwed up their children. And he hoped that his grandchildren wouldn't be looking back at him in the same way he was his ancestors.

Within a few seconds, Marcus had climbed up to Jerry Dunn's window, but he couldn't see inside. The glass had been blacked out. He checked the locks. The ones on the inside weren't latched, but there was a keyed padlock on the outside of the window. Maybe Dunn really did exit through the fire escape.

He checked the lock itself—a good brand, Master Lock, the disc-style padlock with a partially hidden shackle to keep people from snapping off the lock with a pair of bolt cutters. The lock plate and fastenings were also sturdy and well made. If he had been merely a would-be burglar, he would have been deterred.

He removed the sound suppressor from the pocket of his leather jacket and threaded it onto the barrel of his Sig Sauer pistol. It took two shots to remove the lock, and the suppressor only muffled the sound of each blast. It didn't silence the sound completely. But in this neighborhood, he wasn't sure that he even needed to use the suppressor.

With the lock gone, he raised the window and slipped inside. He could see from there that the front door wasn't rigged with explosives. But it had been bolted and screwed and secured in ways that seemed to go beyond the realm of extra security into the range of obsessive-compulsive irrationality. There didn't even seem to be a way to open it anymore, at least not without power tools.

He banged on the door and said, "You'll have to come around. It's blocked."

"Okay, wait for me," came the muffled reply from the other side of the door.

Marcus didn't wait, not that Andrew really expected him to.

The apartment was spacious for a single man. A kitchen and dining area accented by blue-and-gold linoleum gave way to a living room. The hallway entrance divided one wall and led down to two bedrooms and one bathroom. Marcus could have seen a family living here: two parents and a new baby or a single mom and a young son. He could imagine memories in these hallways and kids posing for cheesy photos.

Of course, those people probably would have bought some furniture and lights and beds. Jerry Dunn had nothing like that. No furniture. Just some blankets and pillows scattered about. No television. There was a fridge in the kitchen, and dishes stacked in the sink. The place smelled of moldy food and stale piss.

Marcus supposed that the young parents or the single mom who could have lived here would have decorated the walls a bit differently as well.

Jerry had chosen to decorate his walls, every square inch of them, with photos. Printed pictures of different women. It was clear that Dunn had taken the photos himself, and it was clear that the women had no idea that their picture was being taken. They were unloading groceries and walking down the street and closing blinds, and in some, ones which looked to be shot with long-range lenses, the women were in various states of undress.

The pillows and blankets seemed to be arranged around the room's perimeter, as if Dunn's personal life consisted entirely of sitting on the floor alone and staring at his photos.

Marcus wandered all the rooms, giving a cursory scan, but he didn't immediately notice anything that could be of use to them. Beyond analyzing the photos, which was one hell of a big job.

Marcus had noticed a photo printer in the corner of the living room, but he couldn't imagine what Dunn had spent on ink and photo paper.

And, of course, there was no sign of the computer or the camera equipment.

From behind him, Andrew said, "Remember when these kinds of guys would have their own dark rooms and develop their own photos."

"Yeah, they had to. It wasn't like they could get these kinds of photos developed by Kenneth down at the local drugstore."

Andrew nodded. "This conversation is making me feel old."

"I thought it was your gray hair making you feel old."

"And I suppose you don't have gray hairs?"

"I'm like a fine wine. My hair actually gets darker with age," Marcus said.

Andrew laughed, but then his smile faded. He pointed toward one of the picture walls. Andrew said, "That's Debra

Costello. Powell's daughter. Looks like Jerry was fixated on her, just like all these other women. Guess it's pretty clear that he's the one who killed her."

"If she's dead. We don't know for sure on anything yet."

"I hope we find her," Andrew said. "But we both saw her cuts. That was a different level from these other killings."

"Right. She had to be the inciting incident of all this. But why? And why Jerry?"

Andrew shrugged. "He loved her. Blah. Blah. Blah. They were soul mates, and she rejected him. So he killed her, and he's taking it out on the world until we stop him."

Marcus stood back and looked at the photos. There almost seemed to be a pattern or something strange about their arrangement. But he couldn't quite put his finger on what it was.

After a moment, he said, "Let's check the trash. You want the cans up here or the dumpster."

Andrew said, "I better take the cans up here. You know, my leg."

Marcus opened the dumpster, and then he dug into the heap of plastic bags, discarding each bag of refuse until he found Jerry Dunn's trash. The dry cleaner's trash was obvious by the type and size of bag, and he was able to identify the nail salon's offerings by their contents. This narrowed the search down to two possible bags that could have belonged to Jerry. He put them on top of the pile, but he left them inside the dumpster. He had a few things he needed to check before he returned to Andrew.

First, he needed to check around for the real garbage.

Marcus fully expected the trash he had just found in the dumpster to yield no clues. But it still needed to be checked. He had always found that the biggest part of detective work was ruling out possibilities until only one remained.

The problem with this case was that he had entirely too many possibilities and not nearly enough time to rule them all out. What he needed was a little luck, or one slip-up on the part of his opponent.

And that's where the real trash came in.

A perpetrator would often take certain countermeasures to leave no evidence of their crimes. One common mistake on the part of the perp was to dispose of evidence in places geographically close to their home or business or the scene of the crime. Investigators knew to check for possibilities like that. And, if the situation warranted it, investigators would sometimes check all the trash cans within the public domain inside a ten block radius. But all of that took time. Time he didn't have.

Marcus tried to imagine himself in the killer's shoes. If Jerry Dunn was the Judas Killer, then he would have a great deal of evidence to dispose of. And if the Judas was setting Dunn up as a scapegoat, then he could have faked some or all of the apartment's contents. In either case, there was a lot of potential evidence being disposed of by someone who was intelligent, thorough, and well versed in the methods of both killers and those who hunted them.

Marcus tried to imagine himself in the shoes of a man like that. A man who strived for and coveted superiority and prided himself on the ability to plan ahead by many steps and manipulate people into playing his games, his way. He asked himself how a man like that would dispose of evidence, a part of Marcus wishing his brother would have been there to offer guidance.

Judas would want the method to be quick and easy to access and leave no trace. Burning was good in those circumstances, but Marcus ignored burning as an option. If Judas had burned his evidence, then there would have been little evidence left. Better to focus on something that would yield greater rewards. So he considered other methods of disposal.

The next best method for disposing of evidence like that completely would probably be to "flush it" in one way or another, either down the toilet or straight into a storm drain or sewer.

He walked out to the curb to check the sewer first. He didn't remember any manholes, but he did recall seeing a storm sewer. The drain was inset into the curb, right where he remembered it. The metal cover was heavy, but light enough for one person. He hefted up the grated covering and slid it aside. Then he peered into the hole.

Marcus could see some debris that had found its way down the drain and then had lodged itself in the mud covering the bottom of the pipe and surrounding the grate. It had rained some since they had arrived, and the rain would have been pumping water down the drain faster than the storm sewer could have handled. He could imagine Judas stuffing something down this hole and then considering it to be gone forever.

Marcus poked around some with his shoe, but he knew that, unfortunately, he was going to have to get down on the wet ground and ram his arm into that pipe. He got on his knees and shed his leather jacket. The pipe was about two feet in diameter, just right to stick in an arm.

A memory from his younger days came to mind. A scene from a Stephen King movie. A vision of a demonic, supernatural clown ripping off a little boy's arm by pulling him down into a similar sewer.

Marcus stuck his arm in anyway.

He jammed it in all the way up to his shoulder. He felt around the pipe but found nothing. He prayed for a little luck. In his head, Marcus heard John Williams, his real father, saying, *You make your own luck*.

Marcus reached out farther. He stretched his arm out and was rewarded with the feel of plastic and branches and other garbage that had been swept down the drain. It had found its way a few feet into the pipe before the debris had conglomerated into a sticky mess that refused to be carried away. He wrapped his fingers around the plastic and gave it a gentle tug, being careful not to tear the thin membrane of plastic. It was tangled in the twigs and other debris, so he grabbed hold of the mass by its roots and tore the whole thing free of the mud.

Once he had the entire clog out of the drain and lying on the concrete sidewalk, he examined the plastic he had felt. It was a Ziplock freezer bag. The kind with a red pull tab.

Marcus smiled as he held up the bag and examined its contents.

You make your own luck.

Andrew started with the small kitchen and bathroom, since they were the most normal rooms in the apartment. But he didn't find anything useful; just the typical bathroom and kitchen contents, only with an extra layer of grime and filth.

Next, he went around and checked inside all of the heating vents. They were small and brown and rectangular and inset into the floor. He moved to each room, pulled the blankets aside, and popped up the vented registers. People often hid things inside spots like this, and so it had become an SOP for the SO to check the vents when searching a suspect's house.

He was rewarded with a Ziploc freezer bag, the kind with the red pull tab, full of more photos. Wearing his latex gloves, he opened it up and flipped through the photos. They were all of the same woman, but they didn't appear to be any different than the thousands of other photos covering Jerry's walls. Andrew didn't recognize the woman in the pictures. He wondered why Jerry would feel the need to hide these particular photos. They must have been significant or different somehow.

He took the bag into the kitchen and deposited it on the table. Then he looked around and at all the photographs, all the stolen moments with these women that Jerry had shared. Andrew wondered how many of the women in the photos were still alive. He supposed that both he and Marcus should probably do a complete walk-through and scan all the photos. But as he looked around at the walls covered from floor to ceiling, he realized that even a cursory scan of each individual photo would take more time than Marcus would want to devote.

He decided to hold off on the photos.

He moved to the bedrooms with the intention of checking

the closets. There would have to be clothes and personal items inside. There were no dressers or other furniture, and so the closets would have to hold Jerry's work uniforms, at the very least.

He checked the smaller of the bedrooms first. Not for any particular reason. Just because it was closer, and Andrew liked to attack things in an orderly, linear fashion. The room smelled strangely pleasant and floral, like Jerry had recently sprayed Febreze in there.

The closet doors were solid-paneled and made from a wood the color of whiskey. Each side of the bi-fold panels had a small knob for a handle. Andrew took hold of the knob and went in hard, fast, and low with his Glock at the ready. The closet was clear. Not only was it clear of any attackers; it was clear of anything at all. It was completely empty. Not even more photo wallpaper.

He made his way toward the master bedroom through the hallway of photos. He tried to ignore the faces of the women staring out at him from the walls and focus on the task at hand. It was important to keep a certain objective distance from the victims.

He moved to the closet and repeated the same procedure, but this time the space wasn't empty. Correctional officer uniforms and some civilian shirts and pants hung neatly in place. Shoes and belts littered the floor. The top shelf held some blue plastic totes, shoeboxes, and other miscellaneous items.

He reached up to pull down one of the totes, figuring it would be the easiest to check first. The tote was taller than the opening, and he had to tilt it down in order to slide it between the shelf and the doorjamb.

When he angled the plastic container toward himself, Andrew felt the weight shift inside of the tote. He felt something slide and something clink and something else roll forward. The sudden shift in weight within the box pushed him off balance and forced him to readjust his hold on it.

And that was when he saw the barrel of the shotgun sliding out of the front of the tote as a hidden panel gave way. The shotgun rolled forward lazily, and he watched in shock and indecision as the weapon came toward his face.

He saw the endless black of the barrel's depths. He felt something hit him, and then he was falling. He saw the muzzle flash. He heard the shotgun blast, and then everything went dark.

Marcus climbed back onto the dumpster and up the fire escape. He had the plastic freezer bag in hand, but he hadn't opened it yet. He had decided to do that in the light and privacy of the kitchen. Furthermore, if this bag contained what he thought it did, then he would have a theory to test inside the apartment anyway.

He slipped in through the window. He didn't see Andrew, and so he walked back toward the bedrooms. He didn't see his partner in the smaller of the rooms and moved on to the master. He crossed the bedroom's threshold just as Andrew was reaching up to grab a large tote made of blue plastic.

As soon as Marcus heard the shifting of the tote's contents, he knew what this was.

He had seen something similar back in his homicide detective days. A drug dealer had used a shotgun and a box and a high shelf to protect his stash. The container was rigged so that a sawed-off shotgun would fire if the box was taken down improperly.

It didn't really surprise him that someone like Jerry Dunn would dream up something similar.

Marcus instantly took a step forward, one long stride meant to close the distance as quickly as possible.

By the time his right foot touched the carpet, Marcus had decided on his plan of attack. He had to knock Andrew clear of the blast. It was too late for a shouted warning. It was too late to divert the box. It was also too late to push Andrew out of the way.

He took one last step and then did what was ingrained in him during high school football. He rolled his shoulder and head to the side and twisted his body and hit Andrew at the knees and drove his partner's legs completely out from under him.

The shotgun fired, and the booby-trapped box fell out of the closet on top of them.

Marcus scrambled to push the tote out of the way.

Andrew wasn't moving. He felt for a pulse. It was there and thumping strongly. He was alive.

Marcus checked Andrew's head. There was a little blood, but it didn't look too bad. Still, Marcus knew better than to allow someone who had sustained head trauma to sleep.

He tapped Andrew lightly on the cheek with his open palm, but Andrew didn't wake up.

So Marcus slapped harder. Not hard enough to leave a welt, but just hard enough to make a noise.

Andrew's eyes fluttered open, and he said, "This can't be heaven if you're here."

As Marcus pulled himself off the floor, he said, "I saved

your ass. Now get up. You've had enough nap time, and I have something to show you."

Andrew had a towel pressed to his bleeding forehead, but he was in a hell of a lot better shape than he might have been. A shotgun blast to the face would have definitely put a damper on his day. He was still pretty shaken up about the whole thing, hands trembling and heart pounding, and Marcus had given him no opportunity to process the fact that he had nearly died. He supposed that might have been for the best.

Andrew stared at the wall of photos and said, "I don't see it."

Marcus said, "You have to look at the big picture. Let your eyes blur and look at the wall like one big photo."

Andrew squinted at the photos and tried to see something. Finally, he said, "I don't know what I see. Just tell me."

"When you step back and look at the wall as a whole, you can see that all of the photos have a similar color, contrast, even the shine of the paper. But then there are some that just look a little different. So I pulled off a few of those, and I was right. The dead spots I noticed had been printed on a different type of paper. Probably on a different printer. And those pictures were all of Debra Costello."

"Maybe he just bought a new printer. Maybe the old one quit on him, and they no longer make that particular model."

"Sure. But then there's this."

Marcus held up a plastic freezer bag. It appeared to have some torn pieces of more photographs inside. Marcus unzipped the bag and, wearing a latex glove, laid the Ziploc's contents out onto Jerry's kitchen table.

As he smoothed out each crumpled item, Marcus said, "These photos match up with the majority of our wallpaper. And I'd be willing to bet that, if you counted up the number of Debra's photos, the count would match the number of photos in this sack."

Andrew handed Marcus the sack he had found. "Maybe when you add these." He went on to explain how he had discovered the bag of pictures.

Marcus laid out the photos from Andrew's bag in a separate grouping. He stood back and looked at the two sets of photos. They weren't all of the same woman. Marcus said, "This is very strange. Why have two Ziploc bags disposed of or hidden in two different spots?"

Andrew said, "No clue. Are we thinking that someone came in here, pulled down Jerry's real photos, and then replaced them with their own photos of Debra. And then tried to dispose of the photos? Why do that? Why make it look like Jerry was obsessed with Debra and killed her?"

"And does this suggest that Jerry is not our mastermind. Is he just a scapegoat? Or is this just more noise to confuse us? Here's what I'm thinking. Lash wants out and saw an opportunity with Foxbury. He saw a way that he could not only escape prison, but also create a distraction that would give him time to escape the country."

Andrew added, "Okay, so he hired someone to set it up for him. This Judas. Our mastermind. Then Judas decides to use Jerry Dunn as his fall guy. Some random crazy bastard he's come across who would fit the mold and play the part. So who's Demon? A partner? Someone Judas hired?"

"I don't think so. He's not part of this. Or at least, he wasn't supposed to be."

"What does that mean?"

"Demon took a lot of risk using the sheriff. With the kind of access Judas has, there would have been other, safer ways of getting into Foxbury. That suggests to me that Demon knows what's going on, but he wants to be inside Foxbury without Judas knowing it. Now why in the world would he need to do that?"

Andrew waited, but Marcus didn't answer his own question. A couple of breaths passed in silence before he realized what Marcus was doing. His partner already had a theory. But Marcus was waiting for him to give an opinion first, and Marcus didn't want his own theory to bias Andrew's suppositions.

Andrew hated when Marcus put him on the spot like this. He rubbed at his temples. His head was still pounding from the earlier blow. He didn't want to think. He didn't want to untangle this perfect storm of narcissism and insecurity back to its source. He really just wanted to go to bed. How long had it been since he'd slept?

Marcus said, "Any theories?"

He tried to think over the pounding in his skull. Why would Demon be separate from and secretive toward Judas?

Andrew said, "Powell's daughter, Debra. That one was personal."

"Exactly. Debra is our inciting incident. She hurt Judas somehow, and he killed her for it."

Andrew took a second to process that and carry out the train of thought. Then he said, "The number one rule as a homicide detective with a female victim."

Marcus smiled. "Do you have a contact person down at the sheriff's station?"

"Yeah."

"Let him know we're on our way and why we're coming."

Andrew pulled out his phone and dialed the stored number for the county impound garage where Bradley Reese's car had been transferred. As he listened to the phone ring, he considered the number one unwritten rule of homicide detectives everywhere: if you have a female victim, find the guy who was sleeping with her, because he's also the one who killed her.

Demon waited for them to be alone before dealing with the young fool. He was nothing if not patient. But the second he was alone with Jerry inside the conference room of Control Center East, he struck the young man in the gut with a blow made all the more painful by the speed and surprise of it.

Demon said, "When I give an order, you obey. You disrespected me in front of our enemies. The Legion demands restitution. Give me your hand."

Jerry caught his breath and met Demon's gaze. Then the young man held out his hand. He had no other choice. Demon had established dominance with Jerry early on, as he did with all his employees.

Dominance and respect were crucial when training wild animals.

From there, Demon was deliberately slow in removing a homemade prison shank the size of a bowie knife and placing it on the conference room table. It was a sharp and sturdy weapon. The evidence of that fact was slowly decaying atop the conference room table.

Demon pressed Jerry's hand down onto the table. He felt Jerry tense up. Not to pull his arm away or attack, just bracing himself for the pain.

At this point, Demon could show mercy to his supplicant, as he often did. He considered this as the Legion of demons screamed all around him. He was so tired of the screaming, of the burning, the blood. He closed his eyes, and when he opened them, a nasty creature that was more teeth and flesh than anything else stood beside him. It was nothing that could have possibly survived in reality. Demon knew that. But there was something about this creature. Something different. And then he realized. The unholy abomination was speaking in Jerry Dunn's voice.

It said, "Sir, I beg for your forgiveness. It will never happen again. Please show mercy."

From its words, Demon was about ninety percent sure this thing wasn't merely speaking with Dunn's voice, but, rather, it was Jerry Dunn. He closed his eyes for a few seconds and looked again. Dunn was back to normal, and Demon was glad for that. He didn't think he could have carried on a normal conversation with such a creature.

He considered Jerry's request. Mercy. Should he bestow his grace on Jerry, his forgiveness?

Demon released his grip on the younger man's arm but, at the same time, he snatched up his blade and slashed it across Dunn's throat.

But the weapon's edge barely touched Dunn's skin. Only deep enough of a cut to draw a few drops of blood.

Demon looked into the young man's eyes and said, "Don't ever forget who and what I am."

He noticed for the first time that there were tears in Jerry's eyes.

He stifled a laugh.

Jerry thought he had been shown mercy and grace. In reality, Demon decided against taking the finger because doing so didn't help his goals. Demon was here for Judas, not this moron whom they had planned to use as a scapegoat from the start. And Jerry still had his role to play. Something as small as having a finger cut off could totally distract some people as weak as Jerry. Retribution against a patsy who didn't even have much longer to live wasn't worth jeopardizing a mission.

Demon said, "Where's Judas?"

"He said that plans changed."

"Did he now? When and where are you meeting him?"

"I didn't know you planned to be here yourself, sir."

"Plans changed."

Jerry said, "Does this have to do with my last mission?"

"I told you earlier. I'm not here for you."

"So you're here because of Judas?"

Demon narrowed his eyes at Jerry. Perhaps the Legion would get their blood after all.

The young man quickly added, "I don't mean to pry into your business, sir. I just wanted to know if I should consider him an enemy."

"You just worry about your mission. I'll worry about the Judas."

"Yes, sir."

"Do you understand everything that needs to be done? Every detail."

"Yes, sir. I'll keep them chasing their own tails in a standoff here and then follow you through the escape route. You don't have to worry about a thing."

Demon checked the time. They were already behind schedule. He said, "I'm going to escort Lash and his crew to the exfiltration point and go out with him. You make me proud here, kid. You keep them off our backs, and we'll see you on payday. Don't make me regret all the second chances I've given you."

"You won't, sir. I promise."

Demon started toward the door, but he stopped dead in his tracks when Jerry said, "Sir, one more thing. The federal agent. The woman. I would like to have her. With your permission, of course. And I'll make sure she is still breathing and still works as a hostage when I'm done."

Demon looked out the window of the conference room at his two hostages who claimed to be federal agents. With the new security system online, the man with no fear would be able to do little to stop Jerry from defiling his "little sister."

Demon smiled. It would be a bit of a parting gift for the fearless from the soulless.

"Fine. She's all yours. Just don't let pleasure interfere with business."

Ackerman had been reading Demon's lips as much as possible during the argument in the conference room. From his angle, he could barely see their faces through the room's window, but he read enough key words and facial expressions to sift out a few nuggets of valuable intelligence. And he didn't like any of the things he had learned.

Demon stepped down the stairs from the conference room and had a brief exchange with Lash. Then the ULF leader and his lieutenants packed up their things and headed toward the elevators. As Demon moved to follow, he matched gazes with Ackerman. The two conversed with their eyes for a moment, and then Demon pulled a business card and a pen from his pocket. He used the pen to write something on the back of the card. No more than a sentence.

Then Demon said, "Just in case," and he laid the card atop one of the control room's workstations. With a wink, Demon headed toward the exit and didn't look back.

Lash had left four of his foot soldiers behind as guards, and Jerry Dunn still stood in the conference room doorway. Ackerman could tell that Jerry's eyes and thoughts were on Maggie. Something about that made Ackerman want to jam hot knives through Jerry's eye sockets.

After a few more long and hungry glances, Jerry retreated into the conference room. No doubt plotting and planning for his impending conquest.

Ackerman heard his father's voice in his head.

Cut out his eyes.

From her position kneeling beside him, Maggie said, "If you're waiting for me to give you the go-ahead, then you have it. Do your thing. Hulk smash. Go get 'em."

"I find those references and your tone to be very offensive. I don't know what you expect me to do. We are restrained by their security system now. I can't act out against any of these men without being pacified from above."

She said, "You always have something up your sleeve.

There's always an angle or weakness you exploit. So I'm telling you, now's the time."

Ackerman could see his old friend, Winston, approaching over Maggie's shoulder. Apparently, Winston hadn't made the cut to accompany Lash. Or perhaps Winston merely had a short amount of time left on his sentence.

The truth of the judicial system was that the participants in this little revolution would end up looking like victims. They would probably get by with no consequences. They may even receive cash settlements. Winston may have chosen to stay behind out of good financial sense. More likely, though, the large black man with the military bearing simply wasn't worth bringing along to the ULF leader. Winston was expendable and easily replaceable, and he was moving toward them with anger in his eyes.

Maggie said, "Do something. We can't let them just walk out of here."

"What precisely did you expect? A Jedi mind trick? Do you want me to tell him that we're not the droids he's looking for?"

"You actually have seen *Star Wars*."

"I told you that I read the novelizations."

Winston stormed up and said, "No talking!"

Ackerman said, "Maggie, have you met my friend, Winston?"

"I said shut up!"

Ackerman gave a nod, and Winston was about to pass by, but then Ackerman leaned toward Maggie and said, "He doesn't look like a Winston. I suppose I instantly picture Churchill, though. Isn't it funny how some people and things penetrate the cultural zeitgeist like that."

Winston kicked Ackerman hard in the chest, and he fell over and started convulsing. The electrical current pulsing through his body was invigorating. Ackerman had triggered it by imagining how he could respond to Winston's attack. Ackerman held onto his aggression for a few seconds longer, riding the refreshing wave of electricity.

Winston started to walk away again, and Ackerman, still on the ground, said, "Where was I? Oh yes, the cultural zeitgeist. For example—"

Winston kicked him again.

And again Ackerman rode the wave.

Then he said, "And speaking of our new friend Winston being a clown and thinking of the cultural zeitgeist, are any of you afraid of clowns?"

He noticed that his words were starting to become a bit slurred from the kicks and convulsions. He continued anyway. "Mr. Powell? Maggie? I've found that there are a disproportionate number of people who are afraid of clowns. I've often wondered if that level of irrational anxiety has always manifested itself in regard to clowns, or did John Wayne Gacy, the infamous serial killer, who used to visit hospitals dressed as a clown and paint—"

Winston kicked him several times. Ackerman lost count of the number of blows. He savored the pain and let the flood gates of electricity wash over him.

When he was done with his tantrum, Winston stepped back and fought to catch his breath and control his temper.

Ackerman laughed as he spit some blood onto the concrete floor. Then he said, "So the question is: Were people always scared of clowns or did Gacy actually penetrate the fears of our society? But maybe there's something much older causing that fear. Are people afraid of mice because of an association with their black-plague-spreading cousins, the rats? Are people afraid of snakes because of the Garden of Eden? All fascinating questions. Here's what I think—"

This time, Winston, apparently smart enough to adapt with greater speed than Ackerman had anticipated, changed tactics. Instead of assaulting Ackerman, Winston backhanded Maggie so hard that she ended up flat on the concrete.

This time, Ackerman didn't say another word.

Winston stood over him and said, "That's what I thought." Winston then grabbed Ackerman by the shoulders and easily placed him back on his knees. The big enforcer repeated the procedure with Maggie and stood over them like a silent stone sentry.

Ackerman had expected to get a couple more kicks out of Winston before things escalated, but he could probably still squeeze out another tantrum from the big man later with some well-placed insults. He was about to comment about Winston resembling a gargoyle when the door to the conference room opened.

Jerry Dunn had apparently finished his preparations. And more quickly than Ackerman had initially estimated.

Dunn set his sights on Maggie and then moved down the stairs toward them. The young man's eyes were glassy but wide and hyper-alert and filled with the most basic of hungers.

Jerry reached them and didn't speak for a moment. He

just stood there, devouring Maggie with those filthy eyes. Dunn said, "Winston, please escort Agent Carlisle upstairs to the warden's office for me."

Winston looked conflicted. Ackerman could see that the big man had at least some moral compass. Winston didn't like the idea of Dunn raping one of the hostages. Winston said, "Sir, I—"

"It's a direct order."

Winston considered that a moment and said, "Yes, sir."

Ackerman watched as Winston hauled Maggie to her feet, and he said nothing. He didn't argue or protest. He knew it would be a waste of breath.

Maggie looked genuinely afraid. She met his gaze and said, "Do something."

He said nothing.

Winston pushed her forward and led her away. She glared at Ackerman over her shoulder.

Jerry bent his knees into a crouch, brought his face close to Ackerman's, and said, "I'm not afraid of you." Jerry traced his finger down the side of Ackerman's face and added, "No big speech?"

Ackerman whispered, "I'm going to call our little game 'A Lesson in Loss.'"

Jerry laughed. "Sounds like my life story."

Ackerman said nothing.

"So what exactly are you going to teach me about loss that I don't already know? Huh, Mr. Consultant? You're nothing but a junkyard dog. And they're not so scary when they're on a leash."

Ackerman said nothing.

Jerry gave a smug little smile and followed after Maggie

and Winston, up the spiral metal staircase to the privacy and comfort of the warden's office.

While Andrew was transferred around by the sheriff's department's switchboard as he tried to reach someone at their automotive impound desk, Marcus reviewed the photos that had been removed from Jerry's walls. He wanted to double check that they didn't contain any evidence that Judas was wanting to erase. But he didn't find anything incriminating. The photos weren't even all of the same woman. They appeared to have simply been chosen at random.

But his search did turn up one clue. A receipt from a place called The Dive Shop was stuck to the back of one of the photos. The total was for several thousand dollars, but it didn't give a description of what was purchased. It did specify that the bill was paid in cash.

Marcus snapped a photo of the receipt and texted it to Stan with the message: *Find out all you can about this ASAP*.

Then he carefully placed all the photos back into the ziplock freezer bag. As he did so, he couldn't shake the feeling that something was off. Something he was missing. Something that was there and shouldn't be or something that should have been there but was now gone.

Andrew placed his phone into a pocket and said, "They're ready for us at the garage."

"How far is it?"

"About ten to fifteen minutes from here. Why?"

"I just want to get back."

"Director just texted that nothing's happening. The negotiator and FBI SWAT just arrived, and this thing could take days."

Marcus said, "I don't think so. We're just in the eye of the storm right now. I want to get back."

"I'm worried about her too, but we're helping in the best way we can. And she does have Ackerman."

"Strange how comforting that is."

"She couldn't have a better protector in there. Well, maybe Arnold from Terminator 2."

"Except my brother's not made of metal. No matter how he acts, Ackerman still bleeds like everyone else. And his lack of fear is going to end up getting him killed. Right now, he's in a very bad situation with some very bad people."

Andrew said, "I'm more worried about what will happen to all those 'very bad' people being trapped in there with Ackerman."

The warden's office was a large, open space surrounded on all sides by viewing windows. This part of the building seemed like an add-on to Maggie. Like some former lord of Foxbury was compensating for something.

Jerry Dunn stood in front of the eastern set of viewing windows. His back was to her. She could easily take him down. She knew that she could, if given the opportunity. But if she tried now, she'd end up convulsing on the floor, courtesy of the wrist and ankle restraints that had been forced onto their group. And they had all stood by helplessly as Jerry had demonstrated the power he now wielded to Marcus.

Maggie waited for what felt like several moments before she said, "Are you just going to stand there looking out the window all creepy-like? You look like Dracula's teenage son standing over there like that."

Jerry said, "I'm watching the sunrise. Would Dracula be doing that?"

The sun was indeed rising in the distance behind Jerry. And it was beautiful. Maggie hadn't noticed and didn't care about the sunrise. Right now, her mind was focused on more important things. Like getting out of Powell's office alive and unmolested.

She knew now that Jerry had become obsessed with her. According to Demon, Jerry was also a rapist. Presumably, he raped the women he obsessed over. Maggie had received a C+ in algebra, but she could still add this all up to mean that Jerry had more planned than watching sunrises.

He said, "Have a seat."

She remained standing.

Jerry limped his way over to Powell's desk, opened a bottom drawer, and removed a large decanter filled with brown liquid. He then pulled two glasses from the same drawer. He filled them both with two fingers of the dark liquid and limped his way over to her. He held out one of the glasses. She took the glass and downed the harsh liquid in one swig. It made her throat and chest feel like she had just drunk dragon piss. She immediately regretted it, although she was relatively certain that it made her look very badass.

Jerry sipped his drink and walked back toward the window. She rolled her eyes and joined him in front of the sunrise.

She tried to think of a way to beat the restraints. She

considered what Ackerman had done in the yard. Although, he hadn't really beaten it. He had merely confused it long enough to get a shot in. So even if she could repeat what he had done, she would only get one opportunity.

"I'm sorry that I deceived you," Jerry said.

"You don't seem sorry."

"How so?"

"You recently had a man executed."

"Yes, but he wasn't a very nice man, and it was necessary."

Maggie said, "I'll say the same thing after I kill you."

"That's unkind of you to say."

Maggie shrugged. "Did I hurt your feelings? Stop being a creepy asshole and people won't treat you like one."

Jerry laughed. "So much fire! I love it. When you walked in here and were standing over there watching me, what were you thinking about?"

"About pushing you out the window."

"No, I meant what were you thinking about me?"

"That I'd like to see you fall out the window."

"I guess it doesn't really matter what you were thinking because whoever you were thinking it about isn't the real me."

"I'd prefer not to meet the real you."

"This character I've been playing since meeting you isn't really who I am. Jerry Dunn isn't even my real name."

"I don't care."

"There's a connection between us."

"Not so much."

"I know you've felt it."

"The only connection I ever felt toward you was that of a little brother, and even that was short lived and a lie."

He slammed a fist against Powell's desk. A picture of Debra fell over, and Maggie heard the glass break.

She said, "What are you going to do, big man? You going to hit me?"

"No."

"Oh, that's right. You love me."

"Stop it."

Maggie stepped closer to Jerry and tried to find something she could use to confuse the system like Ackerman had. Maybe something on Powell's desk? She said, "What's the matter, big man? You can't get it up?"

"Don't talk like that! I can't stand a lady who speaks that way!"

Maggie yelled out a string of the most offensive phrases that came to mind. All of the things she said were vulgar and sexual in nature and, as she had hoped, Jerry Dunn hit her.

What she hadn't expected was the type of blow. She had thought Jerry would start with a slap or a backhand. But he jerked his fist straight back and coiled up the muscle and then let that fist shoot out like it was blasted from a cannon. Maggie went limp and didn't fight the blow. Pain erupted out from her left cheekbone as Jerry's fist connected and drove her back. She tumbled over one of the high back chairs in front of Powell's desk and landed face first on the tile floor. She tasted pennies in her mouth.

She didn't move. She didn't try to get up.

Jerry screamed, "See what you made me do? Why did you do that?"

She spit blood on the tile and flipped over onto her back. She felt blood coming from her nose, but she didn't try to wipe it away. She just let it flow and stared at Jerry Dunn with hatred in her eyes. She spread her legs and said, "What's the matter, Jerry? I thought this is what turned you on."

He held her gaze a moment but then laughed. "Now I see what you're doing. You think that I brought you up here to rape you, but I'm telling you that old man is a liar."

"Maybe. I know one thing. You can't rape me while that security system is on. Otherwise, you would be shocked too as I fought back. And I will fight back."

"Listen to me for just one minute, Maggie. I'm going to make a lot of money off this job. Enough to go anywhere. Do anything. You could come with me. You could be part of that. You could have anything you want."

"First of all, you can't be making that much money off the small part you played on this little job. And second, even if someone is cashing in off this, that someone is not going to be little old you."

Jerry walked around to the rear of Powell's desk and typed some keys on the computer. Then he said, "Princess, that just shows how little you know about what's going on here. We're getting money from some people who want to see this place fail, and we're getting a shit load of money from Lash. And second, I'm in charge here. This job doesn't happen without me."

"You mean you're in charge now that Demon left?"

"That old man is a walking corpse."

"He seemed pretty capable to me. And not that old."

"Demon's on the way out."

Maggie laughed. "And you think you're on the way in?"

"Maybe."

"And I'm sure you actually planned all this. You're the real Judas."

"No, but—"

"They're just using you!"

"Don't yell at me!"

"What's the plan, Jerry? You think you're going to meet up with your buddies later. Face it. They left you behind. They abandoned you."

Jerry reached up and started unbuttoning his shirt. He undid it all the way, pulled it off, and dropped it onto Powell's desk. Then he did the same with his undershirt and dropped it onto the desk. He stood there in the light from the sunrise, and Maggie had to admit that Jerry, beneath the sloppy stoner exterior, had the body of a Greek god, albeit a kind of scrawny one.

Still, he was nothing but muscle. Every section of his torso was chiseled like stone.

He said, "You not only rudely reject me, but then you insult me by thinking that if I turned off the security system in this room that you would be able to overpower me. But like I said before, you don't know the real me."

Jerry stretched and then demonstrated some elaborate jump kicks. He said, "You think that because I'm small and have a limp, and all that is true about how my parents died by the way, but just because I have a slight limp, you think that means that I'm weak?"

"I don't care about your exterior. Or your size or strength. No, I think that you're weak and tiny on the inside, Jerry. Muscles don't matter if you have an ugly soul."

Jerry made a few clicks on the computer and said, "There. Security system is down for this room."

Maggie smiled and pulled herself up to her feet.

Jerry said, "I should warn you that I'm considered an expert in seven types of martial arts."

"Oh yeah, I know a couple types too. But the only form I'm going to use today is the ancient art of kicking your ass."

She wiped away the blood from her nose and said, "Maybe you've heard of that one."

He started to speak and, when he did, she tried to catch him off guard. She went for his right knee—a solid kick with enough force behind it to crush bone, if it had connected. But it didn't connect. Jerry blocked it easily and then landed a kick to the side of her head that made her vision go dark.

The manager of the sheriff's impound unit was a heavyset man with a big-brush-pile mustache that hung over his lips. Andrew greeted the manager first with an outstretched hand. "Mr. Finley?" Andrew said. Then, after a brief exchange of pleasantries, they went to work. And Finley was good at his job. Marcus could tell from his reports and his presentation of the findings. Finley ran through everything with a minimal amount of fuss, but it was also clear that his team had done a thorough job.

Finley said, "Unfortunately, the hair and fiber search didn't reveal any smoking guns, but it's all catalogued and filed. All ready for the trial."

Marcus said, "Thanks, but we need something that will help us right now."

Finley smiled. At least Marcus thought it was a smile. "I might have a couple of solid leads for you," Finley said as he walked over to a rolling tool cart and held up an evidence bag.

Marcus said, "What are we looking at?"

The evidence bag appeared to hold some type of smashed computer components, but he hoped that Finley had more details to share than that.

Finley said, "These are the remnants of an iPhone."

Andrew took the bag in hand and examined the pieces more closely. He said, "How can you tell what kind of phone? There's no way you've had time to have the pieces analyzed that thoroughly."

Finley laughed. "No, but I cheated on that with a little detective work. Amongst those components is a piece from a SIM card. Enough of the digits on the card were readable that the cellular company was able to figure out who it belonged to and what kind of phone."

Marcus slapped Finley on the back and said, "An iPhone. Nice work. I don't suppose you asked the phone company for—"

Finley said, "Yes, sir. I requested the call logs. They are all in my report."

Marcus noticed that Finley had a bit of a speech impediment that caused his words to come out thickly, like tree sap. He wondered if that Sam Elliot mustache hid the evidence of a cleft palate. He noticed a desk in the corner. There were pictures on it, scattered among grime-covered reports and forms. Finley was in the photos with two older men in one and a much younger woman in all the others. Finley had black under his fingernails, which made sense considering his line of work. Finley also had signs of cauliflower ear, a condition often found in competitive wrestlers. Marcus filed all the information away in his mental database. He couldn't help it.

Andrew said, "What about GPS data?"

"I have the list of destinations printed up and sorted by date."

Marcus stuck out his hand and said, "Finley, it's been a pleasure. You do excellent work. I'd give you a kiss but I'm afraid your mustache may bite me."

Finley laughed and said, "He only bites if you ask real nice."

As they were heading out of Finley's office, Marcus dialed Stan and put the call on speaker.

"You are a go for Stan. Please keep your arms and legs inside the vehicle at all times."

Marcus said, "The Dive Shop. What is it?"

He had guessed that the receipt had come from a business that sold climbing gear, assuming that cave diving was the focus of The Dive Shop.

Stan said, "I spoke to the manager, and she was able to pull up more info on what was purchased. Well, rented actually. Our bad guy rented five full sets of scuba gear. Breathing masks, tanks, the whole enchilada. She told me all the technical names for everything. I wrote it all down somewhere if you need that."

"So the place is an actual dive shop? As in underwater diving. In the middle of Arizona."

"Oh yeah, they have pools where they teach diving and a sales and rental shop."

Andrew said, "I'm more concerned as to why our guy needs five sets of diving rigs."

Marcus thought about that. A poison gas? Smoke? But they wouldn't need a full scuba load-out for that. Then he remembered the map of the mine. There had been a section on the map marked as flooded.

The receipt was a good clue. A clue that could have been easily discarded and destroyed but was instead left for them to find. Maybe it was too good of a clue.

Marcus closed his eyes and gritted his teeth. Then he said, "Stan, they recovered the remnants of Debra Costello's iPhone. It was smashed to bits."

Stan said, "That's tough to do. Those things are pretty sturdy. And believe me on that, I have attempted the obliteration of one."

"Exactly. Which suggests that there was something on the phone that someone doesn't want us to see. So here's what I was thinking. On my iPhone, it is set to automatically back up the phone when I plug it in at night."

"Yeah, it backs up to iCloud," Stan said. "Wait, now I'm with you. If I can break into her iCloud account, I can get a fresh copy of her phone. I can then set that up in an emulator, and we'll have access to her phone like it was never gone. But you realize that this will only restore her last backup. The info that made our crazy friend go all Gallagher on that thing may not even be there, if it was new data."

"I understand. It's better than nothing. You have five minutes to resurrect that phone."

"Whoa, just the data download alone will take—"

Marcus hung up the phone and said, "So here's what's bothering me."

"Stan hates it when you do that to him."

"He'll get over it. Do you want to hear it or not? You're always telling me to share information."

"What's bothering you?"

"The photos and the receipts were in sealed, watertight bags. Why?"

"It's all he had. He used it as a garbage bag to clean out his car."

"Then why not just dump the bag's contents into the sewer. Destroy them and scatter them. But he didn't do that. He left the evidence preserved for us to find. And both bags were in places that were difficult to find as clues, but they were in places that good investigators do sometimes think to check."

"Or maybe you're just being paranoid."

"You're not paranoid if people really are after you."

"Maybe Judas just slipped up, and we caught it. Go us."

"Or we're being led. We're still playing his game, by his rules."

Andrew said, "Say that we are. What are we going to do about it?"

Marcus closed his eyes and rubbed his cross tattoo. "Look at the GPS report. Where did he go yesterday?"

Marcus heard the shuffling of paper, and Andrew said, "This is a great report. Finley looked all of them up on Google Maps and made notes. He marked one that looks out of place for Reese. It's a residential address. He had driven to that address three times. Finley checked, and the address Reese put in is the home of Becky Takashima. The report says that Finley sent a uniform to do a stop at her home in order to check on her. She's fine and hasn't seen anything unusual."

"I want to talk to her."

"I figured." Andrew was making notes on a pad of paper. The kind that flipped forward. Spiral-bound. It reminded

Marcus of when he had first made detective. He had never needed to make notes. He had always remembered all the details. But he also didn't want to look out of place or seem cocky, and so he had pretended to use a notebook. He had eventually turned it into an animated flip-book.

Andrew finished his note and was about to say more, but he stopped when he saw Finley approaching them from down the hallway, a cell phone still in his hand. Finley said, "Sheriff just called and wanted me to let you know that they're bringing in Bradley Reese's body. Sheriff said you would want to see Reese and the other body ASAP."

Marcus looked at Andrew, who just shrugged. Marcus said, "What other body?"

Finley said, "They pulled two bodies out of the mine. That's all I know."

Marcus asked, "Where are the bodies now?"

Maggie leaned against the high-back leather chair and tried to catch her breath. She hurt all over. Jerry was only toying with her, but she guessed that so far he had shattered her ribs and dislocated her wrist.

Jerry laughed as he flexed his muscles in the light from the nearly risen sun. He said, "I thought you'd be tougher than this. Federal agent and all. Thought you'd put up more of a fight."

"Did the others fight you, Jerry? Is that how you like it? Does it take beating up a woman to turn you on?"

"It wasn't supposed to be like this."

"How was it supposed to be? Did you think you would declare your love for me, and I'd run away with you?

Number one, I don't even know you, and you don't know me."

Jerry spun on his left foot and roundhouse kicked half the contents off Powell's desk. "You didn't want to know me! You're just like the others. You feel the connection, but you ruined it. You think you're too good for me, so you won't accept that you've found your soulmate."

"And how many 'soulmates' have you had, Jerry? How many women have you raped and murdered?"

He kicked out her feet and pummeled her torso with his fists. She thought that he had called her Amy at one point, but it could have just been a scream. He did a lot of screaming. And a lot of punching. When he was done, she was in a lot of pain.

But during his tirade, she had managed to roll closer to the window sill where Jerry had laid her Glock 19 pistol.

She knew now that she couldn't take Jerry in a straight-up fight. He was skilled enough at hand-to-hand to give Marcus or even Ackerman a challenge. He probably spent hours every day on his body and his technique. The more she saw of his shirtless torso, the more she thought that his muscles were defined to the point of being disgusting, like his skin had been stretched over a bag of coiled snakes.

Jerry stopped his barrage and started pacing and mumbling to himself. His limp had grown even more pronounced. She made out the word "ruined" but could understand little of the rest.

Not that she really wanted to understand.

The problem was that Jerry was doing his pacing between her and the Glock.

She spat blood on the floor. She knew that Jerry would end up beating her to death, raping her, or some combination of the two if they continued on like this. She had to end this fight quickly and decisively.

Something about the nature of what was happening seemed familiar. She considered what she knew about Jerry. The limp. The beating. Rape.

She said, "You're the San Diego Strangler. I read your case files."

"I never liked that name. It's not original enough. When I choose my code name, I'm going to pick something that will be legendary."

"So you don't have a cool serial-killer nickname like Judas and Demon? You're not a full member of the squad yet? Oh, that's sad."

"I'll be a senior vice president when Judas takes over. And there's nothing little about Demon or his influence. You have no idea. No clue the level of players you're rolling with."

"I'm starting to understand. Maybe we can still get to know one another better. Maybe we can start over. Tell me about how big of a player you are."

Maggie took a few steps closer to Jerry. She hated standing within kicking distance, but her Glock was directly behind him, and she had to reach that gun.

She closed the gap between them to a couple of feet. Jerry had stopped pacing and mumbling, but he still had that feral, chemically stimulated look in his eyes. She did her best to seem a little flirtatious without being obvious about it. She wasn't very good at flirting and using her feminine wiles for her gain, and she was pretty sure that she wasn't being very sexy as she forced a smile and batted her eyelashes. She had actually received a bit of formal instruction on acting but had never taken to the craft. It was a good thing that guys were so easily enamored by pretty much anything that any woman did with even the slightest hint of sexual implication.

Jerry said, "I thought maybe you would skip this step."

"What step? What are you talking about?"

"Usually the women I kill go right down this list of ways they can try to distract me or confuse me. Flirting. Attacking. Bargaining. Pleading. Threatening. Trying to reason with me. Trying to humanize themselves. But you see, Maggie. None of that works. I thought maybe you realized that I'm too smart for all that."

"I'm not trying to trick you. This job doesn't pay very well, and it's killing me. The way I'm headed, I'll end up as one of those strange old cat ladies. If I live that long, which is unlikely. I think maybe I should consider your offer."

She took another step toward him. He was a bit shorter than her, but she was hunched over and clutching her wounded ribs and struggling to breathe, which brought them eye to eye.

Jerry met her gaze and whispered, "The only thing on your mind is the pistol behind me."

He kicked her in the stomach, and she flew backward and landed beside Powell's desk, the wind knocked out of her.

Jerry picked up the gun and said, "I'm going to rape you now, Agent Carlisle. You were meant to be my soulmate, but it's too late for that. Now, I will taste your soul, and then I'll make sure that no one ever tastes it again."

★★★

The medical examiner's office was, thankfully, adjacent to the garage, which was connected to another larger building that likely held the administrative offices and county jail. The buildings were made from a textured adobe the color of sand, but they were mostly glass with large, expensive looking foyers and facilities. The whole place looked brand new. And, according to Andrew, Sheriff Hall had a few offices like this scattered throughout his jurisdiction.

Travis Hall and his department were no backwoods operation.

As Marcus made his way from the county garage to the county morgue, he couldn't help but think of the money and resources Hall had at his command. But he didn't envy the sheriff one bit. All he saw when he looked at these new facilities were headaches and responsibilities. He saw mayors breathing down his neck and politics and hundreds of thousands of taxpayers seeing him, as sheriff, as the face and hands of justice. All those people looked to Hall's department to hold society together. All those victims. All of their parents. Their spouses. Children. All looking to him to do what was right.

Marcus didn't envy the sheriff in the slightest. He could barely manage a small team of investigators and a son. Sheriff Hall probably had ten kids and managed a few hundred people and millions upon millions of dollars in resources.

The medical examiner's office was much like the others he had seen. Metal examination tables. A rolling cart containing the tools of the trade. A wall of pull-out body trays retracting back into refrigerated storage. All very clean. Very sterile.

Unfortunately, they had arrived before the bodies.

As they waited, Andrew asked, "How do you think Maggie's holding up in there?"

"As well as could be expected under the circumstances."

"You know what I mean. Is she going to freak out and go off like she did in Pittsburgh?"

"And do what? Go on a killing spree?"

Andrew said, "No, but she could get a lot of people hurt."

"It wasn't that big of a deal."

"She stabbed that killer in Pittsburgh eleven times. I could guess the order of the stab wounds when I saw the photos. She kept stabbing him even after he was dead."

"So she got caught up in the moment. That guy had just tried to kill her. She was scared and fighting for her life."

"Then why did you cover for her? Why did you lie?"

"I don't know. It's what I do. I didn't want any of you questioning her like you are now. I wanted to protect her. I didn't want her to feel like a freak. Like she was going crazy and everyone knew it."

Andrew said, "Is that how you feel?"

"Sometimes. It is what it is. In regard to Maggie, she's going through something. I don't know what it is. I don't know if she knows. I'm trying to be there for her as best I can. And figure it out as we go along."

"You don't have to figure it out alone."

The doors opened and a man and a woman in white coats wheeled in a single body zipped in a dark-green plastic bag atop a metal gurney. The two medical techs looked tired. Their eyes were red rimmed and droopy, like they were the night shift approaching the end of their day. They took their time with everything they did. One guided the way while the other pushed.

Marcus supposed they had no reason to hurry. Their patients were already dead. But he was thinking about the people who were still alive. The ones counting on him to keep them that way.

He walked up to the first body bag as soon as they stopped. He had no idea whose remains he would find inside, but not because he had no theories. Simply because he couldn't tell from the bag's shape if this was the male or female body.

Marcus knew that one of the bags would contain the remains of Debra Costello, Powell's missing daughter.

The other would be a decoy. A body that Reese had placed at the bottom of that pit.

Marcus now believed that Bradley Reese was Judas, and Reese had faked his own death in order to manipulate them.

He unzipped the first bag to reveal the bloody remains of a woman. She had been deceased for several days. Marcus could tell. Andrew could probably explain the telltale signs, but Marcus just knew approximately how long she'd been dead because he had seen enough bodies in his time to get a feel for such things.

He recognized the woman from the pictures on Powell's desk. He had been correct in his assessments. It was Debra. Although being right didn't feel like a win. He had assumed from the facts that Debra was dead. He had even expected to find her body here. But the confirmation still felt like a major loss.

Andrew whispered, "Damn it. There's one mystery solved. What do you think we'll find in the other bag?"

"My guess, as much as I hate to guess, is that it's some homeless guy or target of opportunity that Reese used as a decoy."

"You think that Reese faked his own death? That he's Judas?"

"I think that Judas is the codename for a mercenary and serial murderer who was paid to orchestrate all this. I think he came here, analyzed the situation, and decided that the quickest way to get the access he needed was to manipulate Powell."

"And the quickest way to Powell was through his daughter. If you're a young and attractive guy like Bradley Reese. The timing works. He's only been around for a matter of months, and he's already engaged to Powell's daughter and has become one of his executives with complete access to Foxbury."

Marcus said, "So Reese is using Debra to get close to Powell, but then he actually falls for her. But something happens with her. Who knows what it was. Something sets him off, and he kills her. Maybe that's when he decided to pin it on Jerry and fake his own death. Reese is the only one who makes sense for all of it. And honestly, I've always had a feeling about him. My instincts say it's Reese. I'm as sure about this as I've ever been about anything. He faked his own death. He's our killer."

Andrew nodded. "I'm with you. I just wonder if there's a piece to the puzzle we haven't seen yet."

"Let's hope not." Marcus looked to the double doors and

said, "Did they go all the way back to the mine for that body? We're wasting time here."

Andrew said, "Patience."

"That's your job. My job is to find the shortest path to our bad guy. Sometimes that involves busting some heads, and if those two are out there taking a smoke break, I swear to all that is holy that I will—"

The double doors swung open and the two techs wheeled in the second body bag. The saggy-eyed lab assistants barely acknowledged Marcus and Andrew as they lined up the second gurney beside Debra. The female tech, a twenty-something with a nose ring, said, "The ME is on his way."

Marcus didn't really care about the medical examiner at that point. He simply needed a confirmation. If he was right, then a quick look would tell him that this was not Bradley Reese.

He pushed the techs aside, unzipped the bag, and was greeted by the face of a man who looked like he had fallen down a mineshaft.

Andrew said, "He's pretty beat up, but that sure looks like Bradley Reese."

Marcus realized that all his muscles were trembling. He whispered, "His hands. I noticed ink on them earlier."

He couldn't force his muscles to move. He couldn't get his arms to unzip the bag any farther. Andrew finished unzipping it for him. He looked down at Reese's hands. And there, in the same exact patterns he had captured earlier with his eidetic memory, were the ink stains.

Marcus said, "That's it. I give up."

Then he stormed from the room.

★★★

FILE #750265-6726-695
Zolotov, Dmitry - AKA The Judas Killer
State Exhibit F
Description: Diary Entry

Father caught up to us in front of the clock tower at Kiyevsky Railway Terminal as Stasi and I were waiting for the last train to Vienna. He had his rusty old .38 special in his hand and a murderous gleam in his eye. I had seen that look many times before and, when he forced us into the back of the theater's van, I knew that he didn't plan on bringing the wayward children home like a dutiful father.

He had other things on his mind.

He took us back to the basement of the old theater house. At that time of night, the place was abandoned, and there was no one within earshot to hear us scream.

He tied me up, hanging above the floor by my wrists, my feet dangling. Then he made me watch and look into Stasi's eyes as he raped her and slit her throat.

At that point, he should have killed me . . . because I was damn sure going to kill him.

But he didn't, and it's taken me years to realize why. I used to think that he hated me, but I've come to believe that Father actually loved me in his own way. And it's been my experience that people are far more likely to destroy what they love than that which they hate.

Instead of killing me, he stripped me naked and pulled out a knife and a big, fat rubber band. The kind a schoolteacher may wrap around a thick bundle of markers.

As he stumbled toward me, the smell of vodka strong on his breath, in slurred English, he said, "When I was a boy on our farm outside Osnovo, my brother and I used to take pleasure in castrating the livestock by wrapping a rubber band just like this around their testicles. The animal's nuts would eventually die and fall off. But don't worry, my little Judas, we won't wait for that. I'll finish up the procedure with the knife. After a few hours of excruciating pain to teach you a lesson, of course. I know this may seem cruel to you now. But you will do so much more with your life without worrying about the shlyukhas and children. They will only lead you to ruin. Trust me, my son . . . I'm doing you a favor."

As she lay there on the floor of Powell's office—bloody, beaten, and quickly losing the will to keep fighting—Maggie Carlisle realized that she was going to die at the lowest point in her life. Things were rocky between her and Marcus. The twentieth anniversary of her brother's abduction was quickly approaching, and she was no closer to finding the man who took him than she had been when the SO recruited her. She had been drinking far too much far too often. She felt constantly on edge. And now she had learned that she was unable to have children due to some condition she couldn't even pronounce. She would never hold her own baby in her arms. She would never be able to experience that feeling with Marcus.

She realized that she didn't even care if Jerry ended her.

She almost welcomed it. Her child wasn't dead. It had never even been given a single spark of life. But she couldn't help feeling like she had just lowered a baby into the ground.

Jerry Dunn aimed her Glock and said, "We could have been something special. If you had just . . . "

Maggie then realized that one added bonus to being barren was that, when Jerry raped her, she wouldn't have to worry about getting pregnant. Of course, that really wouldn't be a problem because at some point—before, during, or after—he would also strangle her to death.

She started to laugh, but it turned into a cry. Within a moment, she was weeping. She hated that Jerry would think her tears were born out of fear of him. When, in reality, her tears had little to do with Jerry Dunn, and more to do with her own shortcomings.

Jerry started unbuttoning his pants and said, "I think you're going to be pleasantly surprised."

Maggie was about to tell Jerry where he could stick his pleasant surprise, but another voice from across the room—a man's voice, deep and soft with an edge of menace, and dripping with arrogance—said, "I'm just going to stop you there, Jer Bear. You can keep your pants on for this."

Maggie pulled herself up onto her knees and looked across the room at Francis Ackerman Jr. He stood there by the stairs with a coffee cup in his hand like he was just showing up for work.

She spat blood on the floor and said, "It's about time. How long have you been standing there?"

"Long enough to assess the situation," Ackerman said. "I told you I'd come for you. And I've never lied to you, little sister. At least, not when it really counted."

Jerry Dunn said, "How did you get up here? How did you get past the guards?"

Ackerman took a sip of his coffee and made a face. He said, "This coffee is terrible. And cold. It actually belonged to one of the dead technicians. I figured they wouldn't mind, and I needed a boost. Maybe my age is catching up with me, but I just can't stay up for days on end like I used to. But in regard to your friends, I'm afraid that they have been incapacitated and, even as we speak, Ms. Spinelli is working to retake control of the computer systems."

Jerry raised the Glock and said, "Don't move."

Ackerman appeared to be unarmed. He took another sip of his coffee, made another face, and then raised his hands in surrender.

Jerry made a dash for the computer on Powell's desk. Ackerman didn't move, and Maggie was in no condition to do much of anything. Jerry furiously tapped at the keys of Powell's computer.

He said, "There must have been an error that disabled both the CCE and this office. But I've reactivated all security now. And I have complete control of the system from here. Isn't that right, Agent Carlisle?"

Jerry pressed another key, and Maggie felt an electrical current surge through her body.

Ackerman watched Jerry Dunn's gaze fall to Maggie's writhing form. And again there was that hunger in the young man's eyes. And again Ackerman wanted to pop out Jerry's eyeballs with a spoon.

When Dunn looked to Maggie again, Ackerman tossed

his coffee into the air, pulled both of the Tasers he had tucked into his waistband, and discharged the first into Dunn's chest. The muscular little man trembled and dropped as the barbs penetrated him just like he had planned to penetrate Maggie.

Ackerman calmly walked around Powell's desk and stared down at Jerry Dunn. Maggie had stopped shaking now, but she was still on the ground. He could see her labored breathing. She needed to get those ribs looked at.

Jerry started groaning, and so Ackerman pulled the trigger of the Taser again in order to send an additional shock. Then he said, "See this, it's better to give than to receive. Isn't that right, little buddy?"

Maggie pulled herself up into one of the high-back leather chairs and said, "I don't think you're using that saying in the right context. Better to give doesn't refer to pain."

"I feel it's applicable."

"You could have used that Taser on him before he shocked me."

"I was feeling out the moment. You were never in any danger."

Maggie said, "It felt pretty damn dangerous. I could have some heart defect or—"

"I've seen your medical files. Your heart is fine. What should we do with our friend here?"

To emphasize the point, Ackerman shot Jerry with the second Taser.

Maggie pulled herself up onto trembling legs and hobbled around the desk. She scanned the floor for her Glock. She found it, picked it up, and aimed it at Jerry Dunn's head.

Then Maggie said, "Rape this, you sick—"

She squeezed the trigger.

Ackerman watched her finger, with one twitch of a few muscle strands, pass a death sentence onto Jerry Dunn. He traced her aim. He knew her target. The T-zone. The sweet spots on the skull. She wasn't trying to scare Jerry or prove a point. She intended for that finger to twitch and for him to die.

But that didn't happen.

Instead, the gun made an audible click and then remained silent.

Maggie screamed and threw the gun across the room, and then she dropped to the floor, sobbing. Beneath the blubbering, Ackerman heard her say, "I can't even kill someone right."

Ackerman said, "First of all, there is no right or wrong way to kill someone. It's all just personal preferences. Although, it is kind of a pass or fail thing. And he is still breathing. And I do agree that you should have known the gun was unloaded. He obviously had you under control without it—I mean, look at this guy, he looks like some super-soldier experiment gone awry. He wouldn't have given you the opportunity to overpower him with a gun that he didn't even need or want to use."

Maggie said, "Please shut up."

"Plus, you should have been able to feel it was empty from the weight of it."

"I hate you so much right now."

"I just saved you from being raped and murdered. I didn't expect a medal but—"

"You want to do something for me? Remove this piece of human garbage from my universe. You want to earn my gratitude? Simple. All you have to do is execute Jerry Dunn."

Ackerman considered Maggie's proposal.

On the surface, it was simple enough. He could easily end Jerry's life in a variety of different ways, all with various levels of associated satisfaction. In Dunn's pacified state, Ackerman could snap the man's neck. Or tear out his windpipe with his fingers. Or jam his thumbs straight into those filthy, hungry eyes until he could scrape his fingernails against the backside of Jerry's skull.

He said, "I made a promise to my brother."

Maggie said, "Marcus isn't here and never has to know. This is about me. You'll be doing me a favor."

"Marcus would find out. It's kind of what he does."

"Okay, I'll tell Marcus that I ordered you to do it. I'll tell him that it was all me."

"We may need Jerry."

"He's worthless, and you know it. What's the matter? You suddenly sprouting a conscience? What's one more murder? You already have so much to atone for, what's one more?"

Ackerman considered this and then pulled a prison shank that he had taken from Winston. Jerry was still quivering on the floor. Ackerman grabbed him by the foot and stabbed the homemade blade straight through Dunn's Achilles tendon.

The little man kicked and thrashed, but he was unable to keep Ackerman from repeating the same act of mutilation on his opposite foot.

Ackerman said, "If you recall, I'm going to title our little game, A Lesson in Loss. And trust me on this, Jerry, there is so much more that I can take from you than just your life."

Andrew found Marcus sitting on the curb in front of the medical annex. He walked over and said, "Mind if I pull up a stool."

"Be my guest."

Andrew cleaned off a spot as best as he could and then sat down. "It's not a big deal. You were wrong about Reese. You had a theory, and it was a good one. It just happened to be wrong. And that's okay."

"Is it? When I'm wrong, people die."

"That's not on you."

"And what else am I wrong about? Tell me the truth as a partner and friend. Am I wrong to trust Ackerman?"

"The verdict is still out, if you want my honest opinion. But I don't think we're wrong to find out. I mean, Ackerman is tough as hell, and he can provide insight that can help save lives. We just need to proceed cautiously."

"If you see me doing otherwise, you call me out on it. Iron sharpens iron. My dad used to say that, but I only recently thought about it and realized what he meant. It comes from a Bible verse about guys needing other guys to call them out when they're being jerks. Dad always quoted it in reference to his poker buddies when he was arguing with my mom. I guess what I'm trying to say is that you've made me a better person by being my friend. Like Dad said, 'iron sharpens iron.' I'm not good with this touchy-feely crap, but I want you to know I appreciate you always being there."

Andrew squeezed his friend's shoulder, held the pressure for a few seconds, and then slapped Marcus hard across the face. "Stop talking like they're getting ready to send you off to the glue factory. Reese isn't Judas, but he may lead us to him. And that may lead us to a way to put an end to this standoff and help our friends. So we have two leads just waiting to pan out. Stan will get Debra's phone back, and while he does that, we'll go check out that address Reese kept visiting. What do you say?"

Marcus took a deep breath, then stuck out his arm and index finger, and tucked in the other arm like he was a flying superhero. In his best Adam West voice, Marcus said, "I say . . . to the minivan, Robin."

Andrew said, "I am not the Robin to your Batman."

Marcus slapped Andrew on the shoulder as he stood and said, "Come on, little buddy. You can't fight your destiny."

Then, before Andrew could respond, Marcus headed off toward the van. Andrew frowned and grumbled under his breath, "I'll tell you what you can do with that little buddy . . ." then Andrew yelled after Marcus, "The only one I might give you is me being the Murtaugh to your Riggs."

Andrew didn't think his partner had even heard until Marcus yelled back, "You're getting closer. Maybe you can be Goose to my Maverick."

"No way am I Goose!"

★ ★ ★

Jerry Dunn pulled himself along in a backwards crawl away from Ackerman, his wounded heels smearing blood all over Powell's nice, clean floor.

Ackerman fought the urge to pounce on Jerry and gouge those filthy eyes right out of the little man's head. He had plucked out eyeballs before; he had done damn near everything at one time or another. He could almost feel the vitreous fluid on his fingertips. He could almost taste it from memory. Sort of a salty-sweet.

He didn't hear his father's voice in his head at that moment, but he could feel the old man's presence. Like Ackerman Sr. or Thomas White or whatever name he was calling himself now was watching from the corner of the room and urging him on.

Ackerman took his blade and slashed its edge across his own forearm. He savored the pain a moment, and then, with no warning, he pounced onto Jerry Dunn's chest. Ackerman pinned Jerry's arms and pressed the blade to the little man's windpipe. It would be so easy to puncture it and watch Jerry gasp for air and drown in his own blood.

Ackerman fought the urge.

He said, "I want to kill you, Jerry. It's not just that I would kill you, if you make a move, it's that I'm hoping you will give me the slightest justification to end your life. And, if that should happen, I will make the last minute or so of your life something you'll remember for the rest of eternity. Don't speak. Just blink if you understand."

Jerry blinked.

"Good. I feel it's important for you to understand the distinction, Jerry, because I like to get to know the people

I kill. So here's something you've never heard before: let's talk about you."

Jerry said, "I'm the guy who's going to kill you."

Ackerman laughed and pressed the blade deeper into Jerry's skin. A line of blood started to trickle out and pool around his neck.

Ackerman said, "Can you hear the angels, Jerry? Can you hear them singing? With all the people I've killed, if angels do carry us into the next world, I would have been in the presence of angels many times. I've often wondered what those angels thought about me when they collected those souls. Do they care about the affairs and feelings of men or are they merely automatons with a task to complete? Did they weep for my victims? Do they sing their song of mourning for my soul? Do you hear them, Jerry? Can you hear the angels crying?"

Jerry said, "Please, I'll tell you everything I know about Demon, and his operations. Just don't kill me. I know I hurt Agent Carlisle, but you're federal agents. You can't just kill a suspect in custody."

"A suspect!" Maggie screamed, but Ackerman held her off with a raised hand and bit of nonverbal communication with his eyes.

Ackerman said, "Don't be ridiculous, Jerry. I'm not going to kill you. How would you learn about loss if you're dead?"

Then he grabbed a can of compressed air, which he had noticed sitting atop Powell's desk. It was a simple tool often used for cleaning keyboards and computers that shot out a blast of compressed air, which swept away any dust or lose particles. But Ackerman didn't intend to use as directed. He knew that a can of compressed air had another potential utility.

In one fluid motion, Ackerman flipped the can upside down and placed his pinky over the can's release valve. He grabbed Jerry Dunn by the mop of dark hair atop the little man's head, and then he sprayed the contents of the can directly into Jerry's eyes, making sure to thoroughly douse each eye with the liquid shooting from the can's nozzle.

Jerry released a high-pitched wail of agony. He screamed and cursed and rolled and banged his head on the floor.

Standing aside to watch the show, Ackerman explained to Maggie, "I've always wanted to try this. You see cans like this are actually filled with a fluorocarbon which is a liquid under pressure that quickly turns into a gas at room temperature. If you turn the can upside down, the liquid is released instead of the compressed vapor. The liquid turns to gas which has a cooling effect, condensing water out of the air and freezing it. So essentially . . . I just flash froze Jerry's eyeballs. Does that satisfy your bloodlust, or do I need to cut his heart out and eat it too?"

He looked over at Maggie. She had her hand covering her mouth. Her eyes were wide as she watched Jerry thrash and scream.

Ackerman leaned in close to Maggie's ear and said, "Stop trying to be like me. Or Marcus. We're broken men trying to do the best we can with the cards we've been dealt. You can be better than us. You are better than us. I can't begin to imagine what your constant level of fear must be like. I sometimes forget that not everyone finds all this to be so . . . amusing. I'll try to be more conscious of that in the future. I'll work on that along with my communication skills. But remember this. You may not like it, but we're family now. And wolves protect their pack."

Then Ackerman calmly walked over to Jerry and grabbed the young man by the sides of his thrashing head. He squeezed until he was sure he had Jerry's attention, and then he leaned in and said, "And if your eye causes you to sin, gouge it out and throw it away. It's better to enter eternal life with only one eye than to have two eyes and be thrown into the fire of hell."

With a small smile on his face, Ackerman kissed Jerry on the forehead and added, "You're welcome."

A woman wearing sweatpants and an oversized REO Speedwagon T-shirt opened the door and said, "Someone best be dead."

Marcus held up his credentials and said, "Department of Justice, ma'am. And yes, a lot of people are dead."

"Oh dear, I'm so sorry. How can I help?"

"May we come in, ma'am?"

She introduced herself as Becky Takashima. Marcus knew Becky was fifty-two, but she looked good for her age. She had short blonde hair and a thin physique. The house was dated but had been top of the line to start with and had aged well. Marcus did notice, however, that the newest and most expensive items scattered around the room were speakers of various types and sizes. He supposed she was an audiophile.

Andrew made the introductions and explained the situation while Becky Takashima offered and poured them some much needed and appreciated coffee.

Marcus didn't see a ring on her finger or even an indentation or signs of one, but given her lack of any kind of Asian feature, he assumed Takashima to be a name taken from a former husband. He said, "Mrs. Takashima, do you know this man?" He showed her a picture on his phone of Bradley Reese. Then he swiped through several other photos, including one of Jerry Dunn.

"I don't know any of those men."

"Have you had any strange visitors or seen anyone odd snooping around lately? Anything unusual?"

"Nothing."

Marcus showed her the picture of Reese again. "You're sure you don't know this man?"

She looked hard, took her time, searched her memory. She was trying to be helpful. Marcus could read it all over her features.

She shook her head. "I'm sorry."

He said, "What about Foxbury Correctional? The prison? Any connections there?"

This time she nodded, happy to be able to contribute, and said, "My engineering firm handled part of the original feasibility study for Foxbury."

"Does that mean you have some kind of specialized knowledge of the prison?"

"I have the proposed blueprints with our suggested changes on my computer. And some of the maps and files related to Foxbury Mining Company."

Andrew said, "Back up a bit, why do you have the files at your house?"

"I work from home. But I assure you, my system is very secure."

Marcus said, "What were you saying about Foxbury Mining Company?"

"That was part of the study. A part of what we had to assess. Some of the mine shafts run relatively close to the site of the prison."

"I've been in that mine. It's quite a drive from the prison."

"Driving around the mountain to the mine's entrance, yes. But as the crow flies, or I suppose more as the mole digs, the mine and the prison are almost overlapping."

"Why wasn't the proposal rejected on those grounds? The mine being too close."

"It was just inside the gray area of the regulations. Actually, the only way it made it through the inspections was because the tunnels actually don't go under the prison itself, but run under the manufacturing facility. And the section that does is cut off from the rest of the mine."

Recalling the maps he had seen and the receipt for diving equipment, Marcus said, "Cut off because the tunnels are flooded."

"Yes, an expansion of the mine's middle section accidentally struck an underground tributary. A bunch of miners were cut off. It was a whole ordeal. It's what bankrupted the company and closed the mine."

Marcus said, "And you have detailed maps that show the mine and what tunnels are flooded and where all the tunnels are located in relation to Foxbury's manufacturing facility?"

"Yes."

"Can you show those to me, Becky? Please."

Becky stood up and said, "Of course. I have a big screen, and I can blow them up for you in my office."

"Great," Marcus said. "Go ahead and get the files pulled up and I'll be right behind you."

With a nod, she headed down the hall.

Andrew whispered, "You think this is where Judas got his files?"

"For a professional like our guy, her system here at her house isn't nearly secure enough. He probably learned about the study while gathering intel in the beginning. Then he traced it back here and found a path of least resistance."

"And the recent visits made here with Reese's car?"

"Judas was coming back to tie up loose ends. Why Judas used Reese's car and how that ties in? I don't know. But I do know that if Becky and her files are still here, then Judas slipped up. He wanted her dead, but something stopped him."

Andrew nodded. "Which means Judas doesn't want us to know what she knows. He doesn't want us to know their escape route."

"That's why they needed us out of the manufacturing facility so badly. Judas is going to sneak Lash out through the mine, literally right underneath our noses, and then Jerry Dunn or some other patsy holds us off in a stalemate for who knows how long."

Andrew pulled out his phone and said, "I'm going to have the sheriff meet us at the mine with a tactical team."

Marcus smiled. "My thoughts exactly. I'm going to take a look at Ms. Takashima's maps and plot us a course through the mine. And when Lash and whoever else hits those tunnels, we'll be waiting for them."

★ ★ ★

As Ackerman guided Jerry Dunn down the stairs from Powell's office, he was greeted with gasps. Spinelli was the first to ask, "What happened to him?"

Ackerman dropped Jerry onto the floor beside Winston, who was nursing a broken arm, and said, "See, I told you I was gentle with you."

Winston backed away from the husk that had been Jerry Dunn. Ackerman supposed that the little man did look pretty gruesome. The fluorocarbon spray had, of course, dispersed not merely into Jerry's eyes, but it had also flash frozen the skin surrounding his eyes, nose, and forehead. Essentially, that skin was now suffering from frostbite. It was red and swollen and cracked and bleeding. But the skin would heal. For the most part. Ackerman wasn't so sure about the eyes.

He didn't answer Spinelli's question, instead he asked her, "How are you coming along with retaking your virtual domain?"

"It's taking longer than I expected."

"Take as long as you like, but every moment extra is likely going to cost someone their life."

Spinelli's eyes started to fill with tears.

Ackerman added, "No pressure though; just making an observation."

Spinelli said, "I'm going straight to the source. I'm going to review the code on the server."

Ackerman nodded, and she headed for the hatch leading down to the server room.

Several minutes passed before Maggie limped down the stairs from Powell's office. Powell and one of the guards immediately ran over to help her. They sat her down and elevated her feet and checked her wounds. He walked over and said, "I'm going after Demon."

"Not without me," Maggie replied.

"Let's not do this the hard way. You're in no condition."

"I'm still in charge here. Now, first thing is first," she said. "How the hell did you beat the system?"

"A magician never tells."

Powell, who was feeling Maggie's ribs, said, "Try not to speak, darling. Besides, I can tell you how he did it."

Ackerman raised his eyebrows and said, "Please enlighten us. But be careful, Warden, I get jealous of people stealing my spotlight."

Powell didn't hesitate. He just frowned and said, "He ran the damn batteries out."

Ackerman said, "That is a gross oversimplification. I realized that the batteries on the restraints couldn't possibly hold enough power to cook someone like we had witnessed, so that could only be achieved in areas where there is a wireless electricity hub. And as Mr. Powell explained earlier, there is no hub in the control room. It reminds me of something Alexander the Great once—"

Maggie said, "So you shocked yourself until there was no juice left. And Jerry, who was otherwise engaged, was the one who should have been seeing the alerts you were triggering."

"That was later on. To start with, I hid the electrical discharges in the beatings from Winston."

"Good work," Maggie said. "Now, give me a second to get patched up and await further orders."

"That's it? Good work?"

"I'm sorry. I'm all out of cookies."

"I just thought that singlehandedly outsmarting the prison of the future here would warrant a little bit of—"

Powell said, "You didn't beat the prison. The only way that you were able to bypass the security was because these idiots were at the controls and you're in an area where residents aren't allowed."

Ackerman said, "I could have easily done the same thing with the prison in full swing. It would have simply taken more time to learn the ranges of the magnetic fields in the prison and run down the battery using the mild warnings that don't trigger alarms."

"There's a low power alert that would be triggered."

"Likely triggered at ten percent power. I would take the jolt of the last twenty-five percent all at once to be safe. Just like I did earlier when I overtook Winston and his comrades."

Maggie said, "Children. Please. It doesn't matter. Now, help me up."

She held out a hand, but Ackerman refused to take it. He said, "You're staying here. You would only slow me down and get yourself killed."

"I'm going, and there's nothing you can do to stop me."

Ackerman rolled his eyes. "How about this. Powell still has your .357 tucked into the back of his pants. I'm taking that with me because the assault rifle will slow me down. It's a concealed carry model with only five shots. I'd rather not waste one on you . . . "

"You're saying that you will take that gun and shoot me to keep me from following you."

"Yes, I would shoot you in the leg."

"You're bluffing."

"Maggie, I would think that you of all people would understand how absurd you sound right now. Me, bluffing."

"Excuse me!" yelled a deep voice from across the control room.

They all turned toward the man who had spoken. When he had everyone's attention, Winston continued, "You might as well not shoot each other. There's no point in going after Mr. Lash. He's already long gone."

Demon checked the time. His watch face morphed from digital numbers into tiny centipedes. He looked away for a second and back. Now, the time showed 12:00 a.m. But he knew that wasn't right. He usually didn't have to concentrate quite so hard to dispel the visions, but lack of sleep had always aggravated his condition. He looked away again. He closed his eyes. He looked at this watch. This time, it showed him the correct time of 7:04 a.m.

The plan, which he had helped Judas design, called for the floor of the old storage room on the far side of the manufacturing building to implode at 7:00 a.m. Not 7:30 a.m. or 7:05 a.m., but 7:00 a.m. sharp.

Judas was punctual and obsessive to a fault. There was no way he was late, which meant he was making a statement. Somehow Judas knew Demon was here waiting for him. The question was whether Judas was willing to sacrifice Lash and all the money he was paying their organization. Demon hoped his young apprentice wasn't that far gone. Maybe there was still a chance they could work things out.

An old woman's voice over his shoulder said, "Kill him. He betrayed us."

But Demon, or at least the majority of him, didn't share that sentiment and hoped for reconciliation. After a bloody and painful revenge and punishment was enacted of course.

It wasn't merely out of attachment that he wanted to forgive Judas. He also hated the thought of training another replacement. He had invested thousands of man-hours into his apprentice, and just as that investment was about to pay off, the little bastard went and fell in love.

That was, of course, something that Demon couldn't allow. So he had taken steps to remove the obstacle. But instead of sticking to the plan and offing Debra quietly, the kid went off on a tantrum. Hopefully, a spanking would be enough, and Demon could get back to his true life's work.

A shrill child's voice said, "You're weak and pathetic!"

Demon yawned and was about to check the time again. He figured that if Judas were trying to make him sweat, then the delayed blast would come on a time ending in a five or zero. 7:05. 7:10. 7:15. That was the way Judas's obsessive brain would set the timer.

Then, at what Demon guessed was 7:05 a.m., the floor made a thump and rumble and a four-foot-by-four-foot section fell away into the darkness.

"I thought your guy was always on time," Lash said.

"Don't worry, sir. You'll be sipping mai thais and plowing super models in a non-extradition country before the cock crows another time."

"For as much as the cause is paying for your services, I should expect nothing less."

"The ULF is more than getting its money's worth. And everything is going according to plan. As evidenced by the tunnel that just opened up in what was once touted as the prison of the future. The most secure, non-violent correctional facility ever built. And you wanted to break out of it without anyone knowing you were gone."

"I wouldn't exactly say things have gone according to plan. There weren't any federal agents in the plan. And, not that I'm not graced by the presence of the legendary Demon, but I thought you just brokered the deals and helped with planning. From what I hear, you never get your hands dirty anymore. Makes me ask what went wrong that brought you down into the trenches. Makes me wonder what you're not telling me."

"It's good to get out and stretch your legs now and again. You know, make new friends. See new places. Start a bloody prison revolt and slit some throats. It keeps me young and feisty to get my blood pumping once in a while."

Lash jammed a finger into Demon's chest and started to speak. He didn't finish a single word. Demon grabbed Lash by the wrist in a vice like grip and, with his other hand, he expertly dislocated the ULF leader's finger.

Lash screamed, and the other three men with him stopped what they were doing and raised their weapons.

Demon ignored the others and looked deep into Lash's eyes. "Business is all about respect and reputation. I built those two things in some of the darkest corners of the world. People respect someone who can get things done and provide exactly what they promise. We were contracted to get you to freedom. The contract made no promises about federal agents or time schedules. And it bloody well didn't say that I have to let you treat me like some common thug."

Demon popped Lash's finger back into place and said, "Now, I respect this whole Black Moses meets Osama Bin

Laden thing you have going, so why don't you stick to that. And I'll do what I do."

Lash cradled his hand and flared his nostrils. But after a moment, he gestured for his men to stand down. Lash said, "Get back to work on that rope."

His men eyed Demon cautiously but followed orders. Within a minute, they had secured a homemade rope fashioned from bed sheets and dropped it into the pit.

Demon walked to the edge of the hole. It traveled straight down for several hundred feet. They had commissioned a team from Chile to dig it out from the bottom up. It actually hadn't cost as much as he had thought. The only obstacle had been getting the equipment past the flooded tunnels. They had been forced to pay someone to disassemble and reassemble all of the equipment manually.

This job had been a nightmare from the start. If the ULF hadn't already been a loyal client, Demon would have turned it down at the onset.

Lash shined a light down the shaft. The Chilean team had set up metal rungs for them to climb down, but they, of course, couldn't reach all the way up because there had been several inches of concrete in place only a few moments prior, which necessitated the makeshift rope to reach the first rung.

Demon could see a faint light at the bottom of the shaft. He gestured toward the hole and said, "Freedom awaits, boys. I hope none of you are claustrophobic."

Maggie watched helplessly as Ackerman stormed over to Winston and jerked the big man up by the front of his prison-issued shirt. She pushed herself up onto her feet. Powell tried to stop her, but now wasn't the time to recover, now was the time to push through the pain and destroy yourself, if need be, to get the job done.

She hobbled over in time to hear Winston say, "I overheard Lash tell one of the other guys that they would be exiting Foxbury at 7:00 a.m sharp. The big clock up there says that it's 7:06 a.m. You don't even know how they're getting out. And even if you did, you could never run all the way down there, get past the crew holed up in the chow hall, and catch up to them. The odds on that would be next to nothing."

Ackerman said, "First of all, never tell me the odds. Second, why would you want to help us?"

Winston looked over at Jerry Dunn, who had been sedated and was currently passed out on the floor with his eyes and face in bandages. The big ULF enforcer said, "I don't want to have my soul sucked out through my eyeballs like CO Dunn over there. So I figured it wouldn't hurt to get on your good side."

Ackerman released Winston, looked over at Maggie, and grinned this self-righteous, know-it-all smile, as if he were trying to say how useful it was for him to be a scary wacko.

Maggie kept her disgust in check and said, "It's for the best that they're gone. The most important thing now is to establish contact with the outside and retake the prison. Then we can get the whole united law enforcement community to hunt down Lash."

"We're not far from the border."

"We're several hours away. Our best shot at catching

them now is to do the two things I just mentioned. It's not easy for me to admit it, but I need your help."

Ackerman looked at her a moment with those piercing, gray, cold, analytical eyes. She expected him to protest and make her feel small and threaten to shoot her again.

He said, "Okay, little sister, I'll back your play."

Maggie was dumbfounded a moment, but she said, "Good. Where do you think we should start? There's some kind of jamming in place. We could find that."

Ackerman shook his head. "I would focus on the computer system. In order to regain control, you'll need to convince Ms. Spinelli to quit playing for the other team."

"What does that mean?"

"Haven't you wondered how all of her coworkers were killed, but she survived?"

"You think Demon threatened her? Told her to work against us?"

"No, probably just ordered her not to help us."

She said, "Then why even leave her alive?"

"For the fun of it. For the pure joy of owning someone else's existence."

"So he threatened her?"

Ackerman shrugged. "Probably her and everyone she ever loved."

"Let me guess. That's what you would have done."

"Precisely."

"So she was told by the man who had just murdered all her friends that he would kill everyone she ever loved if she helped anyone restore control."

"Theoretically."

"It's going to be tough to convince her to go against Demon."

"Indubitably."

Maggie said, "Why are you talking like that?"

"I got bored with the conversation, so I started replying in all adverbs. Apologies. What are my orders, ma'am?"

With a couple of frustrated muscle spasms, Maggie kept herself from strangling him. Instead, she said, "I'm going to talk to Spinelli. You just stand right there and don't kill or maim anything until I get back."

She limped toward the back of the CCE and the hatch leading to the server room. She had to go convince someone that monsters and demons weren't real, even though she knew they were.

Demon was the last down the ladder. As soon as his feet touched the soft surface of the mine's floor, he realized another reason he hated fieldwork. He preferred surroundings that he knew and understood. Places where he knew what was real and what was a hallucination. He had forgotten how exhausting it was constantly trying to figure out if a scorpion was real or imagined in a place where they actually had scorpions.

The tunnel smelled of dirt and mold and diesel fuel. It was one of the mine's originals, not something drilled out by the Chileans. Lash and his three lackeys—Demon hadn't bothered to learn their names—stood nearby, shivering from the drop in temperature.

Demon pointed down the ten-by-ten tunnel and said, "Move toward the light."

The group started forward, heading in the direction of the faint light glowing in a tunnel somewhere ahead.

Bony hands reached out of the walls at Demon, but he ignored them.

After what he guessed was a couple hundred meters, they found the source of the glowing light and, with it, their exfiltration point.

The light was battery powered and mounted into the ceiling of what was once a four-way intersection of two tunnels. Now, the tunnel ahead of them sloped down into water, essentially changing the intersection into a T junction.

The sets of scuba gear hanging from the tunnel wall would rectify that. In typical Judas fashion, each wetsuit, mask, flippers, and tank combination was labeled with the associated person's name.

Although his handiwork was present, Judas himself was nowhere to be found.

But Demon saw another light burning down one of the non-flooded shafts. He said, "Get your wet suits and all your gear on, but do not turn on or breathe anything from your tanks until I get back."

Lash still seemed a bit angry from their earlier exchange. The ULF leader simply gave a grudging nod and started getting ready. His followers did what followers did best.

Demon set off down the northern branch of the T junction. The shaft was different from the one they had started in. It was wider with old railway tracks in its center.

He traveled for what felt like a few hundred meters before he reached the light, but this one was only a breadcrumb leading him toward another faint glow down a shaft heading off to the east.

There was a television mounted on the wall. The weather was on. The weatherman had the head of a brown bear. The bear weatherman said, "Chance of showers in the afternoon, but you won't be around to see that. You'll definitely be dead by then, you pathetic fool."

Demon ignored the television. He looked back in the direction he had come, toward Lash and a huge payday and then a return to his life's work. He had noticed an extra set of scuba gear. He could forget about facing down Judas and leave now.

But Demon didn't stop moving forward down the eastern tunnel, toward Judas. He would never stop. He was merely tired and letting his mind wander. He would never let Judas go and, to settle any internal discussion, the dark man stepped from the shadows and headed toward the beckoning light.

Demon followed and eventually came to a large open space or, at least, it was large compared to the tight confines of the mine shafts. The tracks ended in the middle of the room and joined a spinning contraption he guessed was designed to load and unload carts and easily turn them around in the proper direction.

The room wasn't the size of a cathedral, but it was cathedral shaped, and it seemed set apart from the rest of the mine. A sanctuary of sorts.

The old mechanism for rotating the carts had been retrofitted by Judas. Now, the hand crank had been replaced by a whirring motor that was perpetually turning the entire plate and would continue to do so until its fuel source depleted or he walked over and smashed it to bits. Some of the Legion liked that idea—they hooted and howled, but he resisted the urge toward destruction.

In the center of the constantly rotating turnstile sat a small, black table with a large computer monitor resting on its surface. The screen's background was black. The lettering was a flowery script, like it was an invitation to a ball. The message read, "Please take your seat, and the show will begin . . . "

It was at that moment that Demon fully decided on showing Judas no mercy and committed himself to the idea of his apprentice's death. Judas always did have a flair for the dramatic, but this little game had gone far enough.

He was The Demon. He refused to be relegated to a player of any kind in some underling's nervous breakdown.

Plus, Judas knew he didn't like it when things spun. It aggravated his schizophrenia.

He considered kicking over the chair and smashing the monitor to bits. The Legion urged him on. But the dark man stood behind the chair, waiting for him to sit.

As soon as his weight hit the chair's surface, the computer screen came to life and showed the smiling face of his apprentice, a man who had been going by the name of Bradley Reese. Demon couldn't even remember the man's birth name. He only knew him as The Judas.

Maggie found Spinelli staring at a computer terminal and crying. The terminal was mounted to the side of one of three enormous towers of whirring hard drives and processor fans. The floors of the server room were stainless steel. The towers were water cooled and lit with blue LED lights. The whole room made Maggie feel like she was stepping into Tron.

Spinelli didn't notice her approach.

Maggie asked, "How's it going?"

Spinelli jumped and wiped her eyes and said, "What? Excellent. It's going great. I just need to write a recursive algorithm that will—"

"Why are you stalling?"

"I'm not. I don't know what you mean."

"They died and you lived. How is that?"

"I hid."

"You're hiding consisted of talking to yourself. Demon found you. What did he do to you?"

"Nothing. I mean I don't know. What you're saying isn't true. I'm working as fast as I can."

"You're the only person who can restore control of this facility without violence and bloodshed."

Spinelli teared up a little, but she said, "No pressure. Can I get back to work now?"

Maggie stepped up to Spinelli's terminal. It folded down from the tower at standing height but looked adjustable. The whirring and clicking of computer components grew louder. She smelled melting plastic and rushing water. She said, "Go ahead. I'm just going to tell you a story while you work."

"That sounds distracting."

"I think it will help."

Spinelli looked around as if she didn't know what else to do, and then she stepped up to the laptop-style terminal and recommenced her typing.

Maggie said, "I never tell this story to anyone, but I told part of it to Agent William's son, so I guess the floodgates are open now. And you know what, I think maybe I should tell this story more often. It's about a boy and a girl. A little brother and an older sister. And the girl is told to babysit her little brother, but she's really not old enough, but hey, Mom was just inside, folding clothes and watching her programs. Anyway, all those details aren't important for you. What is important is that a monster crept up from the shadows, took the little brother, and told her to be quiet about it with a simple gesture. The point of the story for you is that this little girl followed his instructions and has regretted it for the rest of her life. I've often wondered why he didn't just kill me. Why risk me running inside or screaming? Believe me, I had the lung capacity. But he didn't do that because now he owns me. And it's not a good feeling, is it?"

Spinelli started nodding her head and that turned to weeping. Maggie hugged her for a few seconds and then asked, "What did he tell you?"

"He told me that he would let me live if I followed his instructions."

"What instructions? What did he have you do?"

"That's just it. He didn't want me to do anything. At least, not before 7:30 a.m."

"What happens at 7:30 a.m.?"

"Nothing that I know of. I just assumed it was because that would give him enough time to escape."

"Back up. So he told you not to do anything to help get the system back under proper control until after 7:30 a.m.?"

"Pretty much."

Maggie thought about that specific time. Maybe it was just a precaution of a half-hour buffer for their escape, as Spinelli had assumed, but then why not 8:00 a.m. or 10:00 a.m. Why only a half hour?

"We can't wait until 7:30 a.m., Lisa."

"I have to. The things he told me . . . " Spinelli started to cry again. "He knew my grandmother's name. He knew where she lived. How could he know that?"

Maggie thought for a moment, choosing her words carefully, and said, "Your brother. This group probably blackmailed and made that same threat to your brother. Maybe that's really why he sold out. Maybe they made him an offer he couldn't refuse. If that were the case, it would explain how Demon knew your grandmother's name and address. They have a file on your brother and you."

Spinelli blinked several times in quick succession. "A group of psychos for hire having a file on me doesn't exactly make me feel better. I think I would have rather believed he was psychic."

"Sorry. I just meant that we call them monsters, but they're really just men. Broken, disturbed, and frightening men, but flesh and blood. They don't have any supernatural powers or hold over us."

"I don't know about Demon. He's—"

"Just a man. And we can protect you from him," Maggie said. "But let me play out that original story a little farther. So that girl grows up and starts trying to find the man who stole her brother. The papers have called him The Taker. Every year on the anniversary of the abduction, the families of each of his victims receive a package from him containing a piece of clothing or jewelry or small piece cut from a shoelace. Something from the clothes they were wearing at the moment of the taking. Some of the families received hair. But anyway, the girl works with all the families. A lot of families. A lot of victims. And she convinces all of them to send what they receive on the anniversary to her."

"Why did you do that? I mean, why did she do that?"

"Because I wanted to analyze every clue. Because I was going to catch the Taker."

Spinelli said, "Why are you speaking in the past tense? It sounds like you've given up."

"Honestly, I don't think I'll ever catch him. I used to really believe that I would, but now I'm not so sure. I'll get a new package in the mail next week."

"I'm sorry about your brother."

"Next week's package isn't something of my brother's. It's actually from the family of a little girl. Her name was Elizabeth."

"How often do you get things like that?"

"Too often. I have the dates all marked on my calendar. The point is, Lisa, that he owns me. Even after all these years. No matter how many monsters I catch. He owns me. I did what he said. I followed orders. But I didn't survive because of it. I lost my life that day because I surrendered to my fear. I'm still losing. I'm not free, and I won't be free until he's in a cage or in the ground. And it will be no different for you. I wish I could take this experience back for you, but I can't. It's done. As long as he's out there, he'll have power over you. The sooner we get this security system running, the better chance you have of stopping him and regaining your freedom. You don't want to end up like me."

Spinelli pulled out a handkerchief, wiped away the tears, and blew her nose. Then the young woman stuffed it back into her pocket. The whole experience nearly made Maggie vomit. First of all, she didn't know that people still carried handkerchiefs. And second, the germs. The nose, the face, the pocket. Now, when she looked at Spinelli, she would forever see one of the Garbage Pail Kids, which, for Maggie, was akin to her darkest nightmares.

Spinelli said, "You're right. Thank you."

Then Spinelli reached out for a hug. Maggie tried to ask if they could just fist bump, but she wasn't quick enough. Garbage Pail Lisa wrapped her in a warm embrace and said, "I have some work to do."

Maggie smiled back and said, "Let me know if you need anything." But really all she could think about was a bottle of Germ-X she had spotted up in the control room.

She left Spinelli to her work and climbed the ladder up to the CCE. As she came through the hatchway, she was surprised to see Ackerman sitting cross-legged right beside the hatch's exit.

She jumped and then said, "What are you doing?"

As she climbed the rest of the way into the control room, Ackerman stood up and said, "Eavesdropping."

"Please note that normal people think that eavesdropping is weird and creepy."

"Normal people rely on eavesdropping for the really juicy gossip. I was doing it because I'm watching out for you."

"Don't."

She started to walk away, but he said, "I want to help you find the Taker."

"I don't want or need your help."

"I think you actually believe the first one of those. But the second. You know better. Let me help you. When we get back, show me the case files, and the items he's sent to the victims. Everything you have."

After several seconds, Maggie said, "Okay."

Ackerman said, "But I have one stipulation."

She rolled her eyes. "Of course you do."

"When we find him, and we will find him, I will not kill him for you. No matter what happens, his fate will be in your hands."

She would never have admitted it, but Maggie felt more alive and awake after hearing those words than she had felt in months.

His fate will be in your hands.

She said, "That sounds good to me."

The world was spinning, Judas was smiling, and the dark man was waiting and watching. Demon used every bit of self-control he possessed to keep himself from smashing the computer screen to pieces.

Judas said, "I regret to inform you, old friend, that I will not be in attendance today. I won't be joining you ever again actually because, by the time you watch this video, I'll be dead."

Demon clenched half the muscles in his body and dug his fingernails into the arms of the chair.

"That's right, Demon, not only did I rob you of your

retribution against me, but I did it in such a way that has exposed you and will lead to the downfall of you and your whole organization."

The world spun around Demon, in more ways than one. The computer screen was his anchor point, but figures from his past kept reaching for him out of the swirling darkness. The priest from the orphanage. The head guard from his first juvenile detention center. A man whose face he had cut off in a Glasgow back alley.

But those were just distractions. Demon remained focused on the real ghost right in front of him.

Judas said, "Let me begin with what you do know. You helped me write an approved script for this little production, and I've strayed from it. Calling in federal agents. Escalating things. But that's not really why you came out of your hole. You came out because you knew that betraying me was a mistake."

Demon gritted his teeth. The cathedral storage room around him had grown to the size of an actual cathedral. And it was on fire.

Demon ignored the flames.

Judas said, "Here's what you don't know. Let's start with the obvious one that I just revealed. That's right, old friend, I know that it was by your order that photo was taken."

Marcus was the first to walk up the slope of the flooded tunnel and secure their position. He tossed a small oxygen bottle and mask combination onto the ground. The small amount of oxygen was all they needed to cross through the flooded section of this shaft, and there were other shafts that could be crossed by free swimming without oxygen. Which made it all the more peculiar that Judas had rented full tanks and wet suits.

The others were right behind him. Andrew, Sheriff Hall, and five members of an FBI tactical team out of Las Vegas who had just arrived. They covered the tunnels and readied their gear and, as they did so, Marcus had his first real opportunity to digest the new information Stan had sent just as they'd arrived at the mine.

The text message had read, *Was able to restore Debra's phone. Looking through it now, but I already found this photo. It was sent from Debra Costello's phone to a close friend of hers from church, Renata Navarro. Her message with the photo read, "Look at the little problem I've been dealing with."*

Standing in the cold tunnel, which smelled to him like an open grave, Marcus recalled the photo from memory. It showed a man from the chest down getting out of the shower. The man's pubic region was in full display. He was semi-erect. His face wasn't shown. He didn't appear to be aware he was being photographed. The image was probably similar to a million others available on the Internet. It had taken Marcus a moment to place what was different. Then he saw it. The man in the picture had no testicles.

When Marcus had originally viewed the photo, things instantly clicked into place. It answered a few outstanding questions. The photo was how Debra had betrayed her lover. It also explained why the Navarro's had been targeted. A simple photo, probably snapped from a cell phone, had cost Debra Costello and several other people their lives.

To all that, Marcus had texted back: *K. Get in touch with the ME's office and have them check Bradley Reese's body to see if his testicles have been removed.*

A few seconds later, as he had been coordinating with the tactical unit, his phone had vibrated with another message from Stan: *Something strange. The meta data shows the photo was taken with a model of hidden camera, not a cell phone.*

Marcus didn't hear confirmation on Reese's anatomy before entering the mine and still hadn't decided what to think of the photo being taken with a hidden camera, and unfortunately, now wasn't the time to figure it out.

Once the members of the FBI's Hostage Rescue Team were ready, they led the way down the tunnel. Their destination was clear: a faint light to the north of their position.

It only took a moment for the team to converge on their objective. Marcus had instructed them to tread quietly, and so the team held back when they reached the lighted section.

Around the corner, Marcus saw men in full scuba gear. Leonard Lash and his three ULF lieutenants and bodyguards. Lash was already half submerged into the water of the flooded tunnel.

Marcus gave a nod to the team leader and placed his finger to his lips. The commander gave a nod of understanding in return, and the five members of the FBI team melted out of the shadows. The three lieutenants were just standing in a row and easily accessible. The tactical team subdued them without a sound.

But Lash was actually in a good position in the water. He had full view of the tunnel and one foot out the door.

As soon as he saw his comrades fall, Lash dove under and made a break for it.

Marcus ran forward. He knew that the mine was surrounded, but he didn't want to take any chances. And the place was a warren of tunnels with lots of places to hide.

But the FBI team leader beat Marcus to the escaping inmate, and he only arrived in time to help pull Lash, face covered by a full deep-diving face mask, out of the freezing-cold water.

The ULF leader fought them every step of the way. He thrashed and kicked with all his extremities.

Marcus and the FBI agent threw Lash back up into the tunnel where the others were waiting to help.

But Lash kept convulsing even after they had released his arms.

He fell to the ground writhing and clawed off his face mask. He gasped for breath as he continued to shake. He foamed at the mouth. His eyes were wide and afraid. Marcus smelled the stench as the leader of one of the world's most powerful gangs evacuated his bowels and died in fear, writhing in the mud.

Judas said, "I could forgive you for a lot of things, old friend, but not for this. What you did cannot be forgiven."

The fire raged around them inside the cathedral. Flames licked the stained glass. The saints depicted on the glass came to life, reached for the sky, and screamed as they burned.

Judas said, "You tricked me into savagely killing the woman I loved. I'm not like you, Demon. I never was. I didn't object to murder if it was necessary for a job, but I never loved the killing. At least, not in the way you do. I could have walked away from all that. But I didn't plan on it. I was planning to tell Debra the truth and then convince her to come away with me while I continued to work for you."

The screen seemed to dissolve into darkness, leaving only the torso of his former apprentice hanging on a black background. Then the figure morphed into a person sitting across from him at the table.

Demon said, "I don't want men working for me who want to walk away."

"I assume you saw the money I was stashing. Maybe that was enough, or maybe you also caught me stealing all of your files as an insurance policy against you. But instead of confronting me about it, you decided to sabotage my relationship. You put in a hidden camera at Deb's father's cabin before a weekend we were going up there. Then you created a photo that looked like it was taken in a mirror from a cell phone. From there, you made it look like she had photographed me in order to make fun of me with her bitch friend. But you're an artist and you've taught me so much. You knew my sensitivities. You knew exactly how to push my buttons. You knew what would happen next."

The fire continued to rage inside the cathedral. Pieces of the structure collapsed, and burning debris fell to the ground. And below that, Demon's world continued to spin on the turnstile.

He said, "That's right, boy. I know you all too well."

"So I did as you knew I would. I killed her. And in the

442

moment when I ended her, I loved killing again. She had betrayed me, and I so enjoyed making her pay for that. Except that, later on, I noticed the angle of the picture. I had taken Deb's body up to the cabin to stage a scene for the police, and I went in to use the head, so I checked. And there hidden among some fake flowers was a small hidden camera. And that's when my world came crashing down. Deb hadn't betrayed me. The betrayal was from you."

"You betrayed me first by giving your allegiance to that bitch over me."

Judas continued, "Here's something else you don't know. You know that I murdered my father, but I never told you the full story. After Father mutilated me and murdered the love of my life, I let him live for months. Not out of necessity or to prolong his suffering in some way. I waited out of kindness. Because the premiere of his masterpiece was just around the corner. He would die, but I didn't want to rob him of his dream. That night, the production was an overwhelming success. He had a wonderful party afterward, by his standards anyway. He even sprang for the more expensive prostitute. I smothered him in his sleep. I let him go out on top. That's more than he deserved. But he was all I had ever known. He was my father, and I suppose I owed him that much for saving me from being abandoned in a Moscow dumpster by my shlyukha mother at birth."

The cathedral continued to collapse and burn, and then the stained glass windows exploded soundlessly in slow motion.

Demon ignored it all.

"And who doesn't want to go out on top? You see, that's

what I'm going to do. All this has been of my design. When I discovered the camera, I knew that I would crush you and kill myself in a way that would be talked about and studied by generations to come. I will be forever remembered. And you. My teacher. My friend. My adopted father. You will be erased. I've made my last production such a public spectacle that it can't be glossed over. That's important, because here's something else you don't know . . . "

Judas paused for dramatic effect. Demon hated when the boy did that.

The roof of the cathedral flew away as if devoured by a tornado, and rain fell in torrents and extinguished the flames.

Judas said, "You see, old friend, Deb's father wasn't always in the correctional industry. We knew he was in law enforcement but, in truth, I discovered some files that Powell had kept as an insurance policy against a man named Philip—it's actually what gave me the idea to do the same thing against you—but those files revealed that Powell had once been a member of a group called the Shepherd Organization."

The rain turned to blood.

Demon had heard rumblings of a group by that name.

Judas said, "These shepherds are tasked with hunting the country's worst murderers by any means necessary. They're an elite group with resources and connections and, in Powell's files anyway, they seldom take their suspects alive. These men will hunt you from the shadows. They'll topple all you've built, and if they can they'll remove you from existence. And I've led them straight to you. I would suspect that they're surrounding the mine at this very moment. Or if these shepherds are as good as the files made them seem, then they may already be inside this room."

Demon's gaze traveled around the spinning room. He saw a lot of things moving, but he had no idea what was real.

Judas laughed. "Maybe not. In any case, they will hunt you and destroy you. I'm going to provide them with files on you and your entire network. And I've done all this when I've been dead for hours. You can't get your retribution and satisfy your laws or torture me to find out what I've done with your files. You are completely helpless and at my mercy. And, just as you taught me, there will be no mercy. I betrayed you to your enemies, to your greatest nightmare, and I've outsmarted them all with a body count that could rival anyone. I'm the greatest ever. I—"

This time, Demon couldn't contain himself. With a bellow of rage, he reached for Judas's neck. He found the front of a computer screen instead. He grabbed it by the edges and smashed it against the storage room wall.

The cathedral had faded back into his mind.

He overturned the table and smashed the wooden chair to bits. Then he stood atop the turnstile, panting and literally seeing and tasting red.

He stepped off the spinning table and, once his feet were back on solid ground, he was better able to filter out the hallucinations and know what was real.

Unfortunately, the men with the assault rifles were indeed real.

The man in the center of the group, a man aiming a large, black shotgun at Demon's chest, said, "Keep your hands up and no sudden movements. And just so you know, those shepherds that your friend was talking about . . . We are that good."

After securing the escaping prisoners, Marcus and the tactical team received some unexpected news. Apparently, the other half of their team, the one trapped inside the prison, had secured Jerry Dunn and the control room. Spinelli had opened lines of communication and expected to have the system fully restarted at any moment. The full tactical team was preparing to take the prison and massing in the manufacturing facility.

Andrew had asked, "What do we do with Lash's body?"

Marcus took one look at the dead ULF leader and said, "We'll send someone for him, eventually."

Then the group of eight led their four living prisoners up the makeshift metal ladder and back into the manufacturing facility.

But as they led Demon past Lash's body, Marcus noticed that the killer seemed genuinely surprised that the air tanks had been poisoned.

Once up top, the FBI took their prisoners into custody, and Sheriff Hall and the tactical teams went to work on the planning and preparations for a final push to retake the prison.

Marcus stepped away from the group, and Andrew followed. Marcus said, "Something's not right."

"Too easy? Cause I didn't think it was all that easy. It's been a pretty rough case in my book."

"A few things aren't adding up."

"Like what?"

"In the video, Judas claimed his death total would rival anyone."

Andrew said, "He's up to what now, that we know for sure? Debra, the shooting victims, Ray Navarro, anyone killed inside Foxbury, Lash . . . "

"But most of them weren't by his hand."

"But they were by his design. Plus, he could be referring to killings that took place long before any of this started."

Marcus nodded. "You could be right. But what about Lash and the others? Those tanks or masks, or both, knowing our guy, were laced with some kind of poison."

"Yeah, like he's reaching out from beyond the grave and still killing."

Marcus rubbed at his cross tattoo and whispered, "What if he doesn't want anyone to get out alive? This isn't over. He wants a bigger body count, and I know how he's going to get it."

Ackerman tried to stay busy while Spinelli worked. He had secured the elevator, established and rigged Powell's office as a fallback point, and double-checked the restraints on the prisoners. He was glad when Spinelli finally established communication with the outside world and discovered that Marcus had Demon and the others in custody.

But he was extremely disappointed that he had missed all the fun.

Maggie had really stepped up and was helping to organize and plan the final retaking of the prison. She had Valdas and the Director on a video call on the big screen. Apparently, Spinelli had been able to bypass the frequency jamming by communicating through a hard-wired internet connection.

Ackerman had stepped aside to observe.

There was a large clock on the wall. The kind of white-faced, clearly numbered old clock that hung in prisons and schools across the country. It showed the time as 7:29 a.m. And that made Ackerman think of something Spinelli had said.

He didn't want me to do anything. At least, not before 7:30 a.m.

That had seemed strange to him at the time. Why 7:30 a.m.?

And then another memory came back.

Maggie said, "Why does it matter how they're charged?"

"Because if I had full control and my fingers on the switches," Ackerman said. "And I essentially possessed the power of Zeus within these walls, I know exactly what I would do."

If the old Ackerman had had the same opportunity as Judas, the chance to fry hundreds of people, hostage and hostage-taker alike, with one press of a switch, he would have had just one question: Where's the button?

Ackerman knew then that Judas and Demon weren't done killing. They didn't want a standoff. They wanted to burn it all down and crawl out of the ashes.

He started forward to warn Maggie, but then he stopped when he realized that there wasn't a charging station in the CCE, and so no one here would be killed, merely shocked until their batteries were drained. That was a relief. He had been worried about his little sister for a moment.

Then his brother ran into the room on the other end of

the big display, demanding to speak with Maggie. Marcus came onto the screen and said, "Maggie, he's planning to send out a system wide kill order."

She shook her head. "What? Who?"

"Judas. Bradley Reese. I'm betting that literally any second, a Trojan horse in the code, a fail-safe, will—"

Maggie started shaking and fell to the floor. Her bracelets and anklets had been activated.

Marcus screamed her name.

Ackerman looked around the room at all the other people being electrocuted, which would also include Ms. Spinelli in the room below them.

He stepped forward and placed his shoe on Maggie's chest to keep her from harming herself. He said to Marcus, "Don't worry. There's not a charging station here in the control room. None of the people in this room should die. Except maybe Powell with the whole bee sting thing."

Marcus screamed, "Most of the hostages are being held in the chow hall, which I'm sure does have a charging station."

"Yes, it does."

"So they will die."

"Yes, I suppose so."

"Anything we can do to save them? As in, right now!"

Ackerman considered that. He saw one of the assault rifles lying across the workstation. With a smile, he said, "Back in a sec," and snatched up the rifle.

He ran for the server room hatch, slid the last few feet, and swung himself down through the opening in the floor into the small server area.

Once his feet hit the metal, Ackerman released every ounce of rage he had been suppressing.

He raised the M4A1 and emptied a clip into the first tower. He replaced the mag, slammed a new one in place, and emptied that into the second tower.

With no more magazines, he went to work on the last tower the old fashioned way. He used the assault rifle as a club, and then he used his hands. He smashed and kicked and pulled at every wire he could find. He practiced his Silat moves on the towers, ignoring the pain in his fists, knees, feet, and elbows from striking the metal of the servers and their housings.

When it was done, he stood there, panting and bleeding, and surveyed his handiwork. It looked like someone had smeared the servers with peanut butter and locked a grizzly bear in the room.

But Ackerman knew that it had worked because Spinelli had stopped shaking and was now staring up at him from the floor.

She said, "You could have just unplugged them."

Ackerman said, "Darling, you don't send me when you want something unplugged. You send me when you want it dead." He smiled and gave her a wink. "And that was a hell of a lot more fun."

It was nearly another twenty hours before any of them slept. The medical examiner had confirmed what Marcus already knew. The body in the morgue lacked testicles and was indeed the remains of Bradley Reese or Dmitry Zolotov or Judas or whatever the man called himself. Marcus had then remembered that Reese gave them his computer to use. That had to be checked out and analyzed. Then he had the idea to check the cabin where the picture was taken. He also wanted to get someone pursuing the corporate angle. Plus, they had to retake the damn prison, which didn't prove to be much of a challenge after Winston told them that the remaining ULF members had been told to surrender if the tactical teams came in.

It had been a good day that had felt strange to Marcus because someone's life wasn't on the line every second. Unfortunately, things would return to normal for him, but he had enjoyed the brief respite. A little vacation from staring at crime scene photos and seeing the victim's eyes and knowing that the man he was hunting could kill again at any moment, leaving him staring at more pictures and more bodies of more victims.

He kind of enjoyed hunting a few bad guys who committed crimes for rational, comprehensible motives, like money.

But that wasn't his job. His job was to stop broken people with distorted views of the world by seeing the world through their demented perspectives. And if he didn't do it quickly enough, some living, breathing person with goals and dreams and loved ones would be savagely torn from this world.

He knew some guys were able to compartmentalize all that, and he was trying his best to be like them, but the weight of it all took its toll.

He didn't get to see Dylan that day, and Marcus had fallen into bed feeling like a poor excuse for a father and his own worst enemy.

When he woke up the next morning, he looked for the

hotel alarm clock, but it wasn't glowing beside him on the nightstand. He turned on the lights and found that the clock had been removed completely.

They had a decent-sized suite at a Hyatt near the airport. The space on the other side of his room's door was an open communal area with a full kitchen, dining room, living room, and game room.

From the sounds coming through the door, they were all getting some use.

He pushed himself out of bed. He had kicked off his shoes the night before, but beyond that he was still wearing all the clothes he had on the previous day.

He opened the door and was first greeted by the smell of bacon and eggs. And second by a little boy in swimming trunks, still dripping onto the carpet.

Dylan walked over. He didn't run and dive into his father's arms. He walked over and put his arms around his dad's waist and said, "Will you take me to the airplane museum? Grandpa Will won't take me because he's scared to fly."

The whole comment caught Marcus off guard, and he started chuckling.

Grandpa Will stood beside the pool table, a pool cue still in his hand. Will was in his sixties and had shaggy brown hair that had started sliding up his forehead. He wore an old but now-retro button-down shirt, and a greasy red baseball cap with a Chevrolet emblem on its front.

Grandpa Will said, "You weren't supposed to tell anyone that, kid."

That made Marcus laugh even harder.

He shook Will's hand. He hadn't seen Claire's father in

years, and the awkwardness would have been even greater considering that Maggie had dropped Dylan off with Will and then basically disappeared. Luckily, Dylan had helped defuse that tension.

Maggie was at the stove, which was frightening. She gave him a wink and said, "I told the Director we'd be working from here today. And breakfast is almost ready."

He kissed her on the cheek and whispered, "I love you. And not just because you're cooking bacon."

She looked at him roguishly and said, "I know."

"Careful. You know it makes me hot when you quote the classics."

Dylan said, "Dad, did you see who else is here? They let him out of his box."

The boy then pointed across the room to where Andrew and Francis Ackerman Jr. stood in front of the team's digital OLED display board.

Marcus walked over and said, "Who let you out? I thought the Director was sending you back to your cage."

Ackerman shrugged. "He's getting soft in his old age."

Andrew added, "I talked him into it."

Marcus nodded and squeezed Andrew's shoulder. "You're so much better at that than me."

"The key is not getting angry and throwing things."

"I'll try that next time," Marcus said. "What are you boys talking about?"

Ackerman said, "We were just discussing Judas's files."

"What about them?"

"Where to find them."

"I thought Spinelli found an encrypted folder on Reese's laptop. I figured the files would be there."

"Some of them," Andrew said. "Stan broke the encryption, but it only contains some of Judas's journals. From what I've read so far, the journals do discuss other killers associated with Demon's group. Including one in particular whom we think may have the detailed files. The journals call him the Gladiator."

Marcus said, "Any clues as to how we find the Gladiator?"

"Nothing . . . yet."

Marcus nodded. "We need those files."

Ackerman said, "Obviously. But you should consider something else. This isn't a normal case or a normal killer. Taking on something like this requires more than just dedication and solid detective work. Taking on the Demon will require an obsession. One that will tear you away from everything you love. And I have a bad feeling about all this."

"We already have Demon. Now, we just need to use him to take down his friends."

"Please. A man with the resources, money, and intelligence of Demon's level won't remain in custody for long. And he's the kind of beast that lets you think you're hunting it, when really it's hunting you. He won't hesitate to kill any of us. Including your son."

Marcus looked across the room at Dylan laughing and playing pool with Grandpa Will. Maggie had started whistling at the stove. She looked like she knew what she was doing, but he knew from experience that those eggs would wind up being Cajun style and smothered in salsa or ketchup to mask the taste.

He had a beautiful family. A group of loved ones much like the countless other families that Demon and his friends had torn apart. And someone had to step up and put an end to it.

"Cases like this are why the SO was created. It's our job but, more than that, it's who we are. All of us."

Marcus leaned in close to his big brother and added, "When you look around this room at these people, that feeling of happiness and contentment that you feel . . . That's born out of love. And when you imagine losing all of us . . . That's fear."

Ackerman's head slowly tilted back, and his eyes shifted around the room from person to person. He whispered, "Fascinating," and then, after a moment's hesitation, he added, "If two people are lost in the woods and come across a grizzly bear, and it chases them. Those people only have a few options. They could try to climb a tree, which is not a good idea. Play dead. Try to startle the bear somehow. Or they could run as fast as they can. After all, one would just have to be faster than the other person. Most people would fall into this group. They would run and consider themselves lucky for having made it out with their lives. And then there are some of us out there who would help nature along and trip that other person up a bit, ensuring our own survival. But you, brother, you would turn to face the bear and fight it to the death in order to save your companion. That's who you are."

"You saying I need to eat the bear or the bear's going to eat me?"

"I'm saying that I'm glad that there are crazy people like you in the world."

"Thanks, I guess. And what about you? Which group are you in now?"

"By nature, I would trip the other person. No hesitation. But not to save myself. Simply because it would be fascinating to watch such a gorgeous predator in action. Although, I'm doing my best to stand beside you and fight the bear."

Ackerman then theatrically waved his arm toward the display board covered with photos of people and clues. He smiled and said, "So, if we're all in agreement . . . let's go hunting."

```
FILE #750265-6727-097
Zolotov, Dmitry - AKA The Judas Killer
State Exhibit F
Description: Diary Entry (Final Entry)
```

It's strange to think that through this diary you—dear reader, dear future historian—are studying my words, experiencing my feelings, and learning of my innermost thoughts even while I am long dead. There's a kind of immortality in that, isn't there. Especially in this digital age when no good ideas or heinous sins are ever forgotten or lost to history. Every post. Every tweet. Every selfie. Our grandchildren's grandchildren will go back and study those words and images someday.

Maybe as a school project or a hobby.

In this age of 1s and 0s, all that we are is remembered in the digital signature we have left behind. It's something that has never before been possible in recorded history.

Digital files don't fall to ruin or rot away. They will be accessible in some form forever. Well, at least until our entire modern society falls into ruin itself and all that remains of us is legend and myth and the cycle begins anew. Or someone in the future decides that your life or the lives of your entire bloodline aren't meaningful enough for anyone to care and drops the entire record of your existence into some virtual trash can.

Barring either of those, future generations will be able to piece together our lives based on what we have left behind digitally, and for anyone between the ages of 0 and 50, you've left a record of almost your entire life behind. And for those of you who have been born within the past ten years . . . someday your ancestors will be able to go back and experience your birth, your first steps, your first day of school, your first everything, and they'll be there with you from that first breath up until the moment you die. Every report card. Every bad decision. Every good game. Every moment of brilliance. It's all there, accessible forever if one knows where to look.

Your entire story is being told by you to every generation to come.

Make sure you tell a good one.

ACKNOWLEDGMENTS

First of all, I wish to thank my amazing, awesome, loving God for all of the incredible blessings he has bestowed upon me and for giving me the chance to follow my dreams (and hopefully, honoring Him while doing so).

Second, I want to thank my beautiful, patient, hard-working, devoted, and compassionate wife—Gina—and my children—James, Madison, and Calissa—for their love and support.

And, as always, none of this would be possible without my wonderful agents, Danny Baror and Heather Baror-Shapiro, and my mentor and great friend, Lou Aronica. In addition, I wouldn't be here without the guidance and friendship of all my fellow authors at the International Thriller Writers organization.

A lot of research went into this book, which would not have been possible without the help of Warden Cecil Polly, Stacey Kidd, and my wonderfully talented assistant, Allison Maretti.

Last but certainly not least, without my wonderful group of readers and fans, I'm nothing more than a guy clicking keys and writing about my imaginary friends. But when we share a story, something magical happens. A new world is born. A world that we can both share and enjoy filled with people we can love, hate, laugh with, cry with, and care about. Thank you so much to all of you out there sharing the magic with me, especially the impressive group who have joined my mailing list and Story Army to help make my work even better! I love all of you and consider you to be part of my extended Ethan Cross family.

And remember... Be Blessed, Not Stressed ;-)

ABOUT THE AUTHOR

ETHAN CROSS's Ackerman thrillers are international bestsellers. Before becoming a full time writer, he was a computer programmer, a Chief Technology Officer and a Marketing Director for a New York publisher. He lives in Illinois with his wife, three kids, and two Shih Tzus.

@EthanCrossBooks www.ethancross.com

MOST PEOPLE HATE ME.
BUT EVERYONE REMEMBERS ME.

Read the next Ackerman thriller from
Ethan Cross, conjuring one of the most
compelling cop versus killer confrontations
in the pages of crime and thriller fiction.

1

Francis Ackerman Jr. had lost track of the number of lives he had taken and the level of destruction he had wrought. He barely remembered much of those dark years. They were merely a blur of blood and pain. If a man truly reaped what he sowed, Ackerman knew the kind of harvest he deserved. Still, he couldn't make himself worry about consequences or fear judgment. He had stared into the darkness on numerous occasions and imagined the smell of brimstone and the sound of weeping and gnashing of teeth. But he couldn't harness the proper emotional and physical response. Fear remained as elusive to him as sight to a man whose eyes had been carved from his head.

Ackerman hadn't been born blind to fear and addicted to pain. His own father had subjected him to every form of torture imaginable and forced him to experience traumatic events from the lives of the most notorious killers in the world. When that wasn't enough, his father surgically ravaged the portions of his brain which controlled the response to fear and the fight or flight instincts.

Despite those inherent setbacks, Ackerman was proud of what he'd accomplished so far. He had found his way back to his younger brother and, through Marcus, had gained a family. Since then, he had saved several lives and, by his count, aided in the capture of eight serial murderers. And the biggest catch yet—a man they knew only as Demon who ran a network of sadistic killers for hire—was scheduled for transfer from Foxbury Prison to ADX Florence, one of the most secure correctional facilities in the world.

Ackerman should have been in a better mood. But he couldn't allow himself joy or pride over the capture, since he hadn't directly beaten the Demon. Part of him knew that while they both still breathed, their struggle would never be over.

He watched his brother from the rear of a briefing room with speckled floors and white block walls that stank of cigarettes and gun oil. Special Agent Marcus Williams—Ackerman's younger brother—wore a black suit and a dark-gray dress shirt, no tie, his brother having vowed to never wear one again. Marcus outlined the details of the transfer to the team of law enforcement and correctional officers arranged in a grid of folding chairs crowded into the room's center. Ackerman wasn't allowed to directly participate in the transfer, since his status was merely that of a "consultant." But his skills would be put to use soon enough. What coach left the star player on the bench for long? And if killing were a sport, then Ackerman was certainly the Michael Jordan of murder.

His brother's plan was simple, but had merit. Three teams would leave the staging area at staggered intervals. Each convoy would consist of a forward scout in an unmarked sedan, two patrol cruisers, the armored prisoner transport, two trail cars, and a helicopter on overwatch. In addition, they would have state police diverting traffic to insure that their route was clear of innocent bystanders and potential threats. Each armored transport would be loaded with a hooded man. Not even the guards would know which convoy held the real prisoner.

Marcus would ride shotgun with a state trooper behind the real prisoner, while the others from their team occupied the trail cars of the decoys. Ackerman and Special Agent Maggie Carlisle would be in the overwatch chopper for Marcus's group—him as a special consultant and her as his keeper. Ackerman had grown quite fond of Maggie and considered her family, though his brother had yet to pop the question to his longtime girlfriend and officially make her Ackerman's little sister.

Marcus finished the briefing and motioned for Ackerman and Maggie to join him at the side of the room opposite the exiting officers. Marcus said, "I want you two to be scouting ahead for possible ambush points. We'll send the forward car up to check out any spots that could pose a threat."

Ackerman said, "I still don't think we should be sending him in any of those transports."

"Drop it, Frank. It was hard enough getting all of this approved once. We're not going to do multiple waves. But don't worry. That transport isn't stopping for anything."

Ackerman shrugged. "You're the boss, little brother."

"Don't call me that. At least not in public."

"That hurts my feelings."

"Considering you enjoy pain, you're welcome."

Ackerman smiled. "When do I get to say goodbye?"

"Are you sure that's a good idea?"

"The only ideas I have are good ones."

Maggie rolled her eyes. "Let's just get on with it. I wouldn't mind spitting in that prick's face before he's hauled off."

Ackerman said, "Majority rules."

Marcus shook his head. "This is not a democracy. That being said, I think the three of us could possibly get him to give something away. Some clue to his identity or where we can find his friends. Keep that in mind when we talk to him."

Ackerman's heart rate increased and his anticipation grew at the thought of once again coming face to face with the Demon. The feeling reminded him of the girl who took his virginity, or at least what he felt was his true virginity— all his other encounters being of a forced and violent nature. She had been a Mayan girl he had picked up along the road to Cancun, and she had served as Bonnie to his Clyde. For a time anyway. He now trembled with the same kind of adrenaline he had felt when she had dropped her flower dress from her shoulders.

Marcus led them down a concrete-and-block corridor into a room that smelled exactly as it should: like six men with shotguns in full tactical gear baking in the Arizona heat. Demon was strapped to an industrial dolly in the center of the six men. As they approached, Marcus ordered one of the guards to remove the hood, straps, and bite-stopping mask covering the prisoner's face.

Demon rolled his head from side to side and opened his mouth to stretch out the muscles of his jaw. He had long black and gray hair that hung down over his face. The tissue over his left eye had been melted, and he had no eyebrows. Knife wounds and slashes intersected most of the rest of his face, but the most prominent of the disfigurements was his Glasgow smile—a wound achieved by cutting the corners of the mouth and then torturing the victim. When the victim screamed or moved, the flesh of his face would tear.

Demon's Glasgow smile stretched nearly from jawbone

to jawbone. But it wasn't straight across or turned up like a smile. It looked more as though a giant axe had cleaved the bottom of his head off at a slight angle.

When Demon spoke, his voice flowed out in a mellifluous Scottish brogue. "This is not even close to the level of comfort I'm accustomed to when traveling. I'm definitely going to leave you a bad Yelp review."

Marcus's lips curled back in disgust. "I'll call up the captain and have him send in your wine, jackass."

"You've seen me take life before, Agent Williams, but that was for business. You've never experienced the beauty of what I do for pleasure. I like to lead my subjects through a representation of each level of hell."

Marcus stepped close and whispered, "It's good you're into that kind of thing. Because that's where we're sending you. Hell."

"Are you referring to the prison or a plan to send me to the grave?"

"Pick one."

Demon shook his head, black strands of hair whipping back and forth over his face like inky tentacles. "You've probably heard 'Seek and ye shall find' in regard to the Kingdom of Heaven and God, but that applies in the opposite direction as well. For every thesis, there is an antithesis. If you pursue the devil, he'll find you . . . and everyone you love."

Marcus was about to respond, but Ackerman had sat back long enough. It was time to establish dominance. He punched Demon in the center of his face, snapping the dark-haired man's head back against the metal of the dolly. Demon laughed and spit blood on the floor.

PREVIEW

Ackerman said, "Whoever my brother calls family is my family as well. And I dare any man to try and take what's mine."

"I offered you a way out before, but I'll give you one more chance. Your team can let me go and forget all about me. Or, if you choose to oppose me, I will burn your family alive and shake their dust from my feet as a testimony against them."

Ackerman grinned. "If I was capable of fear, I would be worried."

Demon's gaze traveled from Maggie to Marcus. "This is one of life's binary choices, boys and girls. There's only one path or the other, no in between. It's like choosing whether to believe or not believe or have children or not. Your only options here are to let me go now or face the consequences."

Maggie said, "I've heard enough."

"Then a cloud appeared and covered them," Demon said, "and a voice came from the cloud: 'This is my vessel of wrath, whom I hate. Fear him.'"

Ackerman tilted his head at their prisoner. "I've heard that the Almighty doesn't look kindly upon those who pervert the Gospel."

Demon whispered, "I'm not even sure I believe in all that. But I do know this, my boy. I'm going to give you a tour of hell, and when you ask me for the bread of mercy, I'll give you razor blades instead."

Ackerman chuckled. "Sounds like a party."

2

Special Agent Marcus Williams—a team leader in the Department of Justice's black ops program known as The Shepherd Organization—strapped on his Level-4 tactical gear. The armor had been designed to withstand rounds even from a high-powered rifle. He cycled his M4A1 assault rifle to make sure it was locked and loaded, clean and lubricated. He had a terrible feeling that he would be needing the weapon and the body armor in the next few hours. He had hunted several serial murderers—including, at one time, his own infamous brother, Francis Ackerman Jr.—but Marcus had never encountered anyone quite like the man they knew only as Demon.

Marcus had apprehended Demon just beyond the borders of Foxbury Prison as the madman aided in the escape of the leader of one of the world's most dangerous gangs. He had learned from Demon's former apprentice, the now-deceased Judas Killer, that the Scottish-born man with the scarred face had actually recruited and organized a network of the most depraved members of society and given them direction and purpose. He had banded this interconnected web of psychopaths and malcontents into a money-making machine, which allowed Demon's influence to grow in both power and reach.

It was the kind of case the SO had been created to handle, the sort of work Marcus had been born for.

Ackerman had told him that a man with Demon's resources wouldn't remain in custody for long, but that only led Marcus to take a more personal role in Demon's transport and incarceration. He had succeeded in the apprehension of a killer whose criminal influence spread out like a fibrous cancer across the dark underbelly of society, and Marcus had no intention of letting such a prize slip from his grasp.

He waited in the long dark tunnel leading from Demon's holding area to an armored transport that would carry the criminal mastermind to the supermax prison known as ADX Florence—a modern dungeon surrounded by a barren wasteland which housed everyone from the world's most dangerous terrorists, including Al-Qaeda operatives and Unabomber Theodore Kaczynski, to several organized crime figures. One of those inmates had a very personal connection to Marcus and Ackerman—their own father, the mass murderer known as Thomas White.

His real name was Francis Ackerman Sr., but the SO had kept that information under wraps, allowing the name of Thomas White, the killer's last-used alias, to become his permanent name. Even Marcus had grown accustomed to thinking of his biological father as Thomas White. It made it easier to distance himself from the madman who had used Marcus and his son, Dylan, as test subjects, just as he had done with his brother many years prior.

Marcus had no plans to visit his biological father upon dropping off his current prisoner. He hadn't spoken to

Thomas White since his apprehension, after the madman tried to blow up a group of school children in Kansas City, which only came after his torturing Marcus in a dark hole for months on end. If God answered his many prayers, Marcus would never have to look in the eyes of his biological father again. His brother felt differently, even though Ackerman had endured even more torture at the hands of their sperm donor. Ackerman had gone so far as to request visitations with their father, and the Director had reluctantly indulged his brother's forays into the dark mind of Thomas White.

He wondered if his brother's control and willpower had now surpassed his own. He couldn't stand to be in the presence of the man who had brought him into this world. He had even fantasized many times about his father's violent death and didn't know how Ackerman could look the bastard in the eyes. But he supposed that his brother's total lack of fear helped when facing their own personal monster.

As the guards marched Demon down the long dark corridor of concrete and rebar, Marcus white-knuckled his weapon and resisted the urge to end the mastermind's life. Part of him wished he had killed Demon when he had the chance in the tunnels beneath Foxbury.

"Take off the headgear. I want to say goodbye," Marcus said to the guards.

With the hood and protective mask removed, Demon smiled and puckered his lips as if for a kiss. Grabbing the killer by the throat, Marcus said, "If you try anything, I'm going to put a bullet in you. The biggest part of me hopes that you'll attempt to escape, because nothing would bring me more peace than to have you lying on a slab in some morgue."

Demon, quoting Nietzsche through rancid breath, said,

"Whoever fights monsters should see to it that in the process he does not become a monster. And if you gaze long enough into an abyss, the abyss will gaze back into you."

Marcus looked to the lead guard and said, "Get him out of my sight."

The officers loaded Demon into an armored prison transport, and Marcus took his position inside the rear patrol car. He had tried to plan for the worst and consider all possibilities, but some dark intuition told him it wouldn't be enough.

The caravan rolled out from the holding facility in Arizona early that morning, expecting to arrive at the secure facility at ADX Florence around 11:30 that night. Marcus had actually informed the prison of a much later arrival, but the early departure was another attempt at sabotaging any potential rescue attempts. Demon had the resources necessary to stage a dramatic escape, and unfortunately, any countermeasures he could dream up could be outthought by the opposition. He just hoped he had planned one move ahead of the unseen adversary.

The first eleven and a half hours of their journey proceeded without incident.

Marcus could barely keep his eyes open most of the drive. The Colorado scenery whipping past the window was probably beautiful during the day, but now the view was nothing but vague silhouettes and the occasional flash of an animal's eyes illuminated by the periphery of the convoy's headlights. He nodded off for a moment, always surprised at how much easier it was to fall asleep when he was trying to stay awake. But he sprang to attention as the cruiser bumped its way over a dead animal, some small carcass that flashed out of sight before he could really look. His hand rested on his pistol. He tried to relax while keeping his eyelids from dropping like castle gates.

The state trooper behind the wheel of the cruiser—possessing about as much personality as an earthworm—was little help. The short but muscular man had barely spoken a sentence since they left. Marcus disliked people who were comfortable in their own silence. The quiet moments left more time to think. More time for questions with answers he didn't really want to know.

The cruiser's radio crackled to life and a voice said, "Command, this is Overwatch 2. You've got a car parked along your route about twenty miles ahead."

Before Marcus could give the order, the scout came back with, "10-4. This is Forward 2. Proceeding to intercept."

The next few moments dragged on as Marcus waited for the scout to reach the site of the potential ambush. He held his breath in anticipation. Finally, the senior officer in the scout car reported, "Appears to be a genuine breakdown. Male and a female are outside the vehicle flagging me over."

Marcus grabbed the radio receiver and said, "Go in hot! Take them down and ask questions once they're secured."

"They seem scared to death. If it's a real breakdown, they've been out here for quite some time with no traffic flowing past. They—"

"That's an order. Take them down hard and fast. Apologize later, once the scene is secured."

"Roger, Command."

A moment passed, and Marcus said, "Overwatch, do you have eyes on?"

"Affirmative. The suspects have been subdued."

After another pause, one of the cops in the scout car said, "Command, we've got a nine-month-old baby in the back seat. Should we arrest her as well? I don't think my cuffs will fit."

Marcus gritted his teeth and took a deep breath before responding, "No need for cuffs. But you may want to have the dog sniff the kid's car seat for explosives. Don't forget for a second the kind of people we're dealing with. The type who would slaughter that whole family and wear their blood like war paint if it furthered their cause. Don't let your guard down for a second."

"Roger, Command."

Marcus added, "And the rest of you, remember . . . I don't care if your grandmother or your baby sister is in the middle of that road. We stop for nothing."